INVESTIGATING GOOGLE'S
SEARCH ENGINE

Bloomsbury Studies in Digital Cultures

Series Editors
Anthony Mandal and Jenny Kidd

This series responds to a rapidly changing digital world, one which permeates both our everyday lives and the broader philosophical challenges that accrue in its wake. It is inter- and trans-disciplinary, situated at the meeting points of the digital humanities, digital media and cultural studies, and research into digital ethics.

While the series will tackle the 'digital humanities' in its broadest sense, its ambition is to broaden focus beyond areas typically associated with the digital humanities to encompass a range of approaches to the digital, whether these be digital humanities, digital media studies or digital arts practice.

Titles in the series

The Trouble With Big Data, Jennifer Edmond, Nicola Horsley, Jörg Lehmann and Mike Priddy
Queer Data, Kevin Guyan
Hacking in the Humanities, Aaron Mauro

Forthcoming titles

Human Exploits, Cyberpunk and the Digital Humanities, Aaron Mauro
Ambient Stories in Practice and Research, Edited by Amy Spencer
Metamodernism and the Postdigital in the Contemporary Novel, Spencer Jordan
Herman Melville and the Digital Humanities, Christopher Ohge and Dennis Mischke
Listening In, Toby Heys, David Jackson and Marsha Courneya
People Like You, Sophie Day, Celia Lury and Helen Ward

INVESTIGATING GOOGLE'S SEARCH ENGINE

ETHICS, ALGORITHMS, AND THE MACHINES BUILT TO READ US

Rosie Graham

BLOOMSBURY ACADEMIC
LONDON • NEW YORK • OXFORD • NEW DELHI • SYDNEY

BLOOMSBURY ACADEMIC
Bloomsbury Publishing Plc
50 Bedford Square, London, WC1B 3DP, UK
1385 Broadway, New York, NY 10018, USA
29 Earlsfort Terrace, Dublin 2, Ireland

BLOOMSBURY, BLOOMSBURY ACADEMIC and the Diana logo are trademarks
of Bloomsbury Publishing Plc

First published in Great Britain 2023

Copyright © Rosie Graham, 2023

Rosie Graham has asserted her right under the Copyright, Designs and
Patents Act, 1988, to be identified as Author of this work.

For legal purposes the Acknowledgements on p. xiv constitute an extension of this
copyright page.

Cover design by Rebecca Heselton
Cover image © J614/ Getty Images

A catalogue record for this book is available from the British Library.

A catalog record for this book is available from the Library of Congress.

ISBN: HB: 978-1-3503-2520-3
PB: 978-1-3503-2519-7
ePDF: 978-1-3503-2521-0
eBook: 978-1-3503-2522-7

Typeset by Deanta Global Publishing Services, Chennai, India

Series: Bloomsbury Studies in Digital Cultures

To find out more about our authors and books visit www.bloomsbury.com and
sign up for our newsletters.

This book is dedicated to:

Regenia Gagnier for your fierce intellectualism and encouragement.

Anne and Keith for your love, support, and patience.

Zoe Hope Bulaitis for everything and more.

CONTENTS

Contents

ILLUSTRATIONS

Charts

Figures

Tables

ACKNOWLEDGEMENTS

The seeds of many of the ideas in this book were sown many years ago at the University of Exeter, and I am indebted to those who inspired me to become an academic and whose enthusiasm will always stay with me, particularly Paul Williams, Sinéad Moynihan, Matt Hayler, Corinna Wagner and Derek Ryan. You all make even the most complex of ideas come to life with an urgency that I will always try to capture. I am fortunate that I continue to be surrounded by inspiring friends and colleagues at the University of Birmingham. I am particularly grateful to Rachel Sykes, Amy Burge, Dorothy Butchard, Rebecca Mitchell and Rex Ferguson for your support and wonderful times spent together. My sincere gratitude goes to my PhD students for our enriching conversations and to all the students who attend the Centre for Digital Cultures events and contribute to an exciting intellectual environment at Birmingham. I am particularly indebted to the founders of Play/Pause and Niall Gallen for your academic generosity and boundless enthusiasm: I look forward to seeing your next exciting steps. Thank you to my undergraduate students, especially those who took *Digital Futures* and *The End of Life*, to whom I taught several of the topics in this book. Your curiosity has helped me reflect on the ideas that really matter and your honesty has made me better at explaining them.

I am deeply grateful to all the friends who have helped support me during the writing of this book. In particular, thank you to Jack Griffiths and Zenna Taganey for all the pints in the sunshine; Rob Davy-Cripwell for the fun evenings and Slay the Spire comradery, which made the final editing stages bearable; Tristan Potter, Omid Baherli and Charline Jao for the jazz and socialism; Wren for all your support over the years; Greg for your grounded good humour, as well as your tech wizardry that helped Chapter 3 of this book. Special thanks to Ellie and James Tyndall for your love, support and weekends of laughter.

A number of people have been instrumental in different parts of my life in enabling me to get to where I am now. I am forever indebted to Julian Kendell. Without your support and generosity in letting me into your classroom, I might never have gone to university. My sincere gratitude to Victor Luftig and everyone I met aboard Semester at Sea, you all changed me in wonderful ways. Thank you to Norroy for the spirit towards education that you passed down. Wesley and Zagreus, you were instrumental in your daily reminders that there is more to life than work.

I am particularly grateful to everyone who has directly supported this book, including Anthony Mandal and Jenny Kidd, Ben Doyle, Laura Cope and everyone at Bloomsbury. My deepest appreciation goes to the anonymous reviewers of the first draft of this manuscript. Your generous suggestions thoroughly improved this book, and I am sincerely grateful for the way you gave your feedback.

INTRODUCTION
INVESTIGATING GOOGLE'S SEARCH ENGINE

What do search engines do? And what *should* they do? These questions might read as relatively simple; however, this book aims to show that they are full of urgent social and ethical questions. Furthermore, attempting to answer them forces us to confront our biases about the world, our unspoken expectations of ubiquitous technologies, and our own minds and allows us to consider the kinds of ways we might want technologies like search engines to influence our lives in the future.

The influence of Google's search engine is enormous. Google's search engine does not simply shape how internet users find pages on the World Wide Web, but how we think as individuals, how we collectively remember the past, and how we communicate with one another in a progressively globalized world. Search engines are gateways to the social, political, and personal spheres of daily life and control which kinds of attitudes become amplified and which are buried in obscurity. As one of the technology industry's largest economic powerhouses, Google Search has shaped the agenda of Silicon Valley, including its attitudes towards data collection, personalized experiences, and the politics of algorithmic judgement. This book explores the impact of search engines within contemporary digital culture and, in particular, focuses on the social, cultural, and philosophical influence of Google, the impact of which ripples throughout the world in numerous domains.

Search engines are deeply enmeshed with other developments in digital culture – the rise and fall of platforms, news outlets, and other institutions – as well as being fascinating technologies in their own right. It is also necessary to acknowledge the way that certain institutions, in particular Google, have shaped the web and wider culture around a particular set of economic incentives that have far-reaching consequences for contemporary digital culture. Throughout this book, I argue that understanding search engines requires a recognition of their contemporary context, while also acknowledging that Google's quest to 'organize the world's information and make it universally accessible and useful' (Google 'About') is part of a much older discourse stretching back thousands of years. Balancing these two viewpoints is important: Google shapes contemporary public discourse on a global scale with unprecedented consequences. However, many of the issues addressed in this book would remain centrally important even if Google declared bankruptcy or if search engines were abandoned for an alternative technology. Search engines are a specific technological response to a particular cultural environment; however, their social function and technical operation are embedded within a historical relationship to enquiry and inscription that stretches back to antiquity. This book aims to provide an evidence-based understanding of search engines so that as digital global citizens we might have an informed debate about the impact of contemporary technologies on shared cultural values, forms of discrimination, and global flows of information and capital. The wider questions I raise, such as how the algorithms of Silicon Valley seek to describe and define us, and the purposes of these machines built to read us – these questions – are ones we must answer collectively.

Before exploring these vital debates, this introduction first provides a rationale for focusing specifically on Google, which explains the company's dominance, and, second, a basic outline of how search engines function. Following this, I provide an overview of the critical discussions about Google, including five key academic challenges of studying search engines. Full chapter outlines are provided at the end of this introduction.

Google's dominance

While this book touches on search engines other than Google's, a representative portrayal of the history of the search engine market must place Google at the centre of the picture, for several reasons. Google established the main standards central to how search engines are conceptualized and judged. There have been many approaches to providing access to web pages, but Google's model has set the standard, which now all other engines follow.

Globally, across all platforms, Google have a search engine market share of 91.86 per cent as of June 2022.[1] To use an ecological metaphor, the narrative is a story of many web search engines, around seventy or more, all growing up towards the light and eventually being plunged into darkness by Google's overwhelming canopy. The circumstance of Google's monopoly is not an ancillary part of this history; this is because the greater number of individuals who use a particular search engine, the more informational and financial resources it has to shape its results. In addition, the hegemony of a particular company allows them to fix the cultural expectations for search engine results, which reinforces their position. Writing in 2012, media scholar Siva Vaidhyanathan wrote that 'Overwhelmingly, we now allow Google to determine what is important, relevant, and true on the Web and in the world. We . . . have surrendered control over the values, methods, and processes that make sense of our information ecosystem' (xi). Although Google's search engine has shifted, in terms of both the technologies it relies upon and the ideologies that frame its development strategy, Vaidhyanathan's statement remains as true today as it did ten years ago.

The financial success of Google's search engine has enabled its parent company, Alphabet, to invest significant resources in ways that consolidate their dominance. For example, Google's entry into the smartphone and tablet industry – with their Android operating system – as well as directly paying other companies – such as Apple to keep Google Search the default search engine on their devices[2] – has resulted in Google's

---

[1]See 'Search engine market share Worldwide, June 2022.'
[2]Google pays a yearly fee to various companies as part of a deal to keep Google Search the default search engine on their devices. For example, industry experts estimate that Google paid Apple $12 billion in 2019 to remain the default on iOS the operating system that powers all of their products. See Duffy (2020).

search engine becoming the default on 99 per cent of all mobile devices.[3] This means that as the main way to access the web shifts from desktop to mobile, Google's dominance grows even further. For instance, Google's desktop market share in the United States is 76.99 per cent, whereas its mobile market share in the United States is 93.78 per cent (see 'Mobile Search Engine Market Share in the United States of America, June 2022') and continues to grow. In 2015, Google announced that 'more Google searches take place on mobile devices than on computers in 10 countries including the US and Japan' (Dischler), and in 2016, industry expert Greg Sterling estimated that in the United States overall mobile search, which includes both smartphones and tablets, had risen to '58 per cent of overall search query volume' ('Report: Nearly 60 Percent'). Over the last twenty years, Google's voice has drowned out the sound of its competitors. If the market remains on its current trajectory, the search engine narrative of the next twenty years will be in the form of a soliloquy.

In almost every country, Google have a monopolistic share of the search engine market. There are some exceptions, such as Baidu in China, but these examples usually represent their own monopolies; the only exception is the fairly equal market share, between Yandex and Google, in Russia ('Search Engine Market Share in the Russian Federation, June 2022'). However, in many countries, Google's share of the market sits between 90 per cent and 100 per cent. Because alternatives are the exception, rather than the rule, this book does not compare the results of different search engines. This could be a topic for further study, although if trends continue as they are, the real-world relevance diminishes daily. Another important point to note is that there are fewer alternatives to Google than might be assumed, as Dirk Lewandowski argues:

> many providers of what may appear to be a search engine are simply services that access the data of another search engine, representing nothing more than an alternative user interface to one of the more well-known engines, and in many cases, that turns out to be Google. ('Why We Need an Independent Index of the Web' 51)

For example, Yahoo! is powered by Microsoft's Bing search engine, and various meta-search engines such as DuckDuckGo and DogPile rely heavily on Google's results. Even Bing does not necessarily represent an alternative to Google's results. In Chapter 4, I discuss how in 2011, reports conducted by both Google and outside institutions found evidence that Bing was directly copying Google's results wholesale, claiming them as their own. There are occasions when the term 'Google Search' should not be used interchangeably with the phrase 'search engine' but these are few and far between. This book addresses the social and ethical questions generated by the global ubiquity of Google's search engine. However, to properly engage with these wide-ranging debates,

---

[3]Globally, the current smartphone market share is divided between Google's Android OS (74 per cent) and Apple's iOS (25 per cent).

it is essential to understand the basics of how search engines work; therefore, these fundamentals are the focus of the following section.

The three steps of how search engines work: Crawling, ranking, and query results

Step one: Crawling

At the most basic level, search engines function like an index at the back of a book: a collection of keywords with locations of where to find them. However, unlike an index's usual subject specificity, search engines record every word they find on the web. When a person uses a search engine, they are not searching the web directly; instead, they are searching a particular index of the web. Due to their monopoly of the search engine market, this means that, in practice, the vast majority of searchers only ever query Google's index. Each search engine's index is built in an automated way using simple programs known variously as web spiders, crawlers or bots. These spiders crawl the web by carrying out two simple tasks. First, a web page is chosen at random and the spider records all the words that appear on that page (ignoring very common words such as 'the' and 'and', which are termed stop words). Next, the spider looks for any hyperlinks on that page and follows each of them in turn, repeating the process of recording the words used on each page. The aggregated results of all spiders make up the giant, ever-growing index that gets scoured each time a user submits a search engine query.

From the very first search engines, such as WebCrawler, Lycos, Infoseek, AltaVista, and Inktomi, the foundational principle of how a user's query is interpreted has remained the same.[4] Fundamentally, a query submitted to a search engine is a command to *show me all the instances where these words can be found.* Although search technology has grown in complexity to include metadata and other information, this structure, whereby search queries represent language a user hopes to find, remains the fundamental logic of search engines.

Step two: Ranking

The process of crawling the web with spiders results in a large and crude index of words that might be used in a future search engine query. Therefore, the second key aspect of search engine development is developing ways of valuing some results other others. One of the first search engines to become majorly successful was AltaVista, launched in 1995, three years before Google. The focus of AltaVista's ranking emphasized web page design, such as where and how words were displayed on a web page and their proximity to other related words. This was accomplished by placing a high importance on key elements

---

[4]For more on early developments of indexing, see Lucas D. Introna, Helen Nissenbaum p. 171.

used to format web pages and in particular Hypertext Markup Language (HTML) meta tags. This used the existing format of pages to provide an indication of word importance. For example, if a word in a search query is coded as a title or header of a page, then this page would be ranked higher than another that contained it in the body of the page.

In addition, AltaVista prioritized the distance between various search terms. This allowed the recalling of information from the index to be based on the principle that 'pages where the query words occur near each other are more likely to be relevant than other pages where the query words are far apart' (MacCormick 18). John MacCormick provides an example of a search for [malaria cause] (18), which would trigger a search engine to search its index for the two words separately: malaria and cause. When deciding the ranking of each result, MacCormick invents two possible results: one with the phrase 'the cause of malaria . . .' (19), and the other which starts 'the cause of our expedition was not helped when . . .' (20) and which mentions malaria on the same page but in a later section of the writing (see Figure 1).

Consequently, AltaVista's meta tag algorithm would rank the first result higher than the second, not because the algorithm interpreted the meaning correctly, but because an easily measurable factor, like word distance, correlated with the kinds of judgements an actual user might make. This system of ranking worked better than AltaVista's competitors when it was launched and is still one of the many metrics taken into account by contemporary search engines; however, it was not long before AltaVista was overtaken by Google, which pioneered a different way of prioritizing and ranking pages. Google's primary method is still in use and has not only remained dominant but has shaped the overall architecture of the web, which in turn reinforced its hegemony.

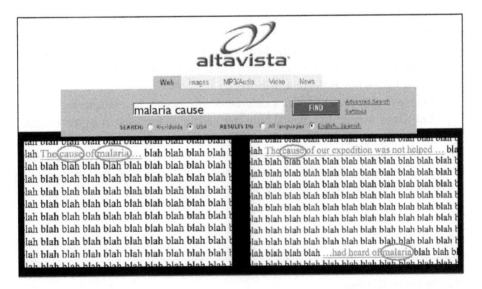

Figure 1 An illustration (drawn by the author) to demonstrate MacCormick's example of how word proximity can indicate probabilities of semantic relevance.

Although there are a number of different reasons why Google became the most dominant online search engine, there was a specific technological difference between its search engine and other competitors.[5] In 1998, Google's founders, Sergey Brin and Lawrence Page, proposed the idea of increasing the importance placed on the hyperlinks between web pages and reducing the significance of the HTML layout of each page.[6] They described this process using the metaphor of academic citation, where a hyperlink would equate to a citation, and the more links to a page, the more important the community had deemed that page. However, as they describe, there are

> significant differences between web pages and academic publications. Unlike academic papers which are scrupulously reviewed, web pages proliferate free of quality control or publishing costs. With a simple program, huge numbers of pages can be created easily, artificially inflating citation counts. . . . Further, academic papers are well defined units of work, roughly similar in quality and number of citations, as well as in their purpose – to extend the body of knowledge. Web pages vary on a much wider scale than academic papers in quality, usage, citations, and length. A random archived message posting asking an obscure question about an IBM computer is very different from the IBM home page. (Page et al. 1–2)

In order to replicate the offline hierarchies, Brin and Page's system prioritized the hyperlinks of pages they deemed to be important or influential. Their measurement of these flows of influence became Google's central algorithm, PageRank, which is still the primary metric used in ranking results. Through this method, Brin and Page created maps of authority that they argued represented 'an objective measure of [a page's] citation importance that corresponds well with people's subjective idea of importance' (109). Conflating existing power dynamics and influence with an aggregation of individual subjective judgements promotes the fiction that Google was giving people what they wanted, when instead they were solidifying old networks of control and authority and establishing themselves as the central broker.

For Google, each hyperlink has a different level of value; for example, an outgoing hyperlink from a page like whitehouse.gov carries more value than an outgoing hyperlink from the page of an amateur blogger. These values get carried over so that any pages with incoming links from whitehouse.gov are consequently awarded a high value. If the whitehouse.gov links directly to the amateur blogger's page, then any outgoing hyperlinks from that page now carry an additional value derived from the previous

---

[5]For a more in-depth account of early search engine development, see Elizabeth Van Couvering 'The History of the Internet Search Engine.'

[6]Documented in Brin and Page 'The Anatomy of a Large-Scale Hypertextual Web Search Engine' (1998) and Page et al. 'The PageRank Citation Ranking: Bringing Order to the Web' (1999).

hyperlink.[7] Therefore, PageRank's logic prioritizes existing hierarchies and thus trends towards a more static informational landscape.

Over time, Google have introduced algorithms that shape results based upon user contexts, such as localization, personalization, and time-dependent variables; however, Google's original design was focused on reflecting an existing order to standardize the web for all users.[8] Page et al. in their 1998 paper describe their initial aim in the following way:

> The importance of a Web page is an inherently subjective matter, which depends on the readers [sic] interests, knowledge and attitudes. But there is still much that can be said objectively about the relative importance of Web pages. [PageRank is] a method for rating Web pages objectively and mechanically, effectively measuring the human interest and attention devoted to them. (1)

Unlike earlier uses of HTML metadata coding, which measured the value of words, their proximity, and the formatting of pages independently of one another, the emphasis of Google's ranking algorithm placed the greatest importance on networks between pages. The coded format of each page was still taken into account, but played a significantly lesser role in establishing the overall information ecology on the web. In 1998, Google established the prevailing logic of the web that reified the influence of existing well-known institutions and gave viability only to parts of the web linked to by those pages with existing authority. It is easy to forget that how the web looks and works today was not inevitable. The establishment of the kinds of pages and sites, voices and spaces, that can be accessed online was not an organic process. When considering the influence of Google's organization and ranking, we should try to consider the kinds of parallel futures and alternative versions of the web if a different system had come to dominate. This is particularly pertinent given that the techniques underpinning Google's algorithms were not created from scratch by Brin and Page, or specially created for the web, but combine traditional methods for dealing with information. In his 2020 historical analysis of the PageRank algorithm, new media scholar Bernhard Rieder explains Google's relationship to previous information systems:

> There is little reason to believe that Google's retrieval engine was initially all that different from the systems that [Hans Peter] Luhn and others had already experimented with in the late 1950s: word frequency counts, processing of document structure to identify 'privileged' text in titles or subheadings, statistical

---

[7] Using a mathematical system called a Markov Chain, these values are standardized as probabilities, in order to prevent feedback loops. For an in-depth mathematical explanation of the PageRank, see Berry and Browne (2005, 84–8).

[8] The degree to which Google ranks search results differently for each user has changed throughout time and is explored directly in Chapter 4.

term-weighting schemes, and other techniques were well-known strategies for probabilistic, content-based indexing and already commonly used in web search. Put simply, the shift in perspective associated with Google Search did not concern retrieval techniques as such but rather the way the collection itself was conceptualized. . . . In this case, PageRank is the mechanism by which the web is no longer treated exclusively as a document repository, but additionally as a social system that is riddled with the very 'socionomic hierarchies.' (285)

Therefore, the difference between the work taking place in the 1950s and Google's early implementations was tied to how the web was radically different from a traditional corpus, such as a library. Throughout the company's history, Google's conception of how and why the web differs from previous bodies of information created a feedback loop, in which their conceptualization actively shaped the web to fit their definition, which in turn provided evidence that this was indeed the fundamental structure of the web. If the world's most dominant search engine had not adapted these particular techniques to fit their idea of the web, but rather developed a different system, the character of the web might be unrecognizably different.

Step three: Query results

Users trust Google's rankings. Chart 1 shows the proportion of which search results are followed by users in 2013 and 2020, respectively. These and many other studies show that users rarely ever venture onto page two of Google and that they choose Google's top-ranking

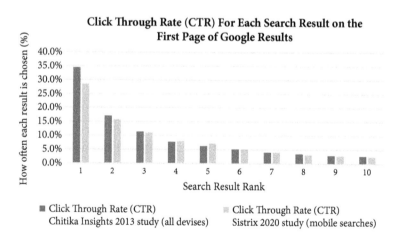

Chart 1 This chart shows the distribution of how often users follow each search result provided by Google, also known as Click Through Rate (CTR) distribution. It shows that users choose to follow highly ranked results and rarely navigate to Google's second page of results. This chart is based on data from a 2013 Chitika Insights study and a 2020 Sistrix study. Note, Sistrix's study only represents mobile searches, which since 2015 overtook desktop as the most common device used for searching.

result most of the time. However, this breakdown of choices – referred to in the industry as Click Through Rate (CTR) – represents a more complex picture than users simply choosing the highest-ranking results. As will be outlined in Chapter 1, Google use a range of metrics to determine the ranking of results, some of the most influential of which measure how other users have previously interacted with a particular ranking. If a majority of users follow the second result, rather than the first, then this becomes a piece of evidence used by Google's algorithms to rank future results differently. In practice, this means that there is an interactivity between Google's ranking and the choices of users that often develops into a feedback loop, stabilizing certain kinds of results. Therefore, it is true to say that users trust Google's rankings, but only because, in many cases, they represent the choices of users. As evidenced in Chapter 4, Google work to personalize and contextualize particular rankings to match the expectations of users in complex ways that are often hard to spot on an individual scale. For this reason, it is even more likely that a ranking specifically curated to match the particular user will reinforce the kinds of CTR distribution evidenced in Chart 1.

The final stage of the search engine process, search query results, is the only aspect of search engines that the vast majority of users interact with. The search box, in particular Google's minimal surrounding layout, has become a ubiquitous part of the web. The early web portals that predate search engines rearticulated an old media aesthetic of a newspaper front page or Teletext offering suggestions and directions to a user. These were populated with news stories, sports scores, and other content that reflected pre-digital curation. Google's web page design was more than simply aesthetic minimalism; it embodies an ideological representation that they work hard to maintain: that of Google Search as an invisible mediator and neutral passageway. Google's homepage gave users no indication of what they might search for, or even how they might search. Ask Jeeves gave suggestions of what to search for, HotBot foregrounded a little insight into how a user's query was being interpreted, Excite offered categories much like a Dewey Decimal system; Google, however, gave users no such direction.

The minimal aesthetics of Google is an important part of their presentation of neutrality and authority. Research shows that trust is intertwined with aesthetics. For example, Erin Klawitter and Eszter Hargittai's 2018 study evaluated how people use search engines to answer medical and health questions and the ways in which they evaluated which sites seemed credible. Those studied overwhelmingly relied on Google over other search engines, in addition, through interviews with the participants Klawitter and Hargittai found that

> Sites that were more organized, less cluttered, and contained fewer ads were deemed as more credible than those with pop-ups and ads, poor usability, and disorganized information. The less savvy approach mentioned that a site looked 'legitimate', 'professional' or 'kosher', but could not explain why. Such assessments relied on layout alone, without a move beyond prominent features to evaluate the information itself. (33)

The main way participants decided the credibility of health claims was through the aesthetic layout of the result pages. Searching Google for symptoms and health information is an extremely common practice where users without specialist medical knowledge must make judgements with potentially life-or-death consequences. The descriptions of the kinds of pages most trusted by the participants – highly organized, with less clutter and advertising that is unobtrusive – perfectly fit Google's search interface. There is a clear interplay between the trust generated from Google's aesthetic and the aesthetics of pages ranked highly by Google that reinforce one another.

Google's aesthetics are also particularly important in the way the company makes money through advertising. The majority of Google's revenue derives from the sponsored links, paid for by companies to be listed at the side or on top of Google's results. Throughout Google's history, these sponsored results have been designed to be as unobtrusive as possible to the extent that – as many studies have shown – most users cannot differentiate between the sponsored results and Google's non-sponsored results, termed 'organic results.'[9] In normalizing their advertising as a central part of their user interface, Google minimalist layout functions to legitimize their business model as neutral. Digital cultures researchers Jonathan Roberge and Louis Melançon argued in 2017 that

> there is a dual aesthetic and ethical aspect in the way advertising is displayed on Google's rather clean interface, whilst it was on the side at first, it moved to the top of the results page in early 2010 [few] see it as something other than indisputable. It's not evil, therefore it's normal. What this moral–aesthetic regime of justification does, in other words, is to reinforce Google's central position as a new form of culture in search of itself. (313)

Google's advertising model is far from ethically neutral; in Chapter 5, I demonstrate how it has actively incentivized the rise of fake news and how Google's economic incentives are exacerbating the decline of linguistic diversity worldwide. Therefore, it is noteworthy that Google manage to portray sponsored advertising as an unavoidable and harmless aspect of their search engine. These examples should show that the aesthetics of Google's search interface are a central part of the way it maintains its authority over the web.

Five key challenges of studying Google's search engine

Search engine studies sits at the centre of an expansive Venn diagram of research. For example, there is a rich literature dedicated to algorithmic critique,[10] automated discrimination,[11] privacy and surveillance, autonomy and digital daily life,[12] and platform

---

[9]See Hillis et al. (2012, 41–2) for a more in-depth discussion of studies that support this conclusion.
[10]For overviews, see Katzenbach and Ulbricht (2019) Kitchin (2017), Gillespie and Seaver (2016).
[11]For overviews, see Mann and Matzner (2019), Equality and Human Rights Commission (2019) West et al. (2019).
[12]For overviews, see Weitzberg et al. (2021) and Lyon (2014).

capitalism[13] that cuts across a large number of academic disciplines. There are a number of practical, legal, and ethical challenges regarding the study of search engines. I outline five important issues below that continue to have significant influence over academic research.

One: Multiple actors: Search engine optimization and economic incentives

Search engines are not singular entities but, rather, assemblages of different technologies, protocols, and stakeholders. Much of Google's work in the regular upkeep of their algorithms represents responses to the wide variety of content on the web, with different authors, conventions, and incentives. One major instance is the multi-billion-dollar industry of Search Engine Optimisation (SEO), in which practitioners are paid to edit web pages to increase or decrease their overall rank in search engine results. In the United States alone, SEO revenue in 2020 was estimated to be $80 billion (see McCue 2018 and Allsop 2022). A 2021 study conducted by Sebastian Schultheib and Dirk Lewandowski, found that 'SEO is not (or no longer) understood as an optional method, but as a necessary standard activity for any website that seeks to achieve visibility' (11). Given that the exact ranking criteria for search engines are closely guarded secrets, SEO employs trial-and-error methods that are updated continually and represent a particular agentic force in how search engines function, that lies totally outside the control of search engine engineers. Therefore, as researchers, we must be careful not to describe search engines and their results as distinct artefacts with clearly defined authors who have sole control over them. As Christian Fuchs, professor of media and communications, writes, these interactions are part of a wider political economy in which each subsystem related to Google's search engine is 'defined and permanently re-created by a reflexive loop that productively interconnects human actors and their practices with social structures' ('A Contribution . . .' 41). Analysing Google's search engine requires an appreciation of this collaborative dynamic in which various actors are jostling for influence and acting in accordance with their own economic self-interests.

Two: Moving targets

As the saying attributed to Heraclitus, philosopher of the sixth century BCE, goes, 'you cannot step twice into the same river' because both you and the river are constantly changing. This description sums up the second of the main challenges inherent in studying search engines. Fergus Henderson, a software engineer at Google for over ten years, described in 2019 that 'Most software at Google gets rewritten every few years' (12), and Eszter Hargittai, professor of Internet Use and Society, reports that Google make around '500-600' ('The Social, Political . . .' 772) changes to their algorithms a year.

---

[13]For overviews, see Mastrangelo (2020), Michael A. Peters (2017), and Fuchs (2017).

Due to these changing factors, the growth rate of the web, and the dynamic processes involved in the ranking process, there is no historical record of search results. Many internet users are familiar with the Wayback Machine, a site run by the Internet Archive, which provides snapshots of web pages throughout time so that users can easily compare, for example, a website like whitehouse.gov as it was in 2001 with how the page looked in 2021. However, due to the dynamic way that search engines function, there is no way of returning to previous search results to see the kinds of web pages ranked for a search term in the past. This makes it impossible for researchers to compare evidence and verify claims made about search engine results. Even when collecting data ourselves, for example, the URLs of a page of search results, these are only ever partial. There is no way to return to that search at a later date to see the results for page two or how the results might be altered by modifying the original search query. This difficult situation is highlighted by search engine scholar Safiya Umoja Noble, whose work explores the racist and sexist results provided by Google and the discrimination its systems embody. Noble writes that 'as I speak around the world on this subject, audiences are often furiously doing searches from their smart phones, trying to reconcile these issues with the momentary results. Some days they are horrified, and other times, they are less concerned' (181). The lack of an historical record for search results prevents a level of accountability that is a serious issue for both academics and the wider public.

Three: Each search a partial viewpoint

In addition to lacking a historical record, even searches conducted at the same time will differ between users. Search results vary between individuals and across various contexts depending on a large number of factors, many of which are kept secret. Every time a query is searched the results are ranked sui generis according to a range of criteria – referred to in the industry as signals – used to predict that specific user's intentions and outlook. Google claim to use around 200 individual signals such as information about the user (their location, the time of day, and their browsing history) as well as information about the pages found (how long a site domain has been registered, the location of the server on which that page is stored, the page's loading time). This means that search engine results can be different between individuals depending on a number of factors. The criteria involved in these 200 signals are complex; the various ways that these signals are given values means that different users will receive different results depending on their context. In fact, although the number 200 is commonly used by Google and the academic community, the number '200' may well be arbitrary, as in 2010 after Bing announced they use 1,000 signals, Google responded that their 200 signals are each made up of 50 sub-signals, thus raising their total to 10,000 (see Sullivan 'Dear Bing').[14] Given this variation, search engine studies is constantly faced with the question

---

[14]For Google's use of 200 signals, see Cutts, and for its widespread adoption in the academic community, see Levy *In the Plex* 49. See Brian Dean's 'Google's 200' for a compilation of the existing evidence concerning

of what should be considered as evidence. As communication scholars Robert Hunt and Fenwick McKelvey argued in 2019, 'No single outcome can be assumed to be indicative of the overall system, and it is impossible for even an expert user to deduce how the algorithm functions in the abstract based on individual results' (322). Therefore, examples of search results, even when collected in large quantities, can never be used to make claims about Google's system as a whole and only represent single snapshots, dependent upon largely unknown factors. As Hargittai argues, this 'poses significant challenges for the replication of search results, which is a basic tenet of scientific investigation' ('The Social, Political . . .' 772). Therefore, search engine research works within the confines of partiality, because such a methodological challenge does not diminish the need to understand and critique algorithmic systems.

Four: No real alternatives

As stated by Lewandowski earlier, there are very few real alternatives to Google's search engine, as their competitors such as Bing, DuckDuckGo, Dogpile, and others actively try to replicate Google's results. While this is appealing to some users who use a non-Google search engine for privacy and data collection reasons but still want the same kinds of results as everyone else, this homogeneity is problematic for researchers and the future of the web. As I detail in Chapter 4, many of the research techniques that would usually be used to judge the organization of a digital corpus or algorithmic ranking system rely upon comparisons to other comparable examples. Without an independent index of the web, search engines that aim to provide a truly alternative set of results, or other non-search engine mechanisms for navigating the web, it is difficult to make both qualitative and quantitative assessments of whether Google's results are fair, biased or diverse. Furthermore, given the lack of appropriate comparisons, it is difficult for users to imagine how Google's results might be different because its monopolistic influence establishes and reifies the expectations of how search engines function. This difficulty in imagining alternatives is reported in 'ethnographies of how people engage with and are conditioned by algorithmic systems[,] . . . their intentions, sense of what is occurring and associated consequences, tactics of engagement, feelings, concerns and so on' (Kitchin 2017, 26).[15] Therefore, the lack of real alternatives hampers research in two significant ways: it prevents comparative analysis between Google's results and something else and limits the possible speculations as to how search engines could be different.

However, creating an alternative to Google is not an easy task. Simply establishing the infrastructure and building up an index of the web, a prerequisite for any kind of search

---

the nature of these signals. However, the exact nature of these signals is not fully known as Eric Schmidt, speaking at the time as the CEO of Google, declared these factors to be 'a business secret of Google' (see Sullivan 'Schmidt').

[15]For examples of search engine research that uses participant observation, interviews, or surveys of user satisfaction with search engine results, see Jutta Haider and Olof Sundin (2019), Erin Klawitter and Eszter Hargittai (2018), Ovidiu Dan and Brian D. Davison (2016), Anne Oeldorf-Hirsch et al. 2014.

engine, is hugely expensive. At present, the only index that covers a large enough portion of the web to be comparable to Google's is maintained by Microsoft. Unsuccessful public, as well as private, attempts have been made; in 2005, a joint German-French project (named Quaero) was established to build a European search engine. The venture failed before even managing to develop an alternative engine, let alone maintain one that would provide enough of an incentive for users to switch from Google.[16] The research and development costs, provided by the European Commission, were €199 million for the French and €120 million for the German development teams. Without an independent index of the web, any attempt to provide alternative search engine rankings requires building and maintaining an index from scratch. Astrid Mager, writing in 2017, argues that the EU's attempt to build its own search engine, as well as its legal challenges brought against Google, stems from strongly held values about 'European identity' in which 'Google was characterized as invading European countries and citizens' privacy' (248). Mager states that such a sentiment is not simply based on economic reasoning but that Google's dominance leads to political and ideological erasure. In the words of Alexander Halavais, a prominent voice in search engine studies, 'the worldviews of those search companies and the engineers who shaped search are made a part of the search process'; therefore, we need alternatives because Google's 'worldviews are not as universal as people within the bubble of Silicon Valley might imagine' (35).

With every passing day, the associated costs of building up an index of the web rise as the web grows larger and the opportunity to challenge the status quo shrinks as Google's profits increase. That, in the search engine market, a multi-trillion-dollar company like Microsoft are the underdog is a telling sign. Although establishing an online landscape of transparency and accountability is overwhelmingly in the global public interest, after Quaero, another attempt at producing a publicly funded search engine seems unlikely.

Five: The myth of black boxes

One of the core difficulties of studying search engines is the degree to which many of the objects of study – the data, algorithms, and ranking metrics – are proprietary, undisclosed or obfuscated. This restricts the kinds of evidence available and claims that can be made by search engine scholars, which has not prevented work in the field but does create challenges. However, it is important not to idealize these kinds of unavailable aspects, not only because much rigorous scholarship has been published without privileged access but also because such an outlook relies on a misconception about the primacy of data. In a 2019 survey of the academic field, Christian Katzenbach and Lena Ulbricht state that 'more recent arguments point out that access to computer code should not become a fetish: absolute transparency is often not possible nor desirable and not the solution to most of the problems related to algorithmic governance, such as

---

[16]See Winkler and European Commission 'State Aid.'

fairness, manipulation, civility, etc.' (6). In this way, many of the arguments, examples or bodies of evidence produced within search engine studies are, by necessity, partial. However, given the range of challenges listed earlier – the multiple actors involved, the constantly changing data and algorithms, the contextual nature of search engine signals, and the lack of comparable alternatives – digital systems like Google's search engine are not static, fully knowable, or wholly explained by access to a secret source of information. In this way, the commonly used metaphor of the *black box* is misleading in oversimplifying the complexity of such sprawling systems. In their 2020 critique, digital media scholars Bernhard Rieder and Jeanette Hofmann argued against the notion that full access to a company's proprietary data or algorithmic systems is necessary or even desirable to regulate platforms and make them accountable. Their critique relies upon the combination of many of the factors I have outlined earlier. They state the following:

> Taken together, research on the properties of algorithms and algorithmic systems suggests that regulatory proposals such as 'opening the black box' through transparency, audit or explainability requirements reflect an insufficient understanding of algorithms and the platform architectures they enable. Algorithms can neither be studied nor regulated as single, clear-cut, and stable entities. Rather, their behaviour and effects result from assemblage-like contexts whose components are not only spatially and functionally distributed but also subject to continuous change, which is partly driven by users or markets facilitated by platforms. Given the ephemeral character of algorithms on the one side and the enormous generative and performative power of algorithmic systems on the other, the question arises what concepts, strategies, and concrete tools might help us to comprehend their logics and to establish effective political oversight. (9)

In many ways, the field of search engine studies, as well as the efforts of this book, is focused on that very question concerning the 'concepts, strategies and concrete tools' necessary to understand algorithmic systems and critique them. This book provides a range of methods that build upon existing techniques and approaches in the field, while adding new methods to the study of search engines, such as the first longitudinal analysis of search results of its kind, provided in Chapter 4. Given the nature of search engines, embracing new techniques, trialling innovative approaches, and adopting an open-minded attitude towards the nature of evidence have been – and will continue to be – an essential part of contemporary research.

Chapter outlines

This book represents a series of investigations that take key topics in search engine studies and redirects them by reframing key assumptions, providing new analysis or tackling previously unaddressed areas of study.

Chapter 1: Understanding Google queries and the problem of intentions

Chapter 1 investigates what people search for, how they do so, and why. In particular, this question of *why* has been a central focus for engineers building search engines and academics studying them. The dominant way of conceptualizing and evaluating search queries is through predicting their underlying intention and categorizing them based on the kinds of actions they facilitate. In this way, much existing scholarship and industry development consider human behaviour, our social context, and epistemological landscape as technical problems that can be solved using computer science. Such an emphasis on intention and prediction distorts the ethical dimension of everyday life. To demonstrate the complex ways that Google controls the behaviour of users, I analyse a range of real examples, from queries about what to feed a pet snake to how people searched about Brexit at the time of the UK's European Union Referendum.

Throughout, I investigate the methods used by search engines to interpret language and how this is used to limit the kinds of perspectives presented to users. In drawing on both information retrieval and philosophy, including the work of Plato, Hans-Georg Gadamer, and Jacques Derrida, I propose a new approach to considering search queries. I do this to shift the terms of the debate away from the perspectives set out by Google engineers, which have been naturalized in the academic field, in order to address a wider set of narratives about how individuals interrogate and navigate the world around them.

Chapter 2: Google's impact on cognition and memory: Histories, concepts, and technosocial practices

How does Google impact our cognition and memory? This question has been raised countless times by the press and in wider public discourse. Chapter 2 intervenes in this discussion by reframing how we might ask this deceptively complex question, while foregrounding the ideological responsibilities of Google's position. I consider contemporary academic evidence alongside a history of mnemonic practices from antiquity to the present. I argue that returning to historically significant shifts in memory practices – for example, the transition from orality to literacy and the influence of practices such as the *Ars Memoria* (influential between 400 BCE and 1600 CE) – helps us to better contextualize the influence of search engines in contemporary life. From the earliest of times, human thought and memory have always been intertwined with technology in complex ways that often become naturalized; however, the ethical responsibilities and nature of Google's influence are truly unprecedented.

In order to better understand contemporary attitudes, I outline Plato and Aristotle's different approaches to conceptualizing knowledge and memory; I argue that they form the conceptual bedrock upon which many epistemological technologies, including Google, have been built. Throughout history, thinkers have interpreted the impacts of technological and social innovation through their own cultural attitudes and biases. Therefore, this chapter uses this historical and philosophical analysis to reframe the current discourse on cognition, memory, and the ethical responsibilities of technology companies.

Chapter 3: Autocomplete: Stereotypes, biases, and designed discrimination

Frequently represented as a kind of digital oracle, Autocomplete produces some of the most pressing ethical issues within the study of search engines, particularly the perpetuation of stereotypes and discrimination. Although widely discussed in popular culture, to date, Autocomplete has received relatively minimal academic attention compared to other aspects of search engines. Therefore, this chapter provides a synthesis of the available evidence to give a detailed account of how Autocomplete functions, in order to support specific criticisms of its inbuilt discrimination. I analyse two different kinds of bias embodied within Autocomplete's suggestions relating to gender, race, sexuality, and nationality. Previous studies have demonstrated the bias of Autocomplete suggestions relating to general words, such as 'women', 'female', and 'girl.' In addition to these, this chapter's case study provides evidence that the aggregated misogyny of Autocomplete suggestions also relates to specific female names, which I refer to as *second-order stereotyping*. This case study demonstrates the insidious ways that discrimination is a central aspect of Google's products.

I relate these findings to the technical and ideological shifts within Google, from 2004 onward, which prioritized neural network and machine learning metrics over existing algorithms for formulating suggestions. I explore how these new methods of automation make this topic even more problematic, considering Google's increasing reliance on machine learning. Therefore, this chapter provides a specific critique of current methods while aiming to open up areas for future research.

Chapter 4: Google's search engine results: What is a relevant result?

Chapter 4 focuses specifically on the kinds of results provided by Google's search engine. Throughout the history of their search engine, Google have stated that its aim is to provide *relevant* results for users. This chapter explores the different meanings ascribed to this term by engineers and critics, while reflecting on the scholarship of personalization, as well as the social implications of tailoring results for different contexts. To relate these discussions to real Google results, this chapter presents the first longitudinal study of search results of its kind, carried out in 2015, 2017, and 2021, documenting how different contextual signals, such as location, language, vocabulary, and phrasing of queries, change the kind of search results provided by Google. This longitudinal study explores queries relating to LGBTQ+ values and shows how contextually dependent results provided by Google portray vastly different moral standards to people searching the same queries in different parts of the world or those using different languages. In addition, my study shows that the minor rewording or rephrasing of queries in the same context can completely change the sentiment or attitudes of the results for queries on the same topic.

Furthermore, the longitudinal aspect of the study provides evidence that the influence of different signals has changed significantly throughout time. During the six years of my study, there were times when the discourse and attitudes of results were consistent between different contexts, while at other points Google's results for the same queries varied dramatically. Using LGBTQ+ queries as my example shows the serious societal stakes in this issue, demonstrating how different contextual signals led some result pages to be filled with homophobia, while others for the same queries provided a wholly positive outlook. I relate these conclusions to existing research that highlights the racism and sexism of Google's results in order to establish the ethical values at stake. Such issues of representation and discrimination are of major significance for Google's role in shaping political attitudes and cultural beliefs worldwide.

Chapter 5: The real cost of search engines: Digital advertising, linguistic capitalism, and the rise of fake news

Chapter 5 explores how Google's method of generating revenue through advertising has a social impact on the web as a whole and wider society. I interrogate Google's two main advertising systems, AdWords and AdSense, and outline how these financial models significantly influence online discourse. In particular, this chapter demonstrates how Google's AdSense programme, along with Google's relationship with Facebook, directly incentivized the rise of fake news in the 2016 US presidential election and continues to do so to this day. In addition to Google's impact on global democracy, I also outline how Google's economic incentives exacerbate the racist and sexist discrimination raised in Chapter 4. Furthermore, I demonstrate how the economics of Google's search engine actively restricts the diversity of online content and accelerates the erasure of minority languages online. In doing so, I draw on the theories of post-Fordism to show how search engines shape the wider state of contemporary digital capitalism, which demonstrates the real cost of search engines on an individual and societal scale.

Throughout, this book develops a framework for attending to algorithmic cultures and outlines the specific influence that Google's search engine has had on the web and continues to have on a global scale. Building on the work of others, as well as introducing methods and approaches new to search engine studies, this book explores what a robust critique of algorithmic technologies looks like. In doing so, I aim to show that the way Google's search engine works is not inevitable and could work differently in numerous ways that would tackle discrimination, enhance public debate, and incentivize a better web for the future.

Notation and examples

Throughout, I follow the standard practice within search engine studies of using [square brackets] to signify when a word or a phrase is being referred to as a search engine query. Note that [sic] applies to these queries throughout, as when using my own examples and those from other researchers, they reflect realistic queries and therefore often lack capitalization, contain slang, and are often grammatically incorrect.

There are times when screenshots of Google searches are used as evidence or examples. All of these searches were performed using a Virtual Private Network (VPN) in order to anonymize search behaviour, prevent results from being personalized, and control other kinds of information sent to Google regarding the search. At times, particularly in Chapter 4, the VPN is used to adopt an Internet Protocol (IP) address from a server in a different geographical location to compare the searches from one country to another.

CHAPTER 1
UNDERSTANDING GOOGLE QUERIES AND THE PROBLEM OF INTENTIONS

Introduction

As described in the Introduction, Google's user interface is a blank slate. What makes the interface of a search engine somewhat unique is the lack of an explicit framework that categorizes topics or provides suggestions for how to search. Web portals, in which the search bar is surrounded by curated information, dominated before the rise of Google and still exist today, for example, see Yahoo! and Lycos. However, the search engine query bar at the centre of the pre-selected content still required the user to begin the process; even with the later implementation of Autocomplete, the drop-down list of suggestions still only appears after the user has initiated the process.[1] In this way, Google stands apart from much of the history of information organization. A survey of pre-digital information technologies – library categorization systems, encyclopaedias, index cards – provides examples of infrastructure in which the information-seeking behaviour might be prompted by a question, but which are organized according to pre-arranged, top-down hierarchies that do not incorporate question-asking behaviour into the system.[2] Google's interface makes no attempt to provide a static categorization of the web. Most previous technologies allow browsing without intent: a user of a library using the Dewey Decimal system can walk to the shelves containing the 300 class books and browse all the social sciences works that that library has; the owner of an encyclopaedia can read every entry that starts with 'A', if they so choose. The fact that every use of a search engine requires some informational input on the part of the user represents a radical shift in technologies used for enquiry.

This unique aspect of search engines has been highlighted since the very beginning of the academic field. In 2005, John Battelle published the first book-length study, titled *The Search*, that considered search engines in light of their social, ethical, and philosophical implications. Battelle was certainly not the first person to study or publish on search engines, but in considering search engines holistically *The Search* established many of the conceptual conventions and topics that became dominant in the field. One of these

---

[1] The history of Autocomplete, as well as the conceptual and ethical implications of its development, is the focus of Chapter 3.

[2] See Chapter 2 for a more in-depth assessment of the history of information technologies, including examples that problematize this characterization, such as oral cultures and the *Ars Memoria*.

was a term he first coined in a 2003 blogpost and which became significantly influential after its inclusion in *The Search*, where it was used to describe what Battelle saw as the fundamental aspect of search engines as representing a 'database of intentions' (2). As he described in his original blogpost,

> The Database of Intentions is simply this: The aggregate results of every search ever entered, every result list ever tendered, and every path taken as a result. . . . This information represents, in aggregate form, a place holder for the intentions of humankind – a massive database of desires, needs, wants, and likes that can be discovered, subpoenaed, archived, tracked, and exploited to all sorts of ends. Such a beast has never before existed in the history of culture, but is almost guaranteed to grow exponentially from this day forward. This artifact can tell us extraordinary things about who we are and what we want as a culture. And it has the potential to be abused in equally extraordinary fashion.

The central claim here is that a search engine's role is that of interpreting intentions, which based on the information aggregated from previous search behaviours, Google might come to know the 'desires, needs, wants, and likes' of humanity. This way of conceptualizing Google's relationship with its users became highly influential, and the term 'database of intentions' has become a dominant context in the field.[3] There are clearly some benefits in conceptualizing Google in this way; it allows us to consider the active aspects of search engine use and its embeddedness in everyday life. In addition, focusing on intentions has been used to highlight the privacy implications for a single company to have access to such a large store of information that is potentially highly personal or revealing. In addition, as I will show in the second half of this chapter, focusing on their dialogic nature also distances search engines from previous static methods of categorizing and cataloguing and allows us to consider them as more akin to the verbal back-and-forth of question and answer.

However, despite these benefits, this chapter argues that the conceptual frame of 'database of intentions' has led search engine research in a problematic direction and established a number of unhelpful conventions that have determined how research has been conducted and what it has looked for. Therefore, this chapter represents an intervention into both the idea of intentions and the resulting schemas that have been used in research to categorize the search behaviour of users. The categorizations that I consider in this chapter developed out of work that uses Transaction Log Analysis (TLA), the conclusions of which have been established as academic norms. In particular, I focus

---

[3]For key examples that cite Battelle, see Frontczak and Trzcieliński, 66 (2007); Duguid, 16 (2009); Pariser, 103 (2011); Hillis et al., 14 (2012); Jarrett 'A Database of Intention?' 17 (2014); Halavais, 37 (2018); Noble, 148 (2018). This list is far from exhaustive and also does not cover the numerous publications that refer to a database of intentions or invoke Battelle's framing of intentions without explicitly citing its origin, which in itself is proof of how ubiquitous the phrase has become.

on three issues with intention: do we always have a clear and unambiguous intention when we search? How significant are the kinds of searches in which a user's intention is changed by what they find? Can any amount of information collected by a search engine truly determine the *actual* intentions of a user, or are such conclusions only ever deceptive and retrospective?

In the Introduction, I explained how search queries are interpreted and how search engines function, but such an understanding does not tell us how people search Google: what people use search engines for and the kinds of queries they enter. Google do not release search records, preferring instead to offer a range of tools listed under Google Trends (formally Google Zeitgeist), which provide some insight into the popularity of search topics, as well as currently searched queries. Although, using Google Trends as a reliable source of insight is problematic for several reasons, which are discussed later in this chapter. While Google have not released any search records, the academic community has had access to publicly accessible logs of actual queries submitted to a range of non-Google search engines between 1997 and 2006.[4] These databases contain information about queries entered, their location, and the URL and rank of the search result followed by the user. Given their age, these databases cannot be used to evidence how people search today. However, the way they were studied between 2002 and 2010 established a key set of norms in search engine studies, which I consider to be problematic and that remain dominant to this day. I will now explain how query logs have been used to categorize search queries and establish prevailing research questions, before offering a critique concerning why we might wish to move away from their framing.

Categorizing how and what people search

Each time someone submits a search query to a search engine, the submission is logged by that company as a transaction and placed in a database. In the early days of search engine studies, several large corpora of non-Google query logs, captured between 1997 and 2006, were used by researchers to provide an evidence-based perspective on the kinds of topics people were searching for, how they phrased their queries, and, based on the user's destination, the assumed intention behind a search. Given that Google have always refused to release query logs of their own, extrapolating from these findings provides a better prediction of the kinds of queries submitted to Google at the time than simple guesswork based on anecdotal evidence of personal search strategies. There are several limitations that prevent us from making conclusions about our present moment,

---

[4]During this time, it was common for search engines to release search query logs to academic researchers and the wider public. However, the last log to be released (by AOL in 2006) did not properly anonymize the data, which led to specific users being identified through their search behavior. The incident became a high-profile scandal for AOL in which multiple employees were fired. Consequently, AOL's 2006 log was the final query log ever to be released by any search engine; for further details, see Silvestri 'Mining Query Logs: Turning Search Usage Data into Knowledge' 11–15.

based solely on these corpora. These search logs cover a time before Autosuggest or Autocomplete tools became a standard part of the query process in 2008, which actively worked to shift and direct how users formulated their queries. Furthermore, these query logs were recorded before mobile searches overtook desktop in 2015 and before the significant rise of voice searches conducted on home smart speakers and mobile virtual assistants such as Siri. These more recent shifts impact both the content of the searches – mobile queries correlate with location-dependent topics compared to desktop queries – and their formal structure in which formulating a query out loud through voice commands leads to more traditional question phrasing than the typically fragmented submissions typed into a search box.

The main way researchers study these query logs is through a set of research methods called Transaction Log Analysis (TLA). TLA research on search engine queries enables researchers to draw various conclusions regarding the following topics: the types of goals or functions queries can be in service of; the kinds of content users search for; the average length of queries; the rate of success of search results to satisfy users queries; and the number of search results that are actually considered by users. These conclusions have shaped the field in significant ways; I outline them here in order to critique the narratives they helped establish. In particular, I focus on how modes of categorizing intentions and search activities misrepresent the complexities of human behaviour. Because of their multipurpose and open-ended nature, search engines accommodate a wide range of behaviour from learning, remembering, and discovering to navigating, purchasing, and problem-solving. Much of the existing research takes the form of sub-categorizing the kinds of queries included in the logs, which generates a body of evidence suitable for analysis but does so at the cost of simplifying behavioural ambiguities. In analysing a particular example, the query [food for snakes], I demonstrate how queries can overlap different kinds of categories and how the process of externally assigning intentions to particular queries misrepresents the active process of searching. In particular, I highlight the difficulties inherent in trying to separate the process of *thinking* from *doing* and *learning* from *acting*.

The roles of search engines and information retrieval's question of why

One way to start thinking about search engine use is to consider the different ways you have personally used a search engine in the last week. Instead of focusing on the frequency, try to reflect on the different kinds of actions and various goals, as well as any instance where you submitted a query without a specific goal or intention in mind. Search engines are open-ended technologies designed to be useful for a range of tasks that continue to grow and change. Search engines are not just portals for asking static questions; search engines are embedded in social life. When preparing to leave the house, I might use Google to find a recipe or cooking times for my evening meal, look up a bus schedule, check the weather, find a picture of my destination, navigate to its homepage, search for a video to watch on the bus, look up information on a film I watched last night and read reviews to decide on films to watch in the future, find out the day's news stories, or search for non-newsworthy topics that interest me personally. Although I might have different strategies for phrasing each kind of query, all of these activities are socially embedded and all use the same technology.

Despite this, there is still a significant tendency within academic research to describe search engine activity in terms of static informational retrieval, separate from the social context of the person searching. My previous list of examples should show how making such a distinction is misleading. Even the most *informational* of these queries have practical implications for my actions during the day, and even the most *practical* searches impact my thoughts and attitudes. However, this reality of messy webs of action and thought is hard to measure with traditional academic frameworks. In the history of search engine research, it has often been the case that particularly methodologies available to researchers have created an unrealistic picture of search queries that are more representative of the frameworks employed than the object of study. A significant part of this discourse regarding web queries comes from the discipline of information retrieval (IR) and as such the dominant academic understanding of web queries is often biased towards particular definitions of information.

Not all IR research discounts the socially embedded nature of information, many studies emphasize the role of embodiment, community, and everyday life.[5] Nevertheless, even the kind of research that critiques particular concepts or metrics often ends up centralizing certain approaches of IR, which further reifies these problematic categories. For example, the research scientist Andrei Broder, who is primarily responsible for establishing many of the frameworks and conventions for analysing search queries, through his pioneering work at AltaVista in the early 2000s, observed how the work in his field misrepresented queries. In a highly influential research paper published in 2002, Broder claimed that the prevailing discipline of IR was biased towards defining search engine queries as 'inherently predicated on users searching for information [even though] the need behind a web search is often not informational' (Broder 3). This was an important observation, but rather than using it to unpick the methods of IR, Broder and the many academics who followed him in the preceding twenty years approached this problem by inventing new categories.

Broder's work at AltaVista combined query log analysis with multiple-choice surveys of AltaVista users;[6] in 2002, Broder concluded that queries could be separated into three kinds: '1. Navigational: The immediate intent is to reach a particular site. 2. Informational: The intent is to acquire some information assumed to be present on one or more web pages. 3. Transactional: The intent is to perform some web-mediated activity' (5).

---

[5] For an overview of such work, see Haider and Sundin pp. 34–37. For search engine specific, see Soo Young Rieh, Pamela McKenzie, and Ralph Schroeder. For more general trends in IR research, see Kimmo Tuominen et al., Annemaree Lloyd, Andrew Cox.

[6] The was carried out while Broder was an employee of AltaVista. It is common for this kind of research to be conducted by employees of particular search engines, as, even before AOL's 2006 scandal, companies had concerns about market competitiveness and potential litigation regarding privacy and the potential to deanonymize data.

Through his log analysis, Broder concluded that AltaVista's sample was made up of 20 per cent navigational searches, 48 per cent informational searches, and 30 per cent transactional searches. This categorization system has become the de facto typology in search engine studies.[7] Over the years, researchers have suggested various subdivisions of each category and highlighted how many queries are difficult to categorize; however, the strict division between these three kinds of search behaviours and a commitment to predicting intentions remain consistent. As Daniel Rose and Danny Levinson argue, 'goal-sensitivity will be one of the crucial factors in future search user interfaces' (13), meaning that search engine success is based on probabilistic assumptions of the goals of users. This kind of attitude draws us back to Battelle's infamous description of search engines as a 'database of intentions' (2) mentioned earlier, an outlook that assumes that the main function of search engines is to correctly guess the intent or goal of a user's query. Consequently, this influential idea of guessing intentions has become firmly embedded in both how search engines are conceptualized within academia and studied by researchers and developers working as search engine employees.

To foreground their assertion that intention is the key factor for successful results, Rose and Levinson present an example of a search for a single word [ceramics], in which, as we will see shortly, such short, open-ended queries are common:

> The 'why' of user search behavior is actually essential to satisfying the user's information need. After all, users don't sit down at their computer and say to themselves, 'I think I'll do some searches.' Searching is merely a means to an end – a way to satisfy an underlying goal that the user is trying to achieve. (By 'underlying goal', we mean how the user might answer the question 'why are you performing that search?') That goal may be choosing a suitable wedding present for a friend, learning which local colleges offer adult education courses in pottery, seeing if a favorite author's new book has been released, or any number of other possibilities. In fact, in some cases the same query might be used to convey different goals – for example, the query 'ceramics' might have been used in any of the three situations above (assuming it is also the title of the book in question). (13)

Although Rose and Levinson stress the importance and ambiguity of search goals, their formulation still sees their categories (informational, navigational, and transactional) as mutually exclusive, which simplifies the actions of individuals as clear, intentional, and rational. Their research is based on the conclusions of TLA studies, which list the queries of users alongside the URL and the rank of the search result that the user followed. This attitude towards queries as clear, intentional, and rational is also an important part of how search engine employees judge the relative success of a set of results for a particular query.

---

[7]For a sample of recent studies that use the informational, navigational, transactional typology, see White et al. (2015); Bute et al. (2017); Mivule (2017); Yusuf (2019); Makvana et al. (2020); Gul et al. (2020); Dou and Guo (2020); Schultz (2020).

The assumption is made that if users generally follow the result ranked first, then the result is a success; if most users choose the second result over the first, then their order should be swapped; and finally, if users are frequently following a low ranking results, then more significant work on reranking should occur.[8] This approach to ranking defines a strict relationship between queries and results.

Although query logs provide information as to the result that a user followed, as well as other information such as how long the user spent on that page and whether or not they returned to perform another query soon after, it is quite an assumption to argue that this provides an insight into the original intention for searching that query. It is easy to propose endless examples of searches where the results shift the user away from their original intention. Perhaps a user searches using the query [watches] intending to look up the history of timepieces but ends up following a high-ranking result to an online watch shop, spends time on the site, and purchases a gift for their partner's upcoming birthday. Transaction log analysis would see this as a success and would categorize it as a 'transactional' query rather than as an 'informational' request that became 'transactional'. Moreover, even categorizing the search as shifting from 'informational' to 'transactional' might be an oversimplification of human behaviour and the interconnected nature of our lives.

A key technological affordance of search engines is their open-ended nature; users do not necessarily need any kind of aim or functional forethought before typing a query. To take a metaphor from quantum mechanics, studies that follow Broder's framework, which use either data collection or user surveys to determine the goal behind a user's query, might collapse a superposition of searching outlooks into an overly neat singular goal that does not fully reflect the overall process. When a user searches an open-ended, short, or ambiguous query the result they follow says a lot more about the overall architecture of the web and the intrinsic biases of search engine ranking than it does the intentions, needs, and desires of a user. However, this method of defining search behaviour as falling into one of three possible categories (either informational, navigational, or transactional) has become the dominant prerequisite for analysis.

The work of Jansen et al. between 2006 and 2011 used Broder's original three categories to structure their TLA findings[9] and suggest that 'more than 80% of Web queries are informational in nature, with about 10% each being navigational and transactional' ('Determining the Informational' 1251), a much more unbalanced split than Broder's findings of 25 per cent navigational, 39 per cent informational, and 36 per

---

[8]There are several different ways search engines carry out these ratings in practice, for example, Google use 'search quality testers' and 'side by side experiments' using human evaluators who follow a set of guidelines, as well as A/B testing, which I cover in more detail in the second half of this chapter; for general descriptions, see Google 'Rigorous Testing'.

[9]For examples, see Jansen and Spink 'How Are We Searching the World Wide Web? A Comparison of Nine Search Engine Transaction Logs.' (2006); Jansen, Booth and Spink 'Determining the Informational, Navigational, and Transactional Intent of Web Queries' (2008) and Jansen et al. 'Real Time Search on the Web: Queries, Topics, and Economic Value' (2011).

cent transactional. I consider this to be evidence that shows how undefinable the category of 'informational' is, rather than a representation of a dramatic change in how people used search engines over a six-year period. Navigational and transactional are much more clearly defined categories than informational, but the significant overlaps have often given way to a tendency for large corpus studies to collapse this ambiguity into the most general of categories, informational, in this case. Many attempts have been made to compare different ways of categorizing behaviour, including IR research that predates Broder, in order to improve ways of analysing search queries. In summary, I argue that analysing research that categorizes queries into types (informational, navigational, and transactional) teaches us much about the nature of search queries, not because these subdivisions work but specifically because they fail to accurately capture the open-ended nature of queries.

Query length and the problems of intention

Search engine companies have consistently described their role of processing queries as the process of guessing a user's intention. This attitude has continued into the present and is one of the main impetuses behind Google's development of neural network technology, which they use to carry out natural language processing of search queries. One of Google's main neural network training methods is a system called 'Bidirectional Encoder Representations from Transformers or as we call it – BERT' (Nayak), the purpose of which is to tackle the inherent tension of search query formulation. The tension, as Google's developers see it, is that search engines process queries as a string of single words, but when a user reframes a natural language question into a string of terms, then the intention behind their query is often removed. In an article explaining the use of BERT, Pandu Nayak, Google Fellow and Vice President of Google Search, wrote the following:

> At its core, Search is about understanding language. It's our job to figure out what you're searching for and surface helpful information from the web, no matter how you spell or combine the words in your query. While we've continued to improve our language understanding capabilities over the years, we sometimes still don't quite get it right, particularly with complex or conversational queries. In fact, that's one of the reasons why people often use 'keyword-ese', typing strings of words that they think we'll understand, but aren't actually how they'd naturally ask a question. . . . BERT models can therefore consider the full context of a word by looking at the words that come before and after it – particularly useful for understanding the intent behind search queries. (Nayak)

There is a kind of irony here, in that search engine users are framing their queries with an implicitly correct understanding of how the technology works, which is preventing Google's engineers from gathering more data on natural language queries, which tend to be longer and contain more information with which to guess a user's intention. As

Table 1 Average terms per query, compiled by the author from various studies. Listed chronologically in order of the 'date of query log collection'.

Study	Date of query log collection	Average number of terms per query
Spink et al. (2002)	Three combined logs: 1997, 1999, 2001 – Excite Logs	2.4
Silvestri (2010)	Two combined logs 1998 – Excite Log 1998 – 'private' AltaVista Log	2.35
Özmutlu et al. (2004)	1999 – Excite Log	2.9
Silvestri (2010)	2001 – 'public' AltaVista Log	2.55
Jansen, Booth and Spink (2008)	2005 – Dogpile Log	2.79
Zhang et al. (2009)	2006 – Dogpile Log	2.9
Pass et al. (2006)	2006 – AOL Log	3.5
White et al. (2015)	2011–2013 'private' Microsoft Log	3.8

has been highlighted in the academic literature, 'query length also plays a major role in any search because the longer and more detailed the search query is, the more it becomes easy for search engines to understand the intent and meaning behind the query' (137, Gul et al.). For example, short queries are inherently ambiguous, such as [burgers], when compared to naturally expressed longer queries, which potentially contain more information about the context or intent of the search, such as [what are the best-rated burger restaurants in London UK]? This issue is important because engineers see their goal as predicting the intentions or context of a user to match the results accordingly.

Without recent releases of query logs, researchers do not have firm evidence about how users currently frame their queries.[10] I have tabulated the available conclusions from the available TLA studies that measure query length (see Table 1). It is clear from statements from Google, such as the previous one regarding BERT, that longer queries framed as questions are an uncommon way of searching. In the most recent TLA study, a team of Microsoft researchers, Ryen W. White et al., found that '3.18% of the queries were written in natural language question form' the average length of which being '7.39 words'. Therefore, although the average query length has increased throughout time, the majority of queries submitted are short strings of separate words or phrases that are not framed as questions.

---

[10]The only TLA research that analyzes more recent logs are ones that have studied the Persian-language search engine Parsijoo, the results and discussion of which have only been published in Persian, see Kaveh-Yazdy et al. (2019).

All information is ethical: Searching for [food for snakes]

As outlined earlier, the primary evaluative metric for search engines is their measurement of search success, which relies upon using the data regarding how a user behaves following their query submission to judge whether or not the ranking algorithms correctly predicted their intention. The assumption that users set out with clear intentions that can be predicted and which do not change during the search is the most sacred belief within search engine development and evaluation. It is a conviction that treats people and their actions as a computer science problem, one which can be solved with enough quantitative evidence and specialized tools. This way of thinking about users eclipses the complexities and messy realities of searching for even the most straightforward of queries. It is not just that intentions can change during a search, or that searches might be a combination of informational, navigational, and transactional behaviours. Rather, it is that any engagement with the world, no matter how mundane, shifts who we are as people: our ethical outlooks, our life choices, and our personalities. To demonstrate this, I present a practical search query example, before moving on to some philosophical positions that aid a reconsideration of the way that query intent is considered by search engine developers and many in the field of IR research.

To provide a particular example, I will analyse one of the real queries submitted to AOL's search engine in 2006 and collected in the 2006 Query Log made available online. The query submitted is [food for snakes] and after making that search, the log shows that the user followed the second given result and visited the site www.applegatereptiles .com.[11] The site in question is the homepage of a reptile breeder that sells snakes online and provides a large number of articles about the care and ownership of snakes. The site is still live and when compared to a 2006 Internet Archive snapshot remains completely unchanged, apart from a short message announcing the retirement of the owners. One of the main articles discusses the need for some snakes to be fed a diet of live prey and describes various methods for stunning mice to avoid them fighting back against the snake:

> we use a quick method to stun I call the 'deceleration method' I throw them at the floor and the sudden stop kills them (please, no tree hugger calls! Man sells poisons that cause rodents to bleed to death internally, or get stuck in sticky stuff and starve to death over several days. Mine die as they strike the floor, so go call someone else!). If a bit squeamish you can put them (it) in a paper bag and hit the bag on a hard flat surface. (Robert Applegate)

Here a search query [food for snakes] that might be classed as transactional has led to an informational result, one that potentially reinforces the intention of the search

---

[11]One of the main limitations of TLA query logs is that the only result URL that is recorded is the page selected by the user. Therefore, it is impossible to know if this result is representative of the rest of the results page as there is no way of returning to historical search states to gather more information.

('no tree hugger calls!') and one that aids future transactional searches (perhaps the user will now be looking to buy paper bags as well as live mice), but nonetheless, given the destination, TLA would consider this as an informational search. Comparing this 2006 search to the same search for [food for snakes] in 2021 the complexities of the example become more apparent. In 2021, the results for [food for snakes] range from informational resources about snakes, links to shops to purchase frozen pet food, to a range of recipes for cooking snakes for human consumption and other recipes for snake-shaped bread and sweets. However, the highest-ranking results are identical in their focus, exemplified by the top result which links to the page 'Feeding Pet Snakes' written by two professional veterinarians, Laurie Hess and Rick Axelson.[12] The page is explicitly focused on persuading the reader not to feed snakes live prey. Overall, the primary focus of Google's results for the search [food for snakes] in 2021 is to take an ethical stance against feeding snakes live prey. Not only is this a complete ethical shift from the result followed in the 2006 AOL query log but it might represent a direct challenge to the user's initial intentions or goals. The user may have intended their query to be transactional – finding a shop to buy [food for snakes] – but instead ended up with a set of informational results that potentially condemned their intentions and ethical values.

Based on the standard methods for measuring and evaluating search success, we cannot know what kind of prey the user intended to find with their search or if these results may have the effect of changing their original intentions. Perhaps they were looking for live food and now settle for pre-killed frozen prey. Or perhaps they were researching snakes before acquiring one as a pet and now, given the graphic and off-putting detail provided in some of the search results, decided not to buy a snake at all. Or in fact, maybe they disregarded all of the results and chose to acquire live prey in person. There are many other ways in which the behaviour following queries can shift and change. Although search engines can record query reformulations, if a user returns to the search bar to change their query, there is no way of measuring how a user's attitudes and values might change, the silent thought processes of users, or their future behaviour after the search. How might success be evaluated in this [food for snakes] example? The conventional wisdom of programmers and TLA researchers would likely count this example as a failure: the user set out with a clear, definable transactional query that did not lead to a successful transaction. I argue that the way we might evaluate this example as individuals would be led from our subjective opinions and personal values, and how we consider the rights of animals and the rights of animal owners. In Chapter 4, I explore the approaches to the question of how much we might want Google's results to change our minds on topics or reinforce our existing system of values. But here I want to emphasize, in particular, how when we gently press on the most simplistic and least challenged norms regarding search engine evaluation, clear-cut categorization gives way to complex ethical considerations and assumptions about our actions online. Therefore,

---

[12]See, vcahospitals.com/know-your-pet/snakes-feeding

the dominant assumption of search engine engineers and many academic TLA studies, which attempt to quantitively predict intentions and evaluate the success of predictions, is anything but robust.

Predicting intentions with a lack of information:
Plato, Gadamer, and Derrida

There is a centrally important aspect of intention that current search engine analysis overlooks. The question is as follows: how can enquirers formulate questions about topics that they are ignorant about? Iterations of this question have been a mainstay of epistemology from the beginning of the Western philosophical tradition. Different approaches to it can help reframe the shortcomings of contemporary conceptions of search engine queries and their relationship to intentions. This next section touches on some key arguments put forward by Plato, Ludwig Wittgenstein, and Hans-Georg Gadamer, which show that the problems with evaluating search engine success raise issues that are far from new. In doing so, I tie search engines back to a long history of enquiry and show that Google's method of treating language and ideas as technical problems to be solved is not only naïve but also an attempt to ignore the ethical dimension of asking and answering questions.

The central paradox of enquiry is how a person can set out to discover something about which they are currently ignorant. A classic exploration of this issue is Plato's 'Meno' dialogue, in which Meno and Socrates discuss the nature of virtue. The dialogue begins with Meno asking whether virtue can be taught which leads Plato's Socrates to begin his characteristic mental midwifery.[13] Socrates is less interested in whether virtue can be taught but rather in how Meno can define virtue in the first place. Meno provides a list of examples that demonstrate virtue, which leaves Socrates dissatisfied. What does virtue *really* constitute, Socrates wishes to know, to which Meno replies: 'How will you look for it, Socrates, when you do not know at all what it is? How will you aim to search for something you do not know at all? If you should meet with it, how will you know that this is the thing that you did not know?' ('Meno' 80d). Learning, for Meno, presents us with a paradox. How does self-education based on questions provide us with new ideas? How can one pose the right questions? And how could one recognize something unknown to us, like virtue, even if we did find it? That this paradox is still highly relevant today establishes some common ground between traditional questions and search engine queries. In fact, due to the way in which search queries are interpreted, as outlined earlier by searching an index for the words submitted, queries are trapped in

---

[13]The role of Socrates in Plato's dialogues is to provoke persistent questions and answers, which is often referred to as the Socratic Method. Socrates describes his role like that of a midwife who, rather than acting as a font of wisdom, would help draw out truths from his interlocutors – a characterization that is also somewhat fitting for Google's search engine.

Meno's paradox at a deep level. Questions function by prompting some aspect of, as yet, unknown dialogue. Search queries, although they might ask any manner of things from the sacred to the profane, rely upon a user's own language and prior understanding. The topics of enquiry and the phrasing of ideas can only build outward from a searcher's personal linguistic framework. At least in Socrates' face-to-face version of enquiry, one speaker could, unprompted, introduce topics or explain unrequested concepts. In the case of Google's blank interface, users must make the first move. Therefore, Socrates' epistemological problem, one of the first in Western philosophy, becomes compounded. To extrapolate Meno's question we can ask, how will a user set out a Google query for virtue? And how will they know which of the search results best represents the unknown concept? A key argument of this book is that a user's search capacity is a representation of their situatedness in language and culture. However, contextual situatedness is not Socrates' solution to Plato's dialogue; instead, his answer is an appeal to the immortality of the soul – based upon the theory of innate knowledge, called anamnesis – which is key for understanding Plato's epistemology and is discussed in detail in Chapter 2. The conclusion that I want to take from 'Meno', at this stage, is that enquiry, through questions and queries, is always limited through a lack of information, personal histories, and subjective positions. The unique perspective each person brings to a search query is not just unknowable for Google but is unknowable to ourselves. To suggest a search engine query could have a clear intention falls into the trap of Meno's paradox, in which to have a clear intention relies upon a fullness of knowledge about the context and alternatives, which would make the initial enquiry unnecessary. Therefore, the very nature of both questions and queries is that they are incomplete, imperfect, and never fully understood by their enquirer.

Search engine users are limited by the language used in their queries, and it is not made clear to them how and why their results might be different if they had used a range of alternative queries. In the context of Google, this matters because much of how specific words are interpreted relies upon the search engine's prediction of intention. A concrete example is whether or not Google chooses to search for synonyms of the words used in a user's query and to what extent these alternative framings feature in the highly ranked results. In practice, the extent to which synonyms are employed depends upon Google's prediction of the query's intention. Sometimes synonyms of query terms feature heavily in results, and for other queries, synonyms feature very little. This also changes throughout time, as shown in Chapter 4. Because these approaches change throughout time and in various contexts, the implication is that users do not know the extent to which their choice of language is framing their results.

Although certain functionality has changed throughout time, Google's main underlying logic remains that formulating a search engine query requires entering words that the user hopes to find on a page. In a very literal sense, search queries embody Wittgenstein's statement from his *Tractatus Logico-Philosophicus* that 'The limits of my language mean the limits of my world' (68). The linguistic nuances of each query, including variations of vocabulary, tone, grammar, and phrasing, shape the kinds of web pages that are provided through search results.

There are many differences between questions and queries, but the way in which queries must mimic the language of their desired answer is of key importance. Even though Google Search employs synonyms by default, the extent to which alternative words and phrasing are used to supply results is highly variable.[14] In Steven Baker's official Google blog post, 'Helping Computers Understand Language', he uses the example of how a search for the query [pictures developed with coffee] is interpreted as representing the same intention as [photos developed with coffee]. Therefore, in this instance, Google's algorithms place heavy emphasis on query synonyms so that both sets of results are similar and draw from pages using either wording. Repeating this comparison in 2021 generates the same similarity with a large overlap, including an identical ranking of the first four results. However, this is not the case for all words nor is it consistent throughout time: the importance assigned to synonyms depends on how Google predicts the intention behind each query and modulates the importance of synonyms depending on the user data of previous searches. You can see this in action by searching a range of queries and changing one word to a synonym and recording whether the results are similar. For some, such as the pictures/photos example earlier, the results are close to identical, while others present totally different sets of results. But Google's ranking metrics are always changing, so it is impossible to know how specific vocabulary choice has influenced a set of results. For example, searching the queries: [being a woman] and [being a female] in 2017 resulted in an entirely different set of page one results, apart from a single overlapping result. The majority of results for [being a woman] were personal accounts, all of which were positive. Results included 'Why I love being a woman – Family Share' and 'The 18 best things about being a woman – Cosmopolitan'. The results for [being a female] were mostly written about women in a more general sense and focused on the negatives. Results included '17 Struggles of Being Female – Puckermob' and '29 Worst Things About Being Female | Thought Catalog'. Google always searches synonyms by default, but in this instance, Google's algorithms determined the linguistic difference between [woman] and [female] was important. However, searching these same queries again in 2021 produces two almost identical results pages, both containing titles that use the words 'women', 'female' and 'girl' interchangeably. These differences demonstrate that sometimes changes in vocabulary greatly influence search results and sometimes they do not. Like much of Google Search's interface, these variations are not explicitly communicated to users.

It is important to note that the example comparing [photos] to [pictures], with its innocuous subject matter and relatively niche impact, is the example used in Google's technical press release on their developer blog. A common theme of such official communications from Google is their use of unambiguous or uncontroversial examples

---

[14]Google explicitly acknowledged that they use synonyms by default in an official blog post in 2010 (see Steven Baker's 'Helping computers'), but the practice is most likely much older, given that it relies on a particular patent filed by John Lamping and Steven Baker and in 2005 (see Lamping and Baker 'Determining query term synonyms within query context').

that shy away from the messiness and ethical dilemmas built into how people use search engines. For my example comparing [woman] and [female], in 2017 Google's algorithms predicted that the specific words searched carried distinct connotations and therefore required different results for each word. In 2021, Google's algorithms decided that the linguistic difference was not significant and provided the same kinds of results. For the kind of examples presented in Google publicity, such as between [pictures] and [photos], the difference is unimportant. But for the example of [woman] and [female], algorithmically deciding whether or not they should have similar or different results is a deeply political question. For example, one of the search results provided by both queries in 2021 is a *Time* article written by Susan Stryker, professor of gender and sexuality studies, titled 'What Does It Mean to Be a Woman? It's Complicated'. The article explores the historical and theoretical relationship between trans identity, sex, and gender and how the words 'woman' and 'female' have been employed in service of affirmation or denial, trans inclusion or transphobia. In the article, Stryker uses the word 'woman' seventeen times and uses the word 'female' only twice. Despite using the word female only twice, Google ranks this page as fifth out of 10,410,000,000 results. If Google's algorithms had chosen not to emphasize synonyms, as it did in my example of 2017, then Stryker's words would not have reached someone relying on the word 'female' over 'woman', which is perhaps exactly the kind of person Stryker's article is written to address. The everyday ways in which vocabulary aligns speakers to particular contexts or reinforces certain discourses are not new. What is new, however, is not knowing when our choice of words has an impact on the discourses we are presented with as users of search engines.

Gadamer's hermeneutics and Plato's fears of deception

The previous examples of how Google changes the interpretations of words on the behalf of a user, depending on their predicted intention, echoes the dynamic of enquiry that takes place between two interlocutors. In communication, the meaning of words used by others is not simply taken to be the same as our own, but based on a prediction of what the other person might take them to mean. The twentieth-century philosopher Hans-Georg Gadamer provides a useful framing for the concept of enquiry as alterity, which sits in stark contrast to the ideas of Plato. For Plato, the world of ideas is fixed and unchanging, so for a definition of *virtue* to be true, it must be true at all times, in all places, and to all people. For Gadamer, alterity – being introduced to something new – should be understood through an historically situated hermeneutics, which means a method of interpretation reliant on context; Gadamer argues that 'We can understand a text only when we have understood the question to which it is an answer' (379). Hermeneutical understanding, then, is a method of formulating the right questions: questions that are inherently part of the text in question. To fully appreciate this claim, it is important to understand *text* in the broadest possible way. In the humanities and social sciences, it is now old news that the word 'text' refers not simply to bound volumes of the written word but to films, objects, buildings, societal conventions, any form of communication, and concepts from the mundane to the abstract. This shared agreement for the capaciousness of the word 'text' developed in part from continental critical theorists such as Roland Bathes, as well as British Cultural Studies and the work of Richard Hoggart, Raymond Williams, and Stuart Hall. Describing non-linguistic objects as *texts* helps to lay the groundwork necessary for interpretation and to show how much of the world around us, if not all of it, represents concentrations of power, representations of ideology, and building blocks of culture in ways that can be interrogated and thereby understood. But this widening definition of *textual objects* does not simply reside in universities and through the practices of critical theory; Google, in its treatment of all things as kinds of information, has spread a similar attitude in which a range of objects (web pages, photographs, locations, businesses, people, laws, music, videos) are all placed within the same category, as *results*. Therefore, this notion that the understanding of a text resides in our ability to comprehend the question to which it is an answer – its reason for existing, its relevance, and context – is now an exceptionally commonplace notion, shaped by the internet's widening borders and Google's voracious appetite. The meaning of a *text* is bound up in its relationship to other texts, people, and behaviours. Hermeneutics can, therefore, offer a way to uncover these relationships.

For Gadamer, the attempt for 'understanding is always the fusion of . . . horizons' (317), by which he means that all understanding emerges in the light of pre-existing prejudices: our situatedness. These horizons are the relationship an interpreter takes to a question, an object, or a text. To properly ask a question is to anticipate and situate one's perspective in line with the area of enquiry as much as is possible. Described in this way, a search engine query represents an even more substantial attempt to align with a horizon. Not only do queries have to foreground unfamiliar ideas but they must do so in the linguistic register that a searcher believes the answer will be written. However, the control of how a user's query is interpreted is out of their hands and dependent on Google's evaluation of the user's intentions.

Gadamer's sense of understanding, which he borrows from the philosopher Martin Heidegger, is that all kinds of knowledge are forms of practical know-how.[15] Finding answers using a search engine relies upon a practical know-how of searching effectively just as much – if not more so – than a fully formed conceptual or epistemological understanding of the search result a user is hoping to find. Here we are drawn back to Meno's paradox and Plato's distrust of the sophists and their routes to false knowledge. The successful approach to formulating a search engine query is by imitating the vocabulary, dialect, and phrasing of the source we want our answer to come from. As Jean Grondin argues:

> For Gadamer, Plato's clear intention was to show that we cannot attain the truth of things by words. By that, he sought to distance himself from the Sophists, who taught that we can be assured of domination over things by mastery of words (or

---

[15]For an in-depth account of how Heidegger conceptualizes knowledge as practical know-how, see Dreyfus.

rhetoric). For Plato, true knowledge should, on the contrary, seek to liberate itself from the empire of words by being directed to things themselves, that is to say, to the Forms.[16] In saying that, Plato did not necessarily wish to deny that true philosophical thought continued to be deployed in language, but his essential point was that access to the truth is not given by words themselves, not their mastery. (131–2)

Plato's concern is that a mastery of language might give a false impression of understanding and shut down productive dialectical enquiry. For Gadamer, because every act of interpretation involves the coming together of different horizons, an attempt to dominate this exchange will always end as a failure in understanding. The pretentious sophist, in masking their ignorance through linguistic mastery, cannot facilitate the understanding of another nor develop themselves because their horizon is not open. This apprehension of illusory knowledge is mirrored in Plato's concerns with literacy, in that a text's failure to be open to questions through active dialogue presents a lack of knowledge. In the 'Phaedrus' dialogue, Socrates outlines his concerns with literacy in the following way:

> writing shares a strange feature with painting. The offsprings of painting stand there as if they are alive, but if anyone asks them anything, they remain most solemnly silent. The same is true of written words. You'd think they were speaking as if they had some understanding, but if you question anything that has been said because you want to learn more, it continues to signify just that very same thing forever. When it has once been written down, every discourse roams about everywhere, reaching indiscriminately those with understanding no less than those who have no business with it, and it doesn't know to whom it should speak and to whom it should not. And when it is faulted and attacked unfairly, it always needs its father's support; alone, it can neither defend itself nor come to its own support. ('Phaedrus' 275 d–e)

The written word cannot talk back and it promotes false understanding. For Socrates, this leads to people who are good at locating knowledge, in the form of the written word, but who have not properly understood that which is easily at their fingertips. For the present context, Plato's notion that writing is a poor substitute for dialogue because it cannot answer back is key to understanding how queries, submitted to a machine, are different from questions directed at an individual.

In Chapter 2, I return to the 'Phaedrus' dialogue in relation to conceptual models of cognition and memory. The purpose of highlighting it in this chapter is to relate it to the various studies that record the behaviour of people when they use search engines, two

---

[16]This is a reference to Plato's Ideal Forms – the unchanging world of ideas mentioned earlier – a concept that will be fully explained in the following chapter.

findings of which speak directly to Plato's concerns. The first is that, in 2010, researchers found that 40 per cent of the time, users entered a search engine query but did not follow any of the links provided (Zhang et al.). Secondly, another group of researchers found that 40 per cent of queries are reformulations of unsuccessful queries (Jansen, Booth, and Spink 'Patterns of Query Reformulation'). Without more recent studies, it is unclear whether this remains the case. However, at least in 2010, many queries led to a results page that left users either stumped or uninterested. So much so that, for whatever reason, a user avoided all of the results provided and instead returned to the search bar to change their query.

If a user is faced with a page of results that do not reflect how they conceived their query, then that text, in a hermeneutical sense, asks a question of that user. This question relies on the user to provide a different query or apply an alternative understanding; search engine results do not help with this process in the way that an individual might. When a user faces a page of results, all of which seem unexpected or unhelpful, they must decide whether the fault lies in their understanding of their topic or the way they have phrased their query. Unlike Socrates, I do not see such a total divide between mastery of language and mastery of knowledge. Yes, this same critique reemerges frequently, that easy access to information causes ignorance, but so much of the contemporary world relies on the know-how of access, rather than the view that understanding requires a solitary thinker, unmediated and pure. Many different contemporary views on cognition – some of which are outlined in Chapter 2 – argue that thinking is not simply contained within the mind but can be embodied, embedded, enacted, and extended and therefore search engine expertise and other methods of locating knowledge are inextricably bound up with Socrates' knowledge of topics.[17] This is why cultivating a deep understanding of how search engines work is key to an informed public and an essential part of digital literacy. Nevertheless, regardless of how we might define knowledge, do Socrates' complaints about writing's passivity hold true for search engines? On the individual scale, once a user is confronted with an unfathomable or undesired page of results, it might seem that such a web page is a mute, static text. However, on a much larger scale, the algorithms that underpin Google's results are not at all as passive as Socrates describes the written word to be.

Google's algorithms and Derrida's monster

In the context of Google Search, each search feeds information back into Google's algorithms at several levels. This feedback of data changes the outcome of future searches as the system has new information for its algorithms to draw from due to the previous investigations. Every query searched draws from Google's ranking system, while at the

---

[17]For various examples of contemporary models of cognition, see *The Oxford Handbook of 4E Cognition*, ed. Albert Newen, Shaun Gallagher, and Leon De Bruin (2018). The following chapter focuses on transactive memory in particular.

same time changing that very same system. The responsiveness of Google Search is due to the constant tests being carried out on its users. As Patrick Riley, a Search Quality Manager at Google, outlines in Steven Levy's *In the Plex: How Google Thinks, Works and Shapes Our Lives*:

> The mainstay of this system [of evaluation] was the 'A/B test', where a fraction of users – typically 1 per cent – would be exposed to the suggested change. The results and the subsequent behaviour of those users would be compared with those of the general population. Google gauged every alteration to its products that way, from the hue of its interface colors to the number of search results delivered on a page. There were so many changes to measure that Google discarded the traditional scientific nostrum that only one experiment should be conducted at a time, with all variables except the one tested being exactly the same in the control group and the experimental group. 'We want to run so many experiments, we can't afford to put you in any one group, or we'd run out of people', says a search quality manager [Patrick Riley]. On most Google queries, you're actually in multiple control or experimental groups simultaneously. Essentially *all* the queries are involved in some test. (61)

As well as each search being part of one or several experiments, every search provides data that is gathered without a specific purpose: information about how long the search took, where in the world it was initiated, what kind of computer and what kind of browser was used, what links (if any) were followed and for how long, as well as information that might be logged that we are not even aware of.

Submitting a query to Google's search engine not only provides a set of results but also changes the data available on which to base these results in the future. However, the opacity of what and how our actions might be changing is troubling for many: when I use Google Search, what is being taken into account? For instance, say a user sits at the same computer, with the same IP address, in the same location and searched the same search term repeatedly over the course of an hour. We might expect the search results to be the same throughout that hour, outside of instances where a breaking news story might concern one of the search terms. Even if the user receives the same page of results each time, the underlying data has been altered and the meaning of that search has changed with each search; even if we try and fix or limit our variables, the action of searching feeds and changes the system as a whole. Every query and every user's response to the results is part of a very literal instantiation of Gadamer's understanding as a fusion of horizons. Through the aggregation of information drawn from each user, the production of search engine results is simultaneously computationally rigid and organically shifting.

Derrida, in the essay 'Typewriter Ribbon: Limited Ink (2)', outlines a position that resonates with the complexities outlined earlier. He writes,

> Will we one day be able, and in a single gesture, to join the thinking of the event to the thinking of the machine? Will we be able to think, what is called thinking,

at one and the same time, *both* what is happening (we call that an event) *and* the calculable programming of an automatic repetition (we call that a machine)? For that, it would be necessary in the future (but there will be no future except on this condition) to think *both* the event *and* the machine as two compatible or even indissociable concepts. Today they appear to us to be antinomic. (72)

The formulation of a search query and using it to query Google's index of the web is not only far from a living dialogue or dialectic, but it also does not express Plato's notion of fixed language, inscribed and final. The two concepts, the singular event and the repeatability of the machine, converge together in Google's search process. Derrida argues that such a convergence would represent 'a new logic, an unheard-of conceptual form. In truth, against the background and at the horizon of our present possibilities, this new figure would resemble a monster' (73). Derrida's coincidental reprise of Gadamer's notion of converging horizons is quite fortuitous. The two notions of understanding broach one another: the hermeneutics of a static text and the dialectic of spoken communication. The logic of Derrida's monster is at work in Google's interface, as each query and every interaction automatically feed into the decision-making of future results. As users try to shape their queries to fit Google's system of interpretation, so too are Google's algorithms learning to better match its results to the expectation of users. In this way, search engines are both tools to interpret the wider world and machines built to read us.

What kinds of things do people search Google for?

So far I have discussed *how* users search, but what evidence exists regarding *what* users search for? Such a question is difficult to answer because search engines have been very reluctant to share information about query content. The kinds of material users might use a search engine to find may well be seriously at odds with the branding and marketing of technology companies. The question regarding what people search for inevitably leads to the kinds of ethical debates Google and others would rather take place more quietly. How many users are searching for Holocaust denial websites, socially unacceptable kinds of pornography, illegal activities, or extremist political forums? Google's stance for the majority of its history has to defend its obligation to provide the most relevant links to people's queries, however distasteful, so long as they do not break the law. Just one consequence of this stance was a 2016 report by journalist Carole Cadwalladr, which highlighted how Google ranked Holocaust denial websites as the top results for queries about the Holocaust. This included the query [did the Holocaust happen?], which led, for a long time, to the first result 'Top 10 reasons why the Holocaust didn't happen'.[18] Google have stated explicitly that it was not up to them to provide editorial direction to results and that if its algorithms decided this result was the most relevant for users then

---

[18]See Cadwalladr's report 'Google is not 'just' a platform. It frames, shapes and distorts how we see the world.' For an academic analysis of this example, see Mulligan and Griffin.

it deserved to be the top result. But we should not be misled. Google does influence the way users search and the kinds of behaviours they might use search engines for in several ways, most notably through Google Autocomplete, which I outline in Chapter 3. For now, I bring this issue up because Google's hands-off stance means that, for the majority of cases, the content users search for is content that Google provides. Therefore, in terms of brand image, providing full knowledge of popular search topics has the potential to drastically damage public attitudes towards technology companies. I now detail the findings from TLA research before moving to more recent insights into search content provided by Google Trends, particularly in regards to searches performed around the UK's EU referendum in 2016.

During the period between 1997 and 2006, TLA literature provides a broad map of the changing nature of the content of users' search queries. In 'How Are We Searching the World Wide Web? A Comparison of Nine Search Engine Transaction Logs', Jansen and Spink provide a five-year overview. Jansen and Spink document that there was 'a steady rise in searching for People, Place or Things and Commerce, Travel, Employment or Economy, with decreased searching for Sex and Pornography and Entertainment or Recreation' (259). The decrease in 'sex and pornography' related queries was also echoed in other studies; however, it draws up a more general difficulty in how changes in query topics can be interpreted. Jansen and Spink conclude that the 'decrease in sexual searching as a percentage of overall Web searching' is part of an overall trend:

> towards using the Web as a tool for information or commerce, rather than entertainment. . . . This analysis certainly confirms survey and other data that the Web is now a major source of information for most people (Cole et al., 2003; Susannah Fox, 2002). There is increased use of the Web as an economic resource and tool (Lawrence & Giles, 1999; Spink et al., 2002), and people use the Web for an increasingly [sic] variety of information tasks (Susannah Fox, 2002; National Telecommunications & Information Administration, 2002). (260)

Jansen and Spink give the impression that a decrease in searches on a topic relates to overall web usage, which is problematic, given the range of web-based activities that do not rely on search engines. In addition, they only outline the percentage changes of topics for search queries, which results in a great deal of guesswork for interpretation. Information regarding wider trends is missing, to take one example, how might we draw conclusions about 'sex and pornography' searches constituting a reduced proportion of overall searches topic? Perhaps during this time, more users became increasingly familiar with the kinds of pornography sites available and navigated directly to them, rather than exploring using a search engine. This result might actually point to the growing sophistication of users' knowledge of the web and sites that are available for such content. Therefore, it is important to avoid using the topics captured in a log of search queries to make conclusions about web usage more generally.

This raises a wider point, even when TLA seems to provide a lot of information, much of the nuance of searching a specific query is lost. It is unfortunate that the only query logs that researchers have had access to are between 1997 and 2006. However, in many ways, TLA oversimplifies many of the complexities of search queries and the data only allow for certain kinds of research questions to be posed. The previous conclusions can serve as a useful guide that can underlie the investigation of search behaviour post-2006. Nevertheless, that studies cannot use TLA to study search behaviour from 2006 to the present frees up, to some extent, the kinds of research questions that can be raised.

Google trends, Brexit, and 'frantically' googling after the EU referendum

The most comparable resource available for Google Search queries is Google Trends (previously known as Google Zeitgeist), which is a service that according to Google's data editor Simon Rogers provides an 'unbiased sample of . . . Google search data' (Rogers). In particular, Google Trends provides a graphical representation of particular search phenomena, such as popular search topics within a time frame. However, the academic value of this service is limited as the 'data' that Google release are based on relative comparisons; all that can ever really be inferred are differences in the volume of particular search topics because the data relating to actual search figures are not released (see Figure 2). Trending is a measurement of how much a topic is being used in search queries compared to other times or other queries. In highlighting changes in usage (rather than absolute volume) trending does not mean that *Stranger Things* (see Figure 2) was the most searched TV show that year, only that the relative difference between that term's use in 2016 is much higher than in 2015. In fact, when comparing them in Google Trend's graph function, Google reports that *Game of Thrones*, listed third for trending, has more than four times the overall search volume than *Stranger Things*.

At best Google Trends is little more than gimmicky self-promotion and at worst it has caused some serious misunderstanding when used as evidence in journalistic claims. An example of this followed the results of the 2016 UK European Union membership referendum, in which several @GoogleTrends tweets (see Figures 3 and 4 for two examples) were used by a range of journalists as a form of evidence. The tweets highlighted the rise of particular Google Search queries following the results of the referendum. These tweets were used by various journalists as 'evidence' that a large number of the British population were uninformed about the EU when voting in the referendum. Example articles include *The Washington Post*'s 'The British Are Frantically Googling What the E.U. Is, Hours after Voting to Leave It' (Fung), *The Independent*'s 'What Happens If we Leave the EU? Google Searches Surge as People Realise They Don't Know What Brexit Actually Means' (Griffin) and the *Mail Online*'s 'Google Search Spike Suggests Many People Don't Know Why They Voted for Brexit' (O'Hare), as well as similar articles by *USA Today* (Blumenthal), the *BBC* (Baraniuk), *Fortune* (Roberts), *Time* (Chan), *NPR* (Selyukh), *Ars Technica* (Walton), *The Huffington Post* (Beres), the *Mirror* (T. Wilson), the *Metro* (Willis), *The Irish Times* (McMahon), and many other outlets. However, because Google Trends only provides the relative differences of search terms it is unclear how many individuals turned to Google for information after they had voted. Data analyst Danny Page published 'Stop Using Google Trends'

See what was trending in 2016 – Global ⌄

Searches		Global News		People	
1	Pokémon Go	1	US Election	1	Donald Trump
2	iPhone 7	2	Olympics	2	Hillary Clinton
3	Donald Trump	3	Brexit	3	Michael Phelps
4	Prince	4	Orlando Shooting	4	Melania Trump
5	Powerball	5	Zika Virus	5	Simone Biles

Consumer Tech		Global Sporting Events		Losses	
1	iPhone 7	1	Rio Olympics	1	Prince
2	Freedom 251	2	World Series	2	David Bowie
3	iPhone SE	3	Tour de France	3	Christina Grimmie
4	iPhone 6S	4	Wimbledon	4	Alan Rickman
5	Google Pixel	5	Australian Open	5	Muhammad Ali

Movies		Musicians		TV Shows	
1	Deadpool	1	Céline Dion	1	Stranger Things
2	Suicide Squad	2	Kesha	2	Westworld
3	The Revenant	3	Michael Bublé	3	Luke Cage
4	Captain America Civil War	4	Creed	4	Game of Thrones
5	Batman v Superman	5	ディーン フジオカ (Dean Fujioka)	5	Black Mirror

See what was trending in 2016 – United Kingdom ⌄

Top trending		News events		Politicians	
1	Euro2016	1	Brexit	1	Donald Trump
2	Pokemon Go	2	US election	2	Theresa May
3	David Bowie	3	Hurricane Matthew	3	Jo Cox
4	Donald Trump	4	Brussels attack	4	Hilary Clinton
5	Prince	5	Zika virus	5	Boris Johnson
		+	SHOW 5 MORE		

Beauty		Famous men		Famous women	
1	How to make your hair grow faster	1	Conor McGregor	1	Meghan Markle
2	How to do a smokey eye	2	Sam Reece	2	Stephanie Davis
3	How to do nail art	3	Paul Pogba	3	Honey G
4	How to make a face mask	4	Wayne Bridge	4	Carol Vorderman
5	How to French braid	5	Kimbo Slice	5	Kesha

Fashion questions		How to cook?		How to?	
		1	How to make batter for fish	1	How to play pokemon go
1	How to get ink out of clothes	2	How to make yorkshire puddings	2	How to lose weight well
2	How to tie a windsor knot	3	How to make mashed potatoes	3	How to stay young
3	How to iron silk	4	How to make meatballs	4	How to go live on facebook
4	How to use a needle threader	5	How to make churros	5	How to vote for EU referendum

Figure 2 Google Trends representing 'what was trending in 2016 (global)' and 'what was trending in 2016 (United Kingdom)', respectively. See Google 'Google's Year in Search 2016'.

Figure 3 @GoogleTrends tweet regarding '+250% spike in "what happens if we leave the EU" in the past hour' after the Brexit Referendum results were announced on 23 June 2016.

in direct response to the widely circulated claims of the previous articles, which outlined the lack of context and transparent data available for such claims to be made. Page's article includes a Google Trends graph (see Figure 5) created by Twitter user @sammich_BLT that demonstrates how even a relative increase of 250 per cent may be extremely small compared to other searches at the time and did not reflect a large number of individuals, as was reported by numerous news outlets. In response to Page's article, Remy Smith used Google's AdWords Keyword Planner, a tool made available to Google's advertising clients, to make a rough estimate of the number of searches represented by the 250 per cent increase publicized by Google. He estimated that the spike following the announcement most likely represented an increase of fewer than 1,000 searches: less than 0.003 per cent of the people who voted (see Smith). Smith's figure is only an educated guess and because Google do not release any figures related to actual search volume, we cannot know how accurate it might be. Therefore, the Brexit Referendum example demonstrates why Google's lack of transparency regarding the content of search queries is such an urgent issue. It also exhibits the way in which many news organizations actively diminish the public's information literacy in their pursuit of maximizing page views, a situation in which Google is complicit, as is outlined in Chapter 5.

Another false flag for understanding the content of search queries submitted to Google is Google's 'Year in Search' videos (previously Google Zeitgeist and Year in Review). These videos are released in coordination with Google Trends and represent Google's

Figure 4 @GoogleTrends tweet listing the 'top questions on the European Union in the UK since Brexit result officially announced' on 24 June 2016.

overall marketing strategy of placing their technology at the centre of world events, rather than presenting insights into how users actually search Google. For example, Figure 6 is a still taken from 'Google – Year in Search 2016' video, in which Google's search bar is superimposed over clips of important world news events. Figure 6 depicts Justin Trudeau marching at a pride parade, a first for any prime minister of Canada, during a year of significant legal victories for Canadian LGBTQ+ communities. The insinuation of the 'Year in Search' video is that Google's search engine was a significant part of those changes. However, by not releasing detailed information regarding how and what users search and what kinds of results Google provided as responses, such inclusion is empty marketing. In 2016, was there a significant amount of people using Google to learn more about LGBTQ+ issues? How did Google's results shape their worldview and, most importantly, what kinds of results was Google providing for homophobic and transphobic queries? Without a way of returning to these results, or at least a breakdown

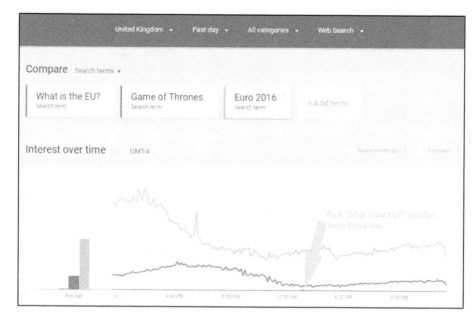

Figure 5 A Google Trends graph comparing the relative search query volume of three search queries [What is the EU?], [Game of Thrones], and [Euro 2016] after the announcement of the UK EU referendum results. Image by @sammich_BLT on Twitter, 24 June 2016 and cited in Danny Page's 'Stop Using Google Trends'.

Figure 6 A still from Google's end of year video 'Google – Year in Search 2016' that shows a search bar superimposed over footage of various world events.

of search behaviour, the history of Google's influence belongs to its own marketing team in ways that ignore the moral responsibilities search engines continue to have today.

Google's marketing identity is based on bombastically vacuous statements, such as 'Information empowers people: We need to protect the free flow of information and help make sure the internet is available to everyone, everywhere' and 'The Internet makes it easy for anyone, anywhere to create, share, and exchange new ideas. It enables everyone to participate without needing permission from a gatekeeper' ('Google: Take Action'). In practice, free-flowing information without gatekeepers facilitates a wide range of racist, sexist, and homophobic views, which Google's algorithms might be helping to support or encourage. In this context, we should recall the earlier discussion of Cadwalladr's reports that Google ranked Holocaust denial websites as highly relevant for users. In that example, it is not a case of Google acting in a hands-off or passive capacity; instead, the promotion of anti-Semitism was entirely dependent on Google's active role as a gatekeeper.

Real insights into search behaviours in 2016 would comprise not only smiling faces and high fives at pride events but also homophobic queries and bigoted results. Chapters 3, 4, and 5 of this book provide numerous examples detailing how Google Search encourages prejudices and discriminatory attitudes towards women, people of colour, the LGBTQ+ community, and a range of other identities. Not only are people searching offensive queries, but Google is helping users to find evidence to support these views, none of which are going to be included in Google's 'Year in Search' videos.

Conclusion

This chapter highlighted some of the key defining features of search engine design, particularly their open-ended nature and requirement for users to enter their own language to generate results. Early on in the academic study of search engines, Battelle's phrase 'database of intentions' (2) came to frame much of the following discourse that emphasized the prediction of users' desires and goals. This influenced the use of TLA for studying query logs and an overarching focus on categorizing queries into mutually exclusive kinds. I argue that these dominant frameworks misrepresent the complexities of human behaviour and have led various academic studies to rearticulate many of the problematic attitudes communicated by technologists in the search engine industry. Defining the queries of users as static, goal-oriented requests enables Google to avoid acknowledging the moral responsibilities of how their results might change people's attitudes and behaviour. By introducing key ideas of Plato and Gadamer, this chapter showed that how people enquire about the world always depends on partial understanding that attempts to locate an unknown horizon of knowledge. Reframing enquiry in this way places the ethical responsibility onto Google, which stands in opposition to the dominant conception that accountability lies with a user and their intentions. Finally, I focused on the way that Google Trends has been used by journalists to blame users and parrot Google's publicity discourse. In framing search queries as isolated topics, mapped by relative frequency, Google avoids presenting the attitudes towards these topics and flattens the difference between historical enquiry and Holocaust denial. Search engines need to be held to account; however, the dominant academic mode that emphasizes user intentions only reinforces the myth that Google is a neutral mediator without ethical responsibilities. Therefore, the ways of categorizing and analysing queries are fundamental in establishing the grounds on which critique can be built. This chapter argues that we should reconsider many of our academic norms that might reinforce Google's mythmaking and focus instead on the kinds of approaches that will enable us to better hold them to account.

CHAPTER 2
GOOGLE'S IMPACT ON COGNITION AND MEMORY
HISTORIES, CONCEPTS, AND TECHNOSOCIAL PRACTICES

Introduction

There is no shortage of popular literature and journalism that make alarmist claims about the impact of ubiquitous computing and the role of search engines; the most infamous and widely shared example is Nicholas Carr's anecdotal approach in his 2008 article 'Is Google Making Us Stupid?' and 2010 book *The Shallows*.[1] His argument in his 2008 article is that the internet 'has been tinkering with my brain, remapping the neural circuitry, reprogramming the memory. . . . I'm not thinking the way I used to think. . . . Once I was a scuba diver in the sea of words. Now I zip along the surface like a guy on a Jet Ski'. Carr concludes his article with a reference to the murderous rebellion of Hal, the Artificial Intelligence of *2001: A Space Odyssey* and with the proposition that 'as we come to rely on computers to mediate our understanding of the world, it is our own intelligence that flattens into artificial intelligence'. These are clearly bombastic claims that aim to be emotional and controversial. However, rather than rejecting the strength of feeling that many have about the centrality of the internet and Google's ubiquity, we can use them as an opportunity to provide new explorations, both intellectual and historical, regarding the influence of search engines. Rather than providing a teleological timeline of increasing technological influence over our minds, such an approach challenges definitions and behaviours we can often take for granted. For example, what is the relationship between memory and cognition? Are they two parts of the same process or are they distinct? To what extent do such processes rely on the world around us? And how have technological developments and social changes influenced the way that thinkers answer these kinds of questions? I ask such definitional questions throughout this chapter because their complexity is essential to understanding how search engines impact the way we think and remember. In understanding how philosophers and scientists throughout history describe

---

[1]Such writing is complete with a number of subgenres, including generalization regarding technology's impact on social change (Andrew Keen's *The Internet is Not the Answer*, 2015); self-help (Cal Newport's *Deep Work: Rules for Focused Success in a Distracted World*, 2016); apocalyptic visions (Gerd Leonhard's *Technology vs. Humanity: The Coming Clash Between Man and Machine*, 2016); and attitudes of determinism (Kevin Kelly's *The Inevitable: Understanding the 12 Technological Forces That Will Shape Our Future*, 2016).

the processes of memory we can see how their conclusions were influenced by their own social and technological context. Such insight can help us to see the biases and expectations that are part of our contemporary approaches to the impacts of search engines.

The chapter outline is as follows. First, I discuss psychological research that explicitly studies search engine use and its potential impact on the information retention of individuals. In doing so, I establish how technological metaphor has influenced the methodologies, questions, and approaches of researchers. Second, I highlight a range of historical examples that highlight the complex interrelation between memory, technology, and social structures to argue that personal memory has always functioned dynamically by relying on external technology and other individuals. This includes particular moments of profound change, such as the birth of literacy and its impact on oral culture, an event that has been used as a parallel for our contemporary shift towards an increasingly digital culture. It is often hard to see the biases and naturalized metaphors we take for granted in our own context. Therefore, this history of memory practices shows our present situation in a new light. Third, I argue that many of the debates regarding knowledge and memory can be framed within the structure of either a Platonic or Aristotelian epistemology. These two approaches, first outlined in the context of a shift from orality to literacy, are developed throughout this chapter in other technological contexts, leading up to the present. Finally, I address the set of technosocial memory practices known as the *Ars Memoria*, which had significant use between 400 BCE and 1600 CE and a form of which is still practised by contemporary competitive memory athletes. The history of the *Ars Memoria* illustrates the tension between Platonic and Aristotelian attitudes, the relationship between logic and mysticism, and the rise of modern science and psychology. This historical and theoretical background provides depth to the initial question of how search engine use impacts memory. Throughout this chapter, I question the way we might usually define cognition, memory, and technology in order to encourage a more imaginative outlook towards our sense of self and the world around us.

Google's impact on cognition and memory

Psychologists who have examined the relationship between search engines and human memory have consistently returned to a particular conceptual framework referred to as transactive memory. Originally established by psychologist Daniel Wegner in the 1980s, the concept aims to describe the process of externally dependent memories, most commonly those memories that rely on interactions with another person. The concept has become influential due to its implementation in various experimental studies, the results of which are often imported into discussions of new technology. A recent example is the 2021 paper by media scholars Paul Atkinson and Richie Barker who consider transactive memory in the context of 'Networked devices . . . such as Google Home and Amazon's Echo, [which might] expand our capacity to find and retrieve digitally encoded information without the deliberation often required by the stand-alone computer' (53). But the applicability of transactive memory to technological relationships is not clear cut. Because of this concept's continuing influence, this section outlines the existing scholarship that supports and disputes how it has been applied to search engines. However, due to their focus on contemporary behaviour, existing considerations of transactive memory often ignore the long history of technological memory practices that stretch back thousands of years. Without considering pre-digital practices, we risk overstating the unprecedented nature of search engines. Therefore, the second half of this chapter relates these contemporary claims to a broader historical and philosophical context.

Sparrow et al., in their 2011 study 'Google Effects on Memory: Cognitive Consequences of Having Information at Our Fingertips', report the findings of four experiments carried out to explore the potential effects of search engines on memory recall. Each experiment tested a different aspect of search engine use: specifically, would participants think about computers when faced with a question? (study one), would participants' memories be affected by whether or not they thought the information would be available in the future? (studies two and three), and would knowing where to find a piece of information influence the memory of that information (study four)? Their results suggested that

> when faced with difficult questions, people are primed to think about computers and that when people *expect to have future access to information,* they have *lower rates of recall of the information itself and enhanced recall instead for where to access it.* The Internet has become a primary form of external or transactive memory, where information is stored collectively outside ourselves. (776, emphasis added)

These studies support the view that the mind makes decisions on our behalf and prioritizes the *how* and *where* of information, rather than the information itself if future access seems likely. Daniel Wegner, one of the researchers in the aforementioned study, first established the term 'transactive memory' in a 1985 study that investigated not computers but the influence of being in a couple: 'Cognitive Interdependence in Close Relationships', written with Toni Giuliano and Paula Hertel. Wegner, Giuliano, and Hertel found that couples interdependently relied on the memories of one another, and through the unintentional practice of various techniques, cueing and re-cueing for example, couples could arrive at information that neither would have successfully recalled alone. Later research (reported in Wegner, Erber, and Raymond 'Transactive Memory in Close Relationships') built on the previous findings that couples rely on the memories of one another, to present evidence that couples unconsciously establish a division of labour regarding the types of things each remembers and forgets. Wegner, Erber, and Raymond argued that this impacted future abilities to recall certain types of information. The central study of 'Transactive Memory in Close Relationships' tested the recall of established couples and impromptu couples (pairs comprised of strangers). These two types of couples were split into two further groups: the first group were assigned particular memory structures –

for example, '1 partner should remember food items, another should remember history items' (923) – and the second were given no such instructions. The results of the study found that 'Memory performance of the natural pairs was better than that of impromptu pairs without assigned structure, whereas the performance of natural pairs was inferior to that of impromptu pairs when structure [*sic*] was assigned' (923). The second part of this finding, which established couples performed worse than impromptu couples when they were instructed to follow specific memory roles, is key to Wegner's definition of transactive memory. Over time, couples establish implicit and unconscious memory roles that, Wenger et al. argue, influence the capacity to form memories and recall them.

With this theoretical background in mind, the assertion of Sparrow et al. that search engine use represents a form of transactional memory is a bold claim. If this is the case, search engine access does not simply provide an added layer of external evidence but rather fundamentally changes how we remember and forget, as people do in long-term relationships. One of their four experiments ran as follows:

> Participants were tested in a 2 by 2 between-subject experiment by reading 40 memorable trivia statements of the type that one would look up online (both of the new information variety, e.g., 'An ostrich's eye is bigger than its brain', and information that may be remembered generally, but not in specific detail, e.g., 'The space shuttle Columbia disintegrated during re-entry over Texas in Feb. 2003'). They then typed them into the computer to ensure attention (and also to provide a more generous test of memory). Half the participants believed the computer would save what was typed; half believed the item would be erased. In addition, half of the participants in each of the saved and erased conditions were asked explicitly to try to remember the information. After the reading and typing task, participants wrote down as many of the statements as they could remember. (776)

They found that 'those who believed that the computer erased what they typed had the best recall . . . compared with those who believed the computer would be their memory source' (777). In addition, there was no statistically significant difference between the groups that were explicitly asked to try to remember the information. Reflecting on the experiment in 2013, Sparrow and Chatman conclude that this result 'suggests this is not a conscious decision people are making' (276), which is consistent with previous findings of Wegner et al. regarding the roles that couples had established but were not aware of.

Another key point of discussion in their 2013 paper was the differences between the particular affordances of search engines as transactive resources and other kinds of transactive memory. In particular, they focused on the process whereby individuals do not remember a piece of information but can remember where this information can be found. Sparrow and Chatman's findings were that

> when we gave people highly memorable trivia ('An ostrich's eye is bigger than its brain') and very unmemorable places the information they were typing would be

stored (things), they tended to remember one or the other. If they remembered the trivia itself, they did not remember where to find it and vice versa. And aside from remembering neither, they were most likely to remember where to find the information. (276)

Highly memorable trivia was, in fact, less memorable than the generically interchangeable folder names, such as 'FACTS, DATA, INFO, NAMES, ITEMS, or POINTS [capitalization used in the original study]' (2011). Sparrow and Chatman (2013) highlight how this kind of memory practice has deep historical roots, but that, given the ubiquity of search engine access, particularly its increasing access on mobile devices, prioritizing where information might be found over the information itself may be much more useful. Sparrow and Chatman also challenge the belief that such behaviours have a negative impact on memory, arguing for three beneficial aspects drawn from their findings. First, they argue that when individuals 'repeatedly visit similar sources of information that arise from online searches' the resulting information may be 'better learned in the long run' but also that individuals 'will selectively learn the information that is relevant in that informational context' (277). Second, they reflect on a related study to their 2011 experiment, outlined earlier, which gave participants a problem-solving activity. They found that in comparing the participants who thought the information was erased with the participants who were informed that it would be accessible, the latter group recalled fewer pieces of information but were better at solving problems.

> Participants who memorized the details, who believed the problem would be inaccessible to them later, did in fact recall more details. But they solved fewer problems. In addition, across conditions, the number of details remembered negatively predicted the number of insight problems successfully solved. This evidence suggests that offloading the remembering of details onto the Internet as a transactive memory partner will in fact aid creative problem solving. (278)

This conclusion provides more nuance to the popular, alarmist claims that search engine ubiquity negatively impacts memory. Finally, Sparrow and Chatman reflect on a very specific aspect of web search engine access: choosing a result. Evidence from their studies demonstrated that when participants selected a search engine query result, their sense of agency and control increased. This was the case even when participants either chose the top results, or their 'choice' actually led to an unrelated result. They found that the more agency participants felt they had exercised in finding a piece of information, the more inclined they were to be critical of that information. Which, as they argue, 'is pretty much the opposite of what most people believe, which is that we, especially if we are children, believe everything we read online without question' (280). It is significant that the structure of search engine enquiry forces users to make a choice, which distinguishes it from other modes of transactive memory. In forms of transactive memory that rely on other individuals, the recalled information is not necessarily scrutinized by the apparent self-doubt directed at search engine results. Sparrow and Chatman argue that 'Because it feels like we are in charge of our web searches, even if we are not as agentic as we believe, the lack of transparency, paradoxically according to our preliminary research on agency and evaluation, results in web users being more critical in the evaluation of what they read online' (281). None of the authors have published any more substantial findings on the relationship between perceived agency and critical scrutiny since 2013; therefore, the findings of these preliminary studies should not be overstated or taken to directly reflect contemporary digital practices. The final chapter of this book, which highlights the extent to which fake news stories are shared by individuals, provides significant evidence of individuals being extremely uncritical of sources. These opposite conclusions most likely evidence the difficulties inherent in defining what *being critical* means. The aforementioned studies ignore the affective or emotional component of evaluation, which is difficult to measure experimentally but is likely a significant factor in the sharing of misinformation and fake news, particularly in the context of the 2016 US presidential election.

Kinds of recall from extended minds to transactive memory

Although no literature disputes the methodology or results of Sparrow et al. and Wegner et al., some have been critical of the interpretative structures used to draw their conclusions. Bryce Huebner's 2016 review of transactive memory, in which he also includes Andy Clark and David Chalmers' extended mind thesis of 1998 and subsequent literature, draws out the theoretical factors involved in making claims that the internet could be used as a site of memory or cognition. Huebner agrees that there is a 'broad and expanding consensus that we often exploit the physical and social structure of our world when we expect that the information we need will be available when we look for it again' (49). However, Huebner argues that defining such activities as memory requires a specific attitude towards the relationship between cognition, agency, and memory. In particular, Huebner draws from John Sutton's *Philosophy and Memory Traces: Descartes to Connectionism* a history of philosophical accounts of memory, which argues that attitudes towards memory can be categorized into two camps: archival and constructive. Huebner sides with the constructivists and contends that memories represent 'skeletal representations' (59) with which individuals flesh out with tacit and general knowledge at the time of remembering. Huebner draws on a body of research concerning false memories and eye-witness accounts, which address the frequency of false details that an individual supposedly remembers. Important to Huebner's argument is that these false memories are often unrelated to the event and, therefore, have been constructed rather than misremembered. The archival approach, which sees memories as far more substantial and static, does not account for such evidence. Huebner argues that using a constructive approach

> to transactive memory systems suggests that Wegner was wrong to claim that our frequent and pervasive use of Google searches and iPhones is sufficient to establish the existence of novel transactive memory systems. In these cases,

the flow of information is unidirectional and exploitative. In these cases, we find a person who uses the informational resources and who encounters information that is structured in a way that makes it a target for exploitation. But exploitation is the paradigmatic relation that obtains between a person and the tools that she uses. (64)

A hypothesis that Huebner mentions in passing, but that is key later in this chapter, is that the increasing use of technology such as Google and smartphones might predispose individuals to model their approach to memory as 'archival' as this 'sits comfortably with an everyday understanding about how digital computers work' (56–7). Therefore, when trying to define the fundamental qualities of the mind we look to our most ubiquitous or naturalized technologies to provide us with models of how individuals make memories. Douwe Draaisma argues in *Metaphors of Memory: A History of Ideas about the Mind* that the line between metaphor and usage is significantly blurred:

artificial memories have not only supported, relived and occasionally replaced natural memory, but they have also shaped our views of remembering and forgetting. Over the centuries memory aids provided the terms and concepts with which we have reflected on our own memory. We have 'impressions', as if memory were a block of sealing-wax into which a signet ring is pressed. Some events are 'etched' on our memory, as if the memory itself were a surface for engraving upon. What we wish to retain we have to 'imprint'; what we have forgotten is 'erased'. We say of people with an exceptionally powerful visual recall . . . that they have a 'photographic memory' [and therefore our] views of the operations of memory are fuelled by the procedures and techniques we have invented for the preservation and reproduction of information. (3)

Draaisma argues that these metaphors are not simply used as models, which come and go, but as structures that have caused historical effects on how we conceive of the mind and consequently the technologies and practices that continue to shift such a definition. More than just descriptions or abstractions, metaphors and our self-conception of the mind change how we think and act. Historically, the rejection of so-called *artificial memory* always relies on a metaphorical conception of *natural memory* modelled on pre-existing technologies.

Technologies are formed as consequences of social attitudes towards cognition and memory and, in turn, shape those attitudes as they become socially embedded. Huebner's contention is that the use of search engines and smartphones as memory prostheses has encouraged the perspective that these activities replicate a model of the mind, that a hard drive memory – measured in gigabytes – might be comparable to human recollection. If this seems overly simplistic – the kind of thinking that only *other people* do – then we should interrogate our own biases further. It is likely that, even if our own conception of the mind is more complex, it relies upon metaphor and analogy. When Draaisma goes on to say that 'The history of memory is a little like a tour of the depositories of a technology museum' (3), he is not arguing that similarities of expression exist but that technologies, metaphors, and practices are deeply enmeshed. Arguing whether or not search engines represent a form of transactive memory depends on a particular definition of memory, which itself is based upon the attitudes and practices informed by ubiquitous computing. However, with this cautionary perspective in mind, I contend that Huebner's definition of search engine use as 'unidirectional and exploitative' (64) is not an accurate portrayal of how search engines function.

First, as outlined in Chapter 1, Google uses search behaviour data to refine and change its results for future users. Every enquiry alters Google's interpretations of words and relationships between sources on the web. The way that user data actively shapes future search experience provides the basis for considering search engine interactions as constituting transactional memory. Second, considering the everyday practices that are intertwined with search engines evidences a kind of conversational structure, rather than search engines acting as mute storehouses of information that either contain the right answer or not. As Jutta Haider and Olof Sundin eloquently put it:

> Due to the ubiquity of search and search engines in parallel with their invisibility, online searching has melted into myriads of social practices. . . . We are gardening, preparing dinner, doing homework, taking care of our health, and search is often enmeshed in these practices. (142)

To properly consider the role of search engines in these everyday practices, it is important to highlight not only the final page of results or outcome of the search but also the process of searching itself. This encompasses the way a user's attitudes and expectations shape what they consider a worthwhile search, based on their previous experiences. Each interaction with a search engine changes these expectations and tacit reliance, in a similar way to how Wegner et al. considered the cognitive interdependence between long-term couples described earlier. It is not necessary to argue that all searches constitute forms of transactive memory but simply that they have this potential, which can be seen in a wide variety of everyday situations.

How do such examples relate to the initial discourse around transactive memory practices? Academic evidence, including the studies of Sparrow et al., shows that thinking we will have access to a piece of information in the future changes our ability to remember it, even if we actively try to remember it. The memories we make and the ways we have access to them depend on the people around us, the strength of our social bonds, and the technologies we are surrounded by. In this way, thinking and remembering are two aspects of the same activity. Considering the mind as deeply reliant on our social and material environment allows us to see that Google is not the first technology to change or challenge how we think or remember. Crucially, even psychological studies that try to standardize and filter out individual factors (such as personality, mood, and emotion) assert that there is no normal way that we 'naturally' think and remember. In the context of transactive memory, I argue that yes, Google impacts cognition and recall in a demonstrable capacity. But I only argue this on the condition that we abandon the idea of a natural or normal function of the mind that exists prior to technology. Doing so requires the rethinking of distinctions between natural/technological, organic/artificial, and original/altered. To support such an argument, I turn now to the birth of the written word. Such an example shows how technologies have altered our minds for millennia and highlights the impact of a particular technological explosion that mirrors the influence of Google's search engine in numerous ways.

Technosocial memory practices from oral culture to digital literacy

Many media theorists have drawn parallels between the shift from orality to literacy and the contemporary shift from a print-based literacy to a form of electronic literacy. Building on the work of Walter Ong,[2] which demonstrated the impact of writing and the alphabetic system upon oral cultures, theorists have claimed that the digital era produces a comparably fundamental shift. Gregory Ulmer, for instance, coined the neologism 'Electracy' (43) (a portmanteau of electronic literacy) building on Derrida's Grammatology to enhance Ong's notion of second orality 'as a hybrid sharing features of literate and oral practices, to be understood as intervening between and mediating the apparatuses of orality and literacy, distinct from its chronological position as coming after literacy' (Ulmer 163–4). In particular, in focusing on the mediation, Ulmer reinforces a Foucauldian emphasis on Electracy as a discourse tied to the institutions that gain power in a digitally mediated space. Another theorist who draws a parallel between the birth of literacy and digital communication is Friedrich Kittler, who emphasizes the open-ended nature of alphabetic encoding, writing that 'for a second time in history, a universal medium of binary numbers is able to encode, to transmit and to store whatever will happen, from writing or counting to imagining or sounding' ('Towards an Ontology of Media' 2–3). Even though the emphasis shifts between theorists, there is a consistency in the claim that discursive epistemes are underpinned by social and technological reciprocity. It is useful to outline the impact that literacy had on oral culture for three reasons. First, such a shift can provide a historical grounding to claims about current technologies such as Google and their effects on language and communication. Second, such a discussion provides a way to outline the epistemological underpinnings regarding the philosophy of memory, through the opposing views of Plato and Aristotle, which will be invaluable for a discussion of the current functions of search engines as memory protheses. Finally, the narrative of literacy leads directly into an important historical precedent for current search engines, the set of memory techniques known as the *Ars*

---

[2]Ong's work relies on the research of Eric Havelock (see *Preface to Plato* 1963), Albert Lord (see *The Singer of Tales* 1960), and Milman Parry (see *L'épithète Traditionnelle Dans Homère: Essai Sur Un Problème De Style Homérique* 1928).

Memoria, which will be discussed later on in this chapter as an historical example that mirrors Google's aims, rhetoric, and influence.

Walter J. Ong's *Orality and Literacy: The Technologizing of the Word* (1982) proposes the argument that literacy marks a significant, if not the first, form of technology that fundamentally alters the way in which humans think. Before entering into greater detail of Ong's line of argument, particularly concerning memory, one aspect should be outlined first. That is, for Ong, literacy fundamentally changes the way people think, and once someone has learned the ability to write they cannot return to their previous cognitive system.[3]

A central example for Ong is that of preliterate texts, known more commonly as oral literature,[4] such as the Homeric epics. In referencing Milman Parry's ground-breaking study of Homeric poetry published in 1928 as *L'Epithete traditionelle dans Homere* (in English: *The Making of Homeric Verse*), Ong states that 'Parry's discovery might be put this way: virtually every distinctive feature of Homeric poetry is due to the economy enforced on it by oral methods of composition' (21). Its form and content are enmeshed in a fundamental way. Ong describes how oral texts can never, due to their medium-specific nature, be reproduced in exactly the same way. Nor can they follow a linear structure of written texts. It is not that oral texts *fail* to be linear but instead that exact sequence has no relevance to oral texts, as Ong explains:

> The singer is not conveying 'information' in our ordinary sense of 'a pipe-line transfer' of data from singer to listener. Basically, the singer is remembering in a curiously public way – remembering not a memorized text, for there is no such thing, nor any verbatim succession of words, but the themes and formulas that he has heard other singers sing. He remembers these always differently, as rhapsodized or stitched together in his own way on this particular occasion for this particular audience. (145–6)

For oral poets, recall represents an awareness of fluid relationships. This covers a range of skills from the knowledge of the length and mutability of stock phases used to complete the metre of each phrase, for instance, dactylic hexameter, up to a macro understanding of themes and tales that might lead into others or create possibility. To use Ong's

---

[3]This was the findings of fieldwork by Milman Parry and Albert Lord, who studied the Serbo-Croat bards of 1930s' Yugoslavia, concluding that once oral poets learned literacy, they lost their ability to compose oral poetry. However, 'it has now been shown that oral traditions, or 'orature,' can interact with literacy in a number of different ways, and they are not necessarily driven out as soon as literacy arrives; in Somalia, for example, oral poets have been able to continue their oral compositions even after acquiring literacy' (Emily Wilson, 12). Rather than invalidating Ong's claims, such evidence further critiques the idea of a *natural* or *non-technologized mind.*

[4]It should be noted that Ong fervently rejects the term 'oral literature' due to the retroactive use of the word 'literature,' which characterizes certain structures and features that rely upon writing, which are exactly what oral texts *can never* be.

terminology, this knowledge develops from interpersonal experience embedded in the human lifeworld. There is not a set of principles taught by oral poets or a correct way that a text should flow but an understanding of context, prior experience of manipulations, and open-ended appreciation of memory as praxis. This understanding of how oral texts functioned also applied to everyday experience. As Havelock asserts, 'in the Greek situation, during the non-literate epoch, . . . the gulf between poetic and prosaic could not subsist to the degree it does with us. The whole memory of a people was poetised, and this exercised a constant control over the ways in which they expressed themselves in casual speech' (134). Oral texts cannot be judged as isolated high-art objects that lie outside of common experience. As Havelock explains, 'Poetry was not "literature" but a political and social necessity. It was not an art form, nor a creation of the private imagination, but an encyclopaedia maintained by co-operative effort on the part of the "best Greek polities"' (125).

When there is no way to store complex assertions or ideas, communication is needed. To communicate ideas in an oral culture is to keep them alive. This is why oral texts are such a key part of oral culture, as they are repositories of knowledge, experience, and heritage. But in the case of new ideas, the bar of entry into a tradition of collective memory is set very high. New thoughts are harder to work through, as Ong argues:

> even with a listener to stimulate and ground your thought, the bits and pieces of your thought cannot be preserved in jotted notes. How could you ever call back to mind what you had so laboriously worked out? The only answer is: think memorable thoughts. In a primary oral culture, to solve effectively the problem of retaining and retrieving carefully articulated thought, you have to do your thinking in mnemonic patterns, shaped for ready oral recurrence. Your thought must come into being in heavily rhythmic, balanced patterns, in repetitions, or antitheses, in alliterations and assonances, in epithetic or other formulary expressions, in standard thematic settings (the assembly, the meal, the duel, the 'hero's helper', and so on), in proverbs which are constantly heard by everyone and so that they come to mind readily and which themselves are patterned for retention and ready recall, or in other mnemonic form. Serious thought is intertwined with memory systems. (34)

The key phrase here is 'think memorable thoughts' (34). As Ong explains, even if types of thought *could* be developed without these mnemonic structures, there would be no benefit for oral speakers as they would disappear, both in their own minds and within the community. Thought must be placed into these formulaic patterns in order to exist. Proverbs and expressions such as '"Red in the morning, the sailor's warning; red in the night, the sailor's delight" . . . are not occasional [in oral culture]. They are incessant. They form the substance of thought itself. Thought in any extended form is impossible without them, for it consists in them' (35). This example leads to Ong's key distinction between orality and literacy. The invention of the written word for Ong and his peers opens up this rigidity. However, this rigidity is a reflection of media-specific characteristics; literacy provides its own formal restrictions and affordances. The shift from print-based literacy to digital literacy also provides its own set of structures. Ong's description that those in oral cultures had to 'think memorable thoughts' (34) maps clearly onto what we would describe as search engine expertise. As established in Chapter 1, formulating an effective search engine query is not a process of properly formulating a traditional question; rather, it is a process of iterating citations of language in which their answer might be written. To search effectively is to have a deep awareness of the language patterns of the source a user wishes to find. Those theorists, Ulmer, Kittler, and others, who argue that digital literacy is a fundamental shift generally describe such a process as one in which distinctions are broken down under the structure of programming. As Kittler articulates it:

> The general digitization of channels and information erases the difference among individual media. Sound and image, voice and text are reduced to surface effects, known to consumers as interface. . . . Inside the computers themselves everything becomes a number, quantity without image, sound or voice. . . . With numbers, nothing is impossible. . . . Instead of wiring people and technologies, absolute knowledge will run as an endless loop. (*Gramophone, Film, Typewriter* 1–2)

Kittler makes an important point about the tendency of the digital to absorb other media. However, in my view, this accentuates, rather than dulls, the characteristics of different media and nowhere is this clearer than when using Google's search engine. A Google search does not simply query an index of text specifically written for web pages. Google's index is filled with raw text and semantic metadata drawn from Google Books, Google Maps, Google Images, Google Shopping, YouTube, and elsewhere. Formulating a query is a process of orientating a word or phrase towards a particular type of media. A version of Ong's 'think memorable thoughts' (34) is in operation with query formulation when a user adopts the dialect to suit their frame of reference. This is not to say that all users are explicitly thinking through the framing of their queries so that they follow how they might be phrased in a book rather than a blog. One of the lessons to be learned from Ong is that individuals in an oral culture need not be aware of the epistemological constraints that they are under in order to be affected by them.

The legacy of naturalized technologies

In the last chapter, Meno's paradox was outlined in the context of how people can form questions about subjects of which they are ignorant to demonstrate the inherent paradox at the heart of enquiry. However, Plato's Socrates proposes a model of thought, anamnesis, in which Meno's statement is not paradoxical. Socrates outlines the basis of anamnesis in the following way:

> As the soul is immortal, has been born often, and has seen all things here and in the underworld, there is nothing which it has not learned; so it is in no way

surprising that it can recollect the things it knew before, both about virtue and other things. As the whole of nature is akin, and the soul has learned everything, nothing prevents a man, after recalling one thing only – a process men call learning – discovering everything else for himself, if he is brave and does not tire of the search, for searching and learning are, as a whole, recollection. We must, therefore, not believe that debater's argument, for it would make us idle, and fainthearted men like to hear it, whereas my argument makes them energetic and keen on the search. ('Meno' 81d)

The idea of an immortal soul does not originate with Socrates. Many pre-Socratics, Pythagoras in particular, believed in similar versions of transmigration, and this accounts for the matter-of-fact way in which Socrates introduces the immortality of the soul. Developing the idea that there is knowledge that transcends individual bodily experience and carries over from life to life, Plato argues for the idea of knowledge as finite as well as objectively structured. This, in turn, relates to Plato's more general concept of ideal forms: the idea that every worldly experience is a mere shadow of a more fundamental abstract concept. Plato's theory of learning as recollection privileges the universal over the particular and downgrades the importance of sensory experience. This attitude is not unique to Plato; the notion of an unchanging world is a key part of pre-Socratic thought, particularly in the thought of Parmenides, for example. The Greek word for truth ἀλήθεια (*aletheia*) translates literally as 'unforgetting' (Scanlan 30). Each life does not provide us with new knowledge but instead opportunities to rediscover the unconcealed or unremembered. However, although the word is used by early Greeks and translates the same, the meaning infused by oral thinking was very different from that of Plato's Socrates. As demonstrated earlier, Homeric thought embodies and can represent oral tradition and its unique thought structures. Christopher Long describes:

> In Homer, truth [ἀλήθεια] grows out of and remains ultimately concerned with the concrete lived experience of human being-with-one-another. From its beginnings, truth has always lived in and from interhuman being-together, even if already at an early age truth begins to stretch itself out toward the world of things. . . . Truth itself does not originally appear as a relation between humans and things; rather, it emerges in dialogue between humans and it announces itself often in the form of a question. . . . [T]hus for early Greeks, truth was at first neither a matter of the mind's relation to nature nor a property of mental representations, but an urgent question bound up with human being-together. (26–8)

Long argues that in Homeric poetry *aletheia* was particularly used in moments of conversation or questioning. In particular, it is used often in personal testimony when another character did not directly witness an event. We can then see how, in translation, *aletheia* might have the same meaning as 'unforgetting' (Scanlan 30) to the Homeric Greeks who predate Plato. Truth in an oral culture, as demonstrated earlier, is established *between* persons. Phrases and proverbs stabilize ideas in the minds of people and between them through communication, but they can never gain a truth outside of the people who have remembered such phrases. Therefore 'unforgetting' to an oral culture refers to an action that, to a modern reader, appears rather literal and therefore less profound than Plato's version; such an attitude demonstrates the influence of a literate bias.

Ong's assertion that people in an oral culture had to 'think memorable thoughts' (34) should highlight that the link between the memorable and the thinkable does not exist today in the same way. In a profound sense, the forgotten in an oral culture is something that ceases to exist. That which cannot be remembered, then, is something that can never exist, or in other words, something that cannot be true. This is very different from Plato's view that all knowledge exists at all times, just elsewhere (in the ideal realm). For Plato 'unforgetting' represents the relationship between an individual (in their many lives) and a wider nonhuman existence. In Plato, the philosophical groundwork of memory shifts from one within community (or, in fact, that which *constitutes* community) to one that is individualistic and aims towards objectivity. Such a shift, argue Havelock and Ong, is due to Plato's indebtedness to literacy. His version of *aletheia*, as well as the fundamental basis of his thought more generally, is due to his technologized mind: his interiority of the written word. It is this, as well as his critique of writing, that we turn to now.

Truth and knowledge for Plato

One of Plato's dialogues that recurs throughout the academic literature concerning technology is 'Phaedrus'. The dialogue principally concerns rhetoric and oration, but it is the final section that philosophers of technology have most frequently addressed. It is in this section that Plato's Socrates recites a story concerning the birth of writing in ancient Egypt. He tells of how Theuth, the god of writing, measuring, and calculation, presents these and other arts to the king of the gods Thamus as gifts for the people of Egypt. Concerning writing Theuth states: 'O King, here is something that, once learned, will make the Egyptians wiser and will improve their memory; I have discovered a potion for memory and for wisdom' ('Phaedrus' 274e). However, Thamus rejects such claims and replies that writing

will introduce forgetfulness into the soul of those who learn it: they will not practice using their memory because they will put their trust in writing, which is external and depends on signs that belong to others, instead of trying to remember from the inside, completely on their own. You have not discovered a potion for remembering, but for reminding; you provide your students with the appearance of wisdom, not with its reality. Your invention will enable them to hear many things without being properly taught, and they will imagine that they have come to know much while for the most part they will know nothing. And they will be difficult to get along with, since they will merely appear to be wise instead of really being so. (275b)

Socrates continues to list the faults of writing, arguing that like paintings written words 'stand there as if they are alive, but if anyone asks them anything, they remain most solemnly silent' and 'signify just that very same thing forever' (275e). Due to this repetition of the same, writing, when 'faulted and attacked unfairly, [will] always need[] its father's support; alone, it can neither defend itself nor come to its own support' (275e).

In summary, Socrates' criticisms are as follows. First, true knowledge can never be outside the mind; like a second-order version of the Cave metaphor, external knowledge will only be a shadow of a truer reality that exists in the mind. Therefore, the difference between written memory and memory within the mind is a difference of *kind* rather than of degree. Second, the illusion of real knowledge, created by writing, will cause ignorance. People will not only become lazy – a moral judgement is clear here – but also their minds will become less capable. Third, the combination of these two factors will produce individuals who are 'difficult to get along with' (275b): bluffing know-it-alls. It is clear that Socrates does not believe in shortcuts to knowledge, in the same section of the dialogue he uses a metaphor of a farmer planting his seeds at the wrong time of year and expecting a harvest in seven days. True knowledge is acquired slowly, and those who have spent sufficient time developing their expertise should be respected. This links to the fourth aspect of Socrates' critique. The written text cannot explain or rephrase itself. Compared with the communication between two interlocutors, this can lead to a text not functioning successfully, not truly getting the intended point across; in addition, a text can bluff: a clever-sounding statement can be written by a fool. This distinction between appearance and truth troubles Socrates and is due to Plato's philosophy of ideal forms. Earthly knowledge is a shadow of objective truth; the human mind mirrors (imperfectly) the realm of forms. Socrates argues that the only true medium for knowledge is the 'living, breathing discourse of the man who knows' (276a) as 'It is a discourse that is written down, with knowledge, in the soul of the listener; it can defend itself, and it knows for whom it should speak and for whom it should remain silent' (276a). The centrality of the soul relies on the previous discussion regarding anamnesis, which suggests that although the external lives of people are temporary and change, the soul has seen everything already in its correct configuration. This is reinforced at the end of the dialogue in which Socrates prays aloud before he and Phaedrus return to the city: 'O dear Pan and all the other gods of this place, grant that I may be beautiful inside. Let all my external possessions be in friendly harmony with what is within. May I consider the wise man rich. As for gold, let me have as much as a moderate man could bear and carry with him' (279c). The interior and exterior should reflect one another. The mind should be as beautiful as the external phenomena it represents, and the external aspects of Socrates should be a reflection of who he is internally. Considering wisdom as wealth uses external metaphors to describe internal realities and foregrounds the notion that wisdom should concern only that which is portable and internalized. Gold stored elsewhere cannot be used at the market, just as knowledge written on paper, stored at home, cannot be described as *your* knowledge.

Aristotle's sensory approach

Aristotle's theory of memory is different from Plato's in two significant ways. First, Aristotle attends to the sensory world, and second, he distinguishes between memory and recollection. The first difference is a reaction to the kind of thinking which underlies Plato's aviary metaphor: 'The metaphor of the storehouse raises the question of how something can be found in the memory which has not entered through the doors of the senses' (Draaisma 28). Aristotle argues that if we think of the mind as acquiring memories that can be recalled, then these must have developed out of our sensory experiences. Rather than seeing ideas as emerging into the mind through anamnesis,

> Abstractions and imprints of objects of perception must be part of the same continuum of perception and cognition. Aristotle asserts that unless one perceived things one would not learn or understand anything (DA III, 8 432a 3f). When one contemplates in the most abstract way one does so from an image. (Coleman 22)

Aristotle's teaching that sensible phenomena were the source of higher concepts became one of the founding principles of the Peripatetic school, fed into Scholasticism, and was rearticulated by Thomas Aquinas as the axiom: 'nothing is in the intellect that was not first in the senses' (2).

Instead of abstractions providing the model for imperfect copies, Aristotle's theory of memory posits an opposite approach. Individual sensory impressions are arranged, extrapolated, and generalized in order to form abstract concepts: the individual images remembered are much more important to Aristotle than to Plato. This brings us to Aristotle's conception of recollection. Recollection for Aristotle is not like natural involuntary memory; it is, rather, 'a sort of reasoning process, described as a search, starting from one's thinking of something rather than from one's perceiving it. It is a deliberate undertaking. It involved a succession of associated ideas [and] is a deliberate, self-motivated, autonomous process of search' (Coleman 23). For Aristotle, the act of recollection is creative. Rather than separating thought, memory, and creativity, recollection demonstrates how our memories are not stable and fixed: our ideas are not a selection of individual birds sitting in an aviary. This idea prioritizes individual agency and celebrates context. In describing recollection as active, Aristotle starts to detail the way in which students might better use their own memories. Aristotle describes the process of recollection as 'starting in thought from a present incident, we follow the trail in order, beginning from something similar, or contrary, or closely connected' (Aristotle, *De Memoria* 451b 18ff, qtd. in Carruthers, *Book of Memory* 79). However, this trail is not automatic and therefore forms the difference between memory and recollection; recollection is a process that can be improved, adapted, and trained. Aristotle's method of recollection was based on *place* (*apo topon*[5]). As Coleman describes:

---

[5]Literally: 'from their sites' (see Lynch 74).

People are therefore thought to recollect, . . . starting from places, and from such a starting point they associate to a succession of other things until they achieve the terminus of their search . . . recollection is the process of finding the next or neighbouring item in a series it derives from the habit of *thinking* of 'things' in a certain order. (245)

Such a description of active and situational recollection directly describes the kind of search behaviours highlighted by Haider and Sundin earlier in this chapter. Although, as stated earlier, Google's overall project – 'to organize the world's information and make it universally accessible and useful' ('Google: About Us') – deploys a certain Platonic logic, the process of *using* Google is much more in line with how Aristotle describes the process of recollection. The kind of memory that was useful in that example was the interrelated links between concepts. The more links a person can make between individual memories, the more useful each memory becomes. For a user of Google's search engine, expertise relies on explicit search tactics and implicitly held expectations regarding the underlying structure of the web, as presented by Google. In addition, the increasing shift towards a predominantly mobile use of Google, on phones and tablets, intensifies the importance of context and place in memory. Users more commonly engage with Google in a range of environmental contexts; the image of a user sitting down at a desk in a hermetically sealed office space, or that cyberspace might exist in a realm divorced from the everyday, is becoming less realistic. However, at the heart of Google's project lies a tension between the philosophical views of knowledge, cognition, and memory proposed by Plato and Aristotle. Such a tension has existed within technosocial practices before; a notable example is that of the *Ars Memoria*, a technique for organizing memory and knowledge, used for two thousand years.

The *Ars Memoria* is a set of memory methods or techniques that originally exemplified an Aristotelian conception of memory, although it predates him by some time. The narrative of the *Ars Memoria* is pertinent to the discussion of Google's philosophical underpinning for a number of reasons; one of these is that, although it initially embodied an Aristotelian attitude towards memory, the practice was taken over by those who wished to demonstrate that through a rigorous application, such a system could exemplify Neoplatonic objectivity. This narrative, which runs roughly from 400 BCE to 1600 CE (see Yates, *The Art of Memory* 29–31), maps onto Google's present situation, as described earlier, in which Google envisions that a complete enough aggregation of personal data (search strategies, book scans, street-view photography, and other methods) could, through its AI, construct an objective collection of knowledge. In essence, Google's epistemological framework aims to transform the Aristotelian into the Neoplatonic; the history of the *Ars Memoria* demonstrates that this path has been trodden before.

Technosocial memory before Google: *The Ars Memoria*

The *Ars Memoria* is the longest tradition of memory training in Western culture. Its use runs from 400 BCE to around 1600 CE, when its formalized practices declined, although it is still the basis of modern mnemotechnics, or memory techniques, used in contemporary memory competitions for recalling decks of cards, strings of binary digits, and random historical dates.[6] Today, displays of prodigious recall may appear disconnected from the practicalities of everyday life; the history of the *Ars Memoria* demonstrates how such an attitude is historically contingent and that attitudes towards memory and cognition develop in concert with technology. The techniques deployed by contemporary memory athletes represent variations on the set of methods outlined in three texts from antiquity: 'Rhetorica ad Herennium',[7] 'Cicero's *De oratore*', and 'Quintilian's *Institutio Oratoria*' (Carruthers, *Book of Memory* 89–90). A central element of the *Ars Memoria*[8] is the skill of building *memory palaces*, a contemporary term many readers may be familiar with. The essentials of the technique consist of calling to mind a real place, often a building, and populating it with images that represent things to remember. The images are made to stick in the memory through a number of sub-techniques where the idea to be memorized is transformed through *personal* association into an image that is often bizarre, lewd, sexual, or comical. The *Ars Memoria* requires explicitly personal associations which are often unexplainable but which inexplicably stick in that individual's mind. A person then mentally traverses the backdrop, or palace, in a consistent order to fix and recall associations between the images that can represent anything at all. One of the main benefits of the *Ars Memoria* is that it can be used to memorize any order of magnitude, from broad conceptual ideas such as political theory or moral arguments down to exact words memorized verbatim. In coordination with the precise principles of moving around the mental space in an exact order, this allowed practitioners to memorize whole books and even whole libraries. Even in situations where scholars had direct access to written texts, they would often memorize them using the *Ars Memoria* so that, in a pre-index or page number age, they could access any part of the library at will and quote from it verbatim. We have evidence of such activities, via historian Mary Carruthers, from the compositions of William of Ockham and John Wyclif. Carruthers details how even though both men were exiled and removed from their libraries, they continued to write as if their libraries were still available to them. While in exile in Munich in the fourteenth century, Ockham is quoted to have told a pupil of his, that 'Complete knowledge about [the subjects of learning] should be patiently extracted and solidly built up' (qtd. in Carruthers, 'How to Make a Composition: Memory-Craft in Antiquity and in the Middle Ages' 25). Indeed, Carruthers comments:

---

[6]See Joshua Foer's *Moonwalking with Einstein* (2012) for a popular account of contemporary memory competitions.

[7]Although this text was accredited to Cicero for many years, modern scholarship has since moved away from this interpretation.

[8]Although repetitive, I continue to use the title *Ars Memoria* throughout this section rather than attempting to replace it for synonyms such as system, method, technique, technology, and so on as the *Ars Memoria* is of interest *because* it cannot be adequately described as any of those.

Ockham did not educate himself with the idea that he might one day be exiled, nor as a student was he the captive of provincial schools, and, in consequence, deprived of ready access to libraries. His whole scholarly life until 1330 was spent in the greatest of European universities, his circle the most academic of the time. And still it is clear that he read to memorize and that in composing he drew extensively on the resources of his mental library. ('How to Make' 25)

In addition, Wyclif's works while in exile in Lutterworth 'are filled with quotations from a variety of sources, too many to possibly be accounted for by the few books he had available' (25). These men were not exceptions, the use of the *Ars Memoria* within scholarly circles was widespread. As Frances Yates, who provided the first and most detailed study of the *Ars Memoria* in modern scholarship, describes: 'Whilst it is important to recognise that the classical art is based on workable mnemotechnic principles it may be misleading to dismiss it with the label "mnemotechnics"' (Yates, *The Art of Memory* 4) for it might make 'this very mysterious subject seem simpler than it is' (4). Memory in historical periods without mass printing or even access to resources such as paper for personal note-taking takes on a moral role intensely related to one's humanity. An example of this discussed already is Plato's metaphor of knowledge as gold that can only be of use if one carries it with them at all times. The *Ars Memoria* was not simply a set of tools or techniques but a way of structuring the mind, one which developed an individual's sense of identity and moral worth. Through its widespread adoption, the *Ars Memoria* established collective memory, norms of thought, and a construction of community and its societal character.

The principles of the *Ars Memoria* foreground a distinction between the memory *of* things and associative links *between* things; doing so emphasized the order and relationships between groups of things, particularly those relationships important for a specific individual. Yes, the *Ars Memoria* not only enabled the memory of whole books and entire libraries but also encoded the perspectives and attitudes that particular scholars took to these works. The texts held in the mind were not ordered within a system that aimed towards neutrality, such as an encyclopaedia or a library cataloguing system, but depended on the sensory life experiences of an individual tied up with their personal reflections and dispositions. As Carruthers states: 'The true force of memory lay in recollection or *memoria*, which was analysed as a variety of investigation, the investigation and recreation of knowledge. . . . To achieve this power, people educated themselves by building mental libraries' ('How to Make' 16). This reference to recollection refers to Aristotle's schema, in which recollection is highlighted as creative use of memory rather than rote recall. As highlighted earlier, Aristotle's view of knowledge is tied inextricably to sensory inputs. Therefore, the mechanics of the *Ars Memoria* embody Aristotle's conception of knowledge. The memory palaces of the *Ars Memoria* cannot be shared. Many people memorized the same ideas, texts, or objects, but the *Ars Memoria* only set forth a system of guidelines. Each individual use of the *Ars Memoria* would have been different: personal, emotional, practical, and subjective in numerous ways. When knowledge is so intertwined with a person's personality and sense of self, it is easy to see how this could be tied to moral development. Even though the *Ars Memoria* is not widely used in our contemporary period, much of this moralizing can be seen in the anxieties over search engine use and the ubiquity of using technologies to remember and cognize.

The science and magic of search

After its use in Ancient Greece, the *Ars Memoria* was passed down into Roman culture and survived the sacking of Rome exclusively in the *Ad Herennium,* the other two texts becoming temporarily lost. Its techniques were then detailed and expanded upon by 'Albertus Magnus and Thomas Aquinas [who] certainly knew no other source for the rules' (Yates, *The Art of Memory* 57) than the *Ad Herennium.* The influence of the *Ars Memoria* continued as it was adopted into the practice of the Dominican Order. This adoption was significant for the *Ars Memoria*'s later direction into mysticism, which derived – at least in part – from Magnus's influence within the Dominican Order. However, the most important figure in the history of the *Ars* Memoria and its relevance for understanding search engines is Ramon Llull. Llull was a thirteenth-century Neoplatonist and a member of the Franciscan Order. He spent much of his life on religious missions in North Africa to convert Muslims to Christianity. His importance to this study is due to his creation of a system developed throughout his life and formalized as the *Ars generalis ultima* (*The Ultimate General Art*)[9] (1305). Llull's *Art* was 'a complex system, using semi-mechanical techniques combined with symbolic notation and combinatory diagrams' (Llull 1), which would organize knowledge, solve questions, and most importantly would be applicable 'to all fields of knowledge' (1). Jorge Luis Borges's often-cited 1939 essay 'The Total Library', which, as the title suggests, describes the idea of absolute knowledge – not just of known topics, but a collection of all permutations of alphanumeric symbols – draws on Theodor Wolff's suggestion that the idea of a total library 'is a derivation from, or a parody of, Ramon Llull's thinking machine' (Borges 214). Drawing a line of influence from the intellectual activities of antiquity towards Google's contemporary mission, Llull's ideas represent a historical convergence of two key discourses. Importantly, Llull takes the *Ars Memoria*, a profoundly Aristotelian method, and reinterprets it along Neoplatonist lines. Llull's *Art* was not just a system of personal recollection but a way of ordering everything in the universe and, in a religious sense, organizing an ultimate truth. In particular, Llull wanted to create a machine, which, knowing the truth of the universe, would convert Muslims to Christianity by providing unequivocal evidence for his religious outlook. In doing so, he wanted to turn disagreements between people of different languages and faiths into objective calculations and logical deductions.

In *Google and the Culture of Search*, Hillis et al. argue that Llull represents an important forerunner of Google's lofty and technodeterministic ambitions. They describe

---

[9]Henceforth referred to as Llull's *Art.*

Llull's *Art* as 'an early attempt to do something now quite widespread – substitute technology conceived as somehow free of human ideologies for the inherently messy and unpredictable ideological political sphere' (93). Hillis et al. also relate Llull's work to the tale of the Tower of Babel, an origin story in which humans who all speak the same language are punished by God for their collective understanding and are forced to speak different languages to prevent an intelligence that might rival their creator. Llull's *Art* not only tries to reconfigure Christian arguments in logical terms but attempts to place all aspects of faith into one language, that of logic: 'his stated goal is the production of "truth", his aim that the *Ars* serve to advance the arrival of something akin to an information monoculture ("one language, one belief, one faith")' (93). The underpinning of this idea is that language creates cultural differences and, in turn, creates inaccurate interpretations of truth. The belief that linguistic variation simply represents a problem that can be overcome by programming is held by many at Google's headquarters and embodied in a number of their products that judge cultural differences as quantifiable and calculate their relevance numerically.[10] Llull's ambitions were never realized as, in 1314, after persistent efforts to disprove the tenets of Islam using the *Art*, he was stoned by a group of Muslims in the city of Bougie and died the following year. Nevertheless, Llull's influence on the development of the *Ars Memoria* continued long after his death and, in part, led to its ultimate decline. This particular shift parallels our current moment. Llull considered the *Ars Memoria* to be neutral, objective, and logical, while using it to enforce ideological oppression of anyone from a different cultural background. Llull harassed the citizens of Bougie and dismissed their grievances by claiming that the results of his technology represented a truth beyond his own personal attitudes. The following chapters of this book highlight multiple ways that Google's technology has produced discrimination and reinforced cultural oppression. The inner workings of search engines are clearly very different to the *Ars Memoria,* but the defence of such automated prejudice and algorithmic intolerance is often made along exactly the same lines.

Yates, in her history of the *Ars Memoria*, argues that 'Though the Art of Lull [*sic*][11] in one of its aspects can be called an art of memory, it must be strongly emphasised that there are the most radical differences between it and the classical art in almost every respect' (*The Art of Memory* 175). Nonetheless, Yates does consider it a defining step of the *Ars Memoria* as it transforms into the version known in the Renaissance. Three main differences exist between Llull's *Art* and the classical *Ars Memoria*. First, as mentioned earlier, Llull draws on a Platonic rather than Aristotelian structure, via Augustine, and as such, 'claims to know first causes' (175). Second, Llull's *Art* does not use images, as the *Ars Memoria* does, and instead 'Lull designates the concepts used in his art by a letter notation, which introduces an almost algebraic or scientifically abstract note into Lullism' (176). The use of images, as described earlier, is too focused on an individual's own memories and emotions to be objective in the Platonic sense.

---

[10]See Chapter 4 for more detail.

[11]Yates uses this spelling throughout so [*sic*] applies to any of her spellings of Llull as Lull.

Third, instead of a static memory palace filled with objects 'Lull introduces movement into memory' (176). Llull built physical machinery with revolving concentric circles, which attempted to reconstruct the motions of the psyche and thought as dynamic and responsive. In this way, 'The first art [*Ars Memoria*] is the more artistic, but the second [Llull's *Art*] is the more scientific' (176). The principles of the *Ars Memoria* dictated how to use Llull's external machine rather than as a system that provided answers itself. The Llullian *Art* was 'intended to construct a world of phantasms supposed to express approximately the realities of intelligible order of which our world is but a distant and imperfect copy' (Couliano 34). In doing so Llull's *Art* presents an attempt at functional Platonism. The earlier classical *Ars Memoria* required an individual to construct their own memory palaces and relied on personal associations at every stage. In this way, the things remembered would be situated within a deeper understanding developed by that practitioner. Success relied on the personal associations of each individual. In particular, lewd and sexual images worked exceptionally well, much to the distaste of the religious orders in which the *Ars Memoria* was used. For this reason, many of the image prompts would stay private and relate deeply to that person's individual fixations, both conscious and unconscious. In contrast, the Llullian *Art* used structures and principles that were hidden from its users. A technical engineer, Llull for example, would answer people's questions using the machine in combination with their mnemonic patterning to produce an answer, which the questioner would be told to accept as *the truth*. Therefore, the answers provided by the *Art* aimed towards objectivity while remaining mysterious. The opacity was a key tenet of why the answers should be trusted, and there was no room for dissent or critique. The contemporary way we would describe Llull's machine is as a black box, that is, a mechanism that takes an informational input and provides an output in the form of an instruction, evaluation, or action that might be visible but which depends on an inner working that is hidden. Although, as outlined in the Introduction, the myth of the black box is a mischaracterization of the unknowns in search engine design, there is a power in mystery that often translates into confidence. If everyone knew the exact calculations that led to a search engine's top result, its authority might well be diminished. If, instead of obligatory blind faith, users could see that a small tweak to the mathematical evaluations buries that same top search result to page 200 of Google's results, its rankings would be revealed as arbitrary. The business model of Google and many other technology companies relies upon obfuscation and ignorance. The behemoths of Silicon Valley are intensely invested in a particular kind of mysticism. It is a mysticism built upon modern science, mathematics, and logical reasoning, but one that is profoundly indebted to the tradition of which Llull is a part.

The point at which Llull's process of mysterious objectivity fully developed into mysticism lies with Giordano Bruno in the sixteenth century. Bruno draws on the classical *Ars Memoria* as well as the mechanics of Llull's system. Yates explains:

> Just as he [Bruno] converts the images of the classical art of memory into magical images of the stars to be used for reaching the celestial world, so the Lullian wheels are turned into 'practical Cabala', or conjuring for reaching the demons, or angels,

beyond the stars. . . . Bruno's brilliant achievement in finding a way of combining the classical art of memory with Lullism thus rested on an extreme 'occultising' of both the classical art and of Lullism. (*The Art of Memory* 211)

Bruno turned the Classical elements of the *Ars Memoria* and Llull's dialectical answering of questions into a system designed to summon demons and contact the dead. As strange as it might seem to a modern reader, there were strong links between mysticism and science in the Renaissance period, particularly among the followers of Hermeticism, of which Bruno was a practitioner. Our contemporary definition of magic is that which is unaccountable, whereas, in the Renaissance, magic could be systematic, practical, experimental, and relied on the use of numbers in a way that draws it close to the scientific method:

> Thus the Renaissance magic was turning towards number as a possible key to operations, and the subsequent history of man's achievements in applied science has shown that number is indeed a master-key, or one of the master-keys, to operations by which the forces of the cosmos are made to work in man's service. (Yates, *Giordano Bruno and the Hermetic Tradition* 147)

Within this context, Bruno links to the scientific tradition and the history of computing. Bruno aimed not only to describe the world with perfect clarity but also to control it and use the underlying structures of number to tame and shape it. In addition, Bruno was one of the pioneers who argued in support of a heliocentric universe, which was part of the reason he was burned at the stake for heresy in 1600. An emphasis on his view regarding the solar system rather than the occult has led to his legacy as a martyr of science: standing up for truth against religious superstitions, a position that is defended in Hilary Gatti's *Giordano Bruno and Renaissance Science: Broken Lives and Organizational Power*. As Gatti argues, 'Bruno remains so much a figure of the modern world [and] was among those who guaranteed the future of the newly emerging sciences' (19). However, an alternative account, exemplified by Yates's critical biography, suggests that Bruno was involved at a much deeper level with Hermeticism and it was this affiliation that the Catholic Church objected to. Rather than describing these two aspects as disconnected, Yates argues that Bruno's scientific method develops from his Hermetic beliefs, in particular, his defence of heliocentrism:

> He patronises Copernicus for having understood his theory only as a mathematician, whereas he (Bruno) has seen its more profound religious and magical meanings. . . . Bruno's use of Copernicanism shows most strikingly how shifting and uncertain were the borders between genuine science and Hermeticism in the Renaissance. (*Giordano Bruno and the Hermetic Tradition* 155)

For Bruno, a scientific or mathematic understanding of the world developed out of the magical aspects of the universe. Far from using science as a tool for debunking mystical or magical experiences, as is commonly held in the popular discourse today, science acted as an extension of existing spiritual beliefs.

This belief of a structured universe that can be understood and controlled by the occult provides a key with which to understand our current rhetoric of modern computing. The ways in which contemporary technologies are often discussed, Google in particular, echo the ties between mysticism and the scientific tradition. John Durham Peters devotes a whole chapter of his *The Marvelous Clouds: Toward a Philosophy of Elemental Media* to 'God and Google' and due to its resonance with the arguments of this chapter is useful to quote at length:

> Sergey Brin famously suggested that 'the perfect search engine would be the mind of God'. This half boast, half ambition puts Google into a long line of hieratic readers of the sky, and has a nice a touch of Kabbalah as well. It shows Google's membership in a distinguished family of religious media. Google's project is to build a temple to meet the sky, anchor remembrance, and serve as a canon of all knowledge. Its aim is nothing less than a metamedium that would be the guide for the perplexed of cyberspace. Google inherits the narrative of the priestly class that discerns the universe, renders order out of chaos, answers our entreaties, and invites us to take part in mantic acts of divination. From the unaccountably vast array of possibles Google provides the answer you seek, rather like fortunetelling and haruspicy or the priests who stood in the *templum* watching the sky for augurs and omens. Google is a clergy defined by its control over the means of inscription and retrieval – as clergies and priesthoods always have been. Google also picks up on the long romance that mathematicians have had with infinite and ultimate things. 'The respective interpretation of the symbols 0 and 1 in the system of logic are *Nothing* and *Universe*', wrote George Boole. This was a variant of Leibniz's view of digital notation as shuttling between creation and the abyss – indeed, in the space where Google likes to shuttle. (333–4)

In addition to the rhetoric of Google's grand ambitions and the all-encompassing nature of its products, the company also employ many individuals who preach the principles of technospiritualism. The futurist Ray Kurzweil, personally hired by Google founder Larry Page in 2012, is Google's head of engineering, as well as a prominent figurehead in the transhumanist community, and a leading exponent of the concept of the Singularity. The Singularity is a technodeterministic and mystical notion that Kurzweil describes as a coming event that he sees as the fifth (out of six) epoch of history, in which the 'universe wakes up' (33). This is the point at which, self-training artificial intelligence will accelerate towards Godlike understanding, surpass humans in every way, and gain the power to shape the universe towards complete order as it sees fit. In many ways, the period between Bruno and the present day, rather than separated by a Kuhnian paradigm shift concerning science and mysticism, might instead be considered as a brief hiatus, a momentary lapse of faith. It is this period that I now turn, to complete this narrative of technosocial memory practices from orality to the present.

Treating the mind as technology: Bacon, Hooke, and modern psychology

The decline of the *Ars Memoria* provides a compelling argument against the technodeterminism of Kurzweil and others. It is a practice that, as Ioan Couliano articulates, 'worked so well that it is astonishing that it fell into disuse in the seventeenth century' (181). The *Ars Memoria* was the most powerful mode of memory, as well as being one of the most dominant, for at least two thousand years.[12] Furthermore, considering that a form of the *Ars Memoria* is used by contemporary mental athletes, these techniques have remained effective despite the wider social changes. For this reason, rather than describing its decline as a lack of usefulness, many critics have attributed its downfall to the iconoclastic activities of the Reformation and Counter-Reformation. As Couliano states, 'The results of this iconoclasm are tremendous if we consider the controversies about the Art of Memory aroused by Bruno in England: ultimately, the Reformation leads to a total censorship of the imaginary, since phantasms are none other than idols conceived by the inner sense' (193). In this way, the disappearance of the *Ars Memoria* represents one of history's most extreme rejections of artificial memory. The lush ornament of the mnemonic techniques, combined with its increasingly occult uses, caused the techniques to be deemed irreligious. These social changes came to influence the development of modern science. Modern science aimed to strip away the subjective, qualitative, and unmeasurable aspects of memory. Designing experimental methods to study and evaluate memory pushed out the aspects that had been so essential for the two thousand years under the influence of the *Ars Memoria*.

An early significant text that outlined and defended the principles of science was Francis Bacon's *Novum Organon* (1620), which was a direct attack on Aristotelian methods, its title being an explicit reference to Aristotle's *Organon*. In laying the foundations for what would become known as the scientific method, Bacon outlined his perspective that subjectivity and sensory experience are inferior to logic and abstract reasoning. Such a perspective not only became highly influential within the experimental sciences but was a framework to structure the interconnected technosocial institutions of the university, curriculum, library, and encyclopaedia. Bacon's approach provided distinctions that can still be seen today, he made:

memory, reason and imagination the basis of his scheme, allocating history to the category 'memory', . . . philosophy to 'reason', and poetry to 'imagination'. An examination of the curriculum, the library and the encyclopaedia in the seventeenth and eighteenth centuries suggests that Bacon's reclassification was the most successful of the various attempts made at this time. (Burke 99)

---

[12]This is based on the time between its first known description *Dialexeis* c. 400 BCE (see Yates *The Art of Memory* 29–31) and Bruno's death in 1600.

This perspective established clear divisions between memory and cognition, sensory experience and external information, and individual memory and collective knowledge. Bacon's scheme came to dominate through its organizing principles self-reinforcing within the network of technosocial institutions of the curriculum, the library, and encyclopaedia. One of its particular influences was on the discipline of history, which alongside the emerging discipline of psychology provided many of the norms and expectations that dictate the kinds of questions that get asked about technologies like Google's search engine.

As John Scanlan outlines, the 'hold of the Baconian view of memory and history began to loosen with the rise of historicism (the professionalization of history as a discipline) in the nineteenth century, but still held enough sway that it could be a target of attack for . . . R. G. Collingwood' (32) in the 1930s. There are significant elements of Baconism still with us today. Although history as a discipline has moved away from Bacon's model, it has done so in a manner that also moves further away from the classical conception, as outlined earlier. The professionalization of history, in Collingwood's view, prioritizes external evidence. Documents and artefacts are better than personal memory and better still are disembodied data. As Bill Schwartz argues, this conception of history is linked to a modern understanding of the past: 'The intellectual practice of history, in its emergent forms was in part devised as a counter to the wayward, indeterminate workings of modern memory. . . . In this scheme of things, subjective time, the time of the everyday and of the self, memory included, could appear *only* as dysfunctional' (43). This increasing prioritization of the impersonal created ripples throughout the early efforts of psychology to measure cognition and memory, from the work of Robert Hooke (1635–1703), an original fellow of the Royal Society and their curator of experiments, to Hermann Ebbinghaus (1850–1909) and beyond. These modes of memory certainly influence the initial studies regarding transactive memory highlighted earlier. Although the studies treat memory in various nuanced ways, as shared and situational for example, the methodologies of Sparrow et al. focus on the recall of trivia and various impersonal facts. That these results can then be measured and tallied numerically for comparison speaks to this historical lineage. The *Ars Memoria* shows us that these divisions are new and are not at all natural. Search engines are embedded into everyday life and rely on highly personal search patterns in which subjectivity and affect are key parts of the process of remembering. The notion that memory can be intertwined with technology in personal and emotional ways is not a new idea nor would it strike a practitioner of the *Ars Memoria* as a strange idea at any point in its two-thousand-year history. But the dominant popular outlook of today is influenced by the early attitudes of the scientific method and separates the interconnectedness of people and technology, individuals and society, and facts and feelings. These false divisions are themselves embodied and re-inscribed within Google's development of the Knowledge Graph, in which individual web pages, written by different people in various contexts, are aggregated into a table of static facts that belong to no one and that are framed as objective and correct. The Knowledge Graph hides the messiness and complexities of how we come to these facts and reinforces the view that knowledge simply requires collecting from out in the world, rather than relying upon production and maintenance.[13]

The history of science and its relationship to psychology is important for three reasons: it helps us to understand Google's epistemological outlook that underlies the development of their products, the wider non-academic discourse and attitudes towards memory held by users and critics in the popular press, and it underpins the research questions, methods, and approaches of contemporary researchers such as Sparrow et al. who I introduced at the start of this chapter. The very first scientific studies of memory carried out by Hooke and his contemporaries aimed to quantify memory. This attitude opened up the possibility of studying the capacities and limits of human memory, as a generalizable category. As Draaisma explains:

> Hooke saw the ideas stored in the brain as truly material entities, and in so doing, introduced a new type of question into theories of memory. For what is the *rate* at which these ideas are formed? What is the *number* of ideas in the memory? And what is their *location*? (57)

Hooke began to ask questions of mental storage, many of which resonate with contemporary digital metaphors for cognition; he concluded that attributing memories a size and location meant that the brain must have a limited capacity. Furthermore, if memory is reliant on attention, then individuals can only make so many memories per day, and by extrapolation, per lifetime. This kind of thinking maintains that memory is quantifiable and, even before computing, can be used to describe anything in terms of its size in the mind. Draaisma notes that Hooke is perhaps the first thinker in a tradition of attempts to calculate the capacity of the mind in quantifiable terms (after many calculations Hooke settles on an estimate that by one hundred years of age an individual might make four million memories). In reference to Hooke's calculations, Draaisma notes that

> anyone tempted to make sarcastic observations on [Hooke's] laborious calculations regarding the number of stored ideas in the warehouse should look at the way in which the number of 'bits' in the human brain is currently calculated. The author of an article giving an overview of the field, Landauer,[14] uses a method essentially identical to Hooke's. . . . Landauer arrives at an 'input rate to long term memory' of 1.2 bits per second, where Hooke's estimate had been one mental image per second. For someone aged seventy that gives a total of 1.8 billion bits. (61)

---

[13]For more information on how Google aggregates information with Knowledge Graph, see Amit Singhal 'Introducing the Knowledge Graph.'

[14]See Thomas Landauer's 'How Much Do People Remember? Some Estimates of the Quantity of Learned Information in Long-Term Memory' (1986).

Hooke's work acts as a catalyst for a certain narrative that sees human memory as computable. Such a framework went on to influence classifications of short-term and long-term memory by experimental psychologist Hermann Ebbinghaus (1850–1909) and, in turn, established the kinds of methodologies for studying memory. The quantifications of memory research valued disembodied charts, tables, and graphs over qualitative values of memory that the *Ars Memoria* depends on. The kinds of technologies borne out of these methods then became the dominant metaphors for describing the mind and its processes of remembering, which further naturalized such metaphors. For example, in outlining the differences between short- and long-term memory, neurobiologist Steven Rose refers to the influence of the information or computer model for cognitive science. Rose writes that:

> The temporal distinction between short-term and long-term memory, the evidence that short-term memory is labile and easily disrupted, whereas long-term memory seems relatively protected, suggested that it must depend on some structural remodelling of the patterns of neural connections within the brain, engraving memory in the brain in a manner analogous to that of inscribing a magnetic trace on a tape or a CD that can subsequently be replayed, invoking the original material. The seductive metaphorical power of computer 'memory' has been influential in shaping thought on this question. (202)

The metaphor of electronic storage and the stability of memory is rather misleading. As Rose goes on to argue, long-term memory has proven in many experiments to lack the stability that it is often credited with. In a review of the history of psychology of cognition, Sutton et al. describe several critiques of the established modal model – the term used for distinguishing long- and short-term memory – stating:

> Despite the widespread adoption of this basic computational view of memory, recent theory and research recognize that memory is more complicated than this model might suggest, especially memory of personal experiences or emotional material. . . . [M]emory has broader functions, such as maintaining our sense of self, regulating emotion, motivating and directing future action, and helping us to promote and maintain relationships with others. (213)

Such an attitude draws us back around to the psychological studies with which this chapter opened, in which the methodologies for studying transactive memory prioritized the memorization of discrete facts that could be stored either in folders on a computer or in the mind. This connection should not be viewed as a dismissal of the work of Sparrow et al. and other transactive memory researchers, instead, it should illustrate that technological metaphors are intertwined at all levels with attempts to describe the mind and its functions. It also foregrounds the way in which available methodologies shape the kinds of behaviour that can be studied. The previous quotation by Sutton et al. regarding the broader functions of memory articulates the expansive nature of memory in oral culture, the use of the *Ars Memoria*, and the role of search engines in the present day.

Conclusion

A survey of the way various thinkers have conceptualized and studied memory shows that we cannot conceive memory without technological metaphor, however implicit or seemingly invisible. In turn, a historical assessment shows that fears regarding the technologization of memory have been with us a long time, especially at times when the *natural memory* that is held up by critics is itself already technologized. If we think back to Carr's question, 'Is Google Making Us Stupid?' with which I opened this chapter, we can see how erroneously formulated such a claim is, how blind it is to our history, and naïve it is in postulating a natural, normal, or non-technological form of memory.

In many ways, contemporary approaches to memory have come full circle in emphasizing many of the bodily, affective, and subjective aspects of memory that would fit with an Aristotelian worldview actualized in the practice of the *Ars Memoria*. However, the contemporary tension between this outlook and the computational one held by many technologists mirrors the tension between a Platonic and Aristotelian epistemology and its conceptual ground that has been trodden many times before. It is important to remember that our evaluative frameworks are always determined by our conceptual map of the world. The initial experimental studies that investigated Google's potential impact on our ability to remember provide some useful conclusions. However, they also demonstrate an approach in which memory can be considered separately from technology and social practices, which speaks to a specific cultural orientation that has not been consistent throughout time.

Because Google Search is a multipurpose and open-ended technology, it is responsible for organizing our personal narratives, the attitudes and norms of a wider culture we are situated within, while at the same time attempting to provide objective truths in the form of the Knowledge Graph. Google Search overlaps these various domains that we often treat separately. The history of the *Ars Memoria* and the rise of modern science shows that the interconnectedness of subjective personal recollection with wider norms through technology has been the dominant mode of conceiving of memory, cognition, and a sense of self. Just because Google's ancestry stretches back thousands of years and has many nodes of its family tree, does not mean that it is exempt from its present social responsibilities. We need to take seriously the conclusions of transactive memory studies, even if their interpretive frameworks are bound by implicit computational attitudes. For example, if individuals have a tendency to forget information that they think they will have access to later on, even if they actively try to remember it, the consequences for informed debate are paramount. Users do not have control over how Google will structure the search results of the future, nor significant agency to push back and edit the biases we might find in its algorithmic worldview. Therefore, being sceptical of alarmist claims does not mean that the contemporary situation does not present us with important challenges.

This chapter highlights that memory has always been described and defined through technological metaphor, whether that of a wax tablet, an aviary, a codex, a photograph, magnetic tape, a CD, or a hard drive. It is clear that conceptualizing something so abstract as memory depends on allegory and scholarship of new technology needs to acknowledge these underlying attitudes. Such self-enquiry should also be required of management executives, engineers, and marketing teams of technology companies that perpetuate similarly inherited conceptual frameworks. Although Google often presents itself as free from ideology, its attitudes towards, and effects on, memory are situated in a long philosophical tradition. Due to its global influence, Google have the power to dictate the kind of behaviours that search engines enable; should this ubiquitous technology be optimized for recall or discovery, should it direct users towards ideas and issues that fit neatly into their existing epistemological landscapes, or should they provide heterogeneous perspectives? These vital questions will be further explored throughout the following chapters. In particular, Chapter 3 explores Google's Autocomplete tool as a kind of collective memory, and Chapter 4 returns to the distinctions between Platonic and Aristotelian thought, in order to better understand the values of particular search engine results.

CHAPTER 3
AUTOCOMPLETE
STEREOTYPES, BIASES, AND DESIGNED DISCRIMINATION

Introduction

Search engines represent and amplify particular voices. Google's emphasis of some voices over others is not neutral and clearly represents specific biases. Chapter 1 outlined these influences in the formulation of queries and Chapter 2 showed how the process of enquiry has been socially and technologically situated throughout history. However, some key features set search engines apart from their technosocial ancestors. One of the most influential of these features is Google's tool, originally known as Google Suggest, later as Google Autosuggest, and today as Google Autocomplete.[1] The tool comprises a drop-down menu of suggestions from which a user can select to either complete or replace their initial query stem when using Google Search (see Figures 7 and 10 for replacements and Figures 8 and 9 for completions).

Google Autocomplete is a compulsory tool that activates whenever a user begins their query; all other search engines such as Bing, Yahoo!, Baidu, Yandex, and even meta-search engines, such as Dogpile, have copied the functionality of Autocomplete in their search engine interfaces. In fact, it has become a staple for all web-based search (for example, search bars on the websites of Facebook, YouTube, Wikipedia, LinkedIn, and Twitter, all of which provide input-text suggestion tools, visually similar to Google Autocomplete's drop-down box, which was the first of its kind). Autocomplete has, therefore, entered a realm of ubiquity throughout various digital contexts and the notion of suggestions and corrections as we type into a search box is now expected as the default. But where do these voices come from? Whose voices are they? And what kinds of values do they support? The answers to these questions are complex and reveal Autocomplete to be one of the most ethically problematic parts of the search process.

Autocomplete attracts the largest public interest of all the aspects of Google Search; however, it has received minimal academic attention. Google provides very little information about how the tool functions, which has led to a number of misconceptions to be established and perpetuated through public and academic discourses. These misconceptions are important to address not only because Autocomplete is a widely

---

[1]For simplicity, the designation Autocomplete will be used throughout this chapter, although this phrasing is anachronistic at times.

Figure 7 An example of an Autocomplete suggestion completing the stem [Google and I are so close we fi]. Search performed on 15 November 2015.

Figure 8 An example of Autocomplete suggestions for the stem [when will]. Search performed on 9 August 2017.

used tool on the web, but also because judging Google's liability for Autocomplete's suggestions should be tied to an accurate picture of how they are generated. Currently, academic discourse focuses on two topics: reviews of court rulings regarding Google's legal liability for specific defamatory suggestions for individuals and the wider societal impact of Autocomplete's perpetuation of stereotypes. What often gets ignored is how these Autocomplete suggestions come to exist in the first place: this key question is addressed in this chapter.

Figure 9 An example of Autocomplete suggestions for the stem [when will]. Search performed on 16 April 2021, during the global Covid-19 pandemic and United Kingdom lockdown.

The structure of this chapter is as follows. First, I survey the significant public interest in Autocomplete within popular culture and the disproportionately minimal academic attention. Second, this chapter details the ethical issues produced by Autocomplete's suggestions, particularly those that reify and perpetuate negative stereotypes. Many of the existing criticisms of Autocomplete's stereotypical and offensive suggestions make the assumption that these reflect the most popular search queries actually searched by users. Consequently, Google is blamed for highlighting the existing prejudices of its users. However, this chapter aims to redirect this discourse regarding Google's ethical responsibilities. I present evidence that suggests that Google's application of machine learning within Autocomplete may in fact be *producing* stereotypical suggestions that do not stem from actual user queries, a possibility that has not been explored elsewhere. Third, I explore the origins and development of the tool while analysing information provided by Google regarding how Autocomplete operates. This enables me to show its relationship to Google's ideological changes throughout the past fifteen years; in particular, I focus on its shift away from traditional probability programming towards a greater dependence on neural network machine learning initiatives, which supports

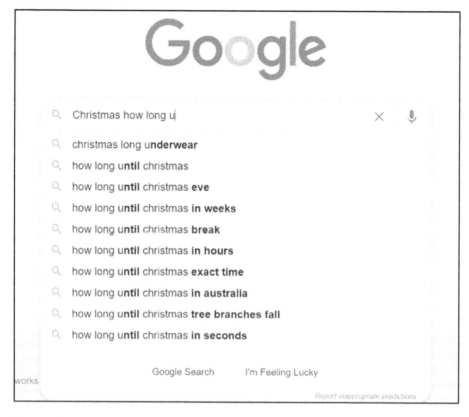

Figure 10 An example of Autocomplete suggestion that rephrases a stem to more accurately reflect grammatical word order. Suggesting a replacement of [Christmas how long u] for [how long until christmas]. Search performed on 15 April 2021.

my claims regarding Autocomplete's production of stereotypes. I specifically focus on RankBrain – Autocomplete's machine learning component – and how it constructs suggestions for queries. Finally, this chapter analyses the importance that speed plays in Autocomplete, particularly in regard to notions of play and critique within contemporary capitalism. I discuss the ideological relationship Autocomplete has to related Google projects, such as Google Instant, and its influence on Google Now, 'the feed' and Google Discover. During this discussion, I reflect on the broader ethical implications of tailored results and introduce Google's criterion of *relevance*, which is the primary focus of the following chapter.

The desire for a digital oracle

A key aspect of this chapter is that the public, the media, and academics have almost unanimously perpetuated a false understanding of what Autocomplete suggestions represent; it is erroneously repeated over and over that Autocomplete suggestions are a reflection of the most searched queries.[2] Such a claim has been reinforced by the lack of information released by Google about the tool. However, Google have never stated that the suggestions are based solely on the metric of search query volume. In fact, in 2020, Danny Sullivan, Google's official Public Liaison for Search, wrote in Google's developer blog: 'We don't just show the most common predictions overall. . . . Autocomplete is a complex time-saving feature that's not simply displaying the most common queries on a given topic.' This was a rare direct admission and I will discuss later in this chapter how Google benefits from the widespread misconception that Autocomplete suggestions purely represent search volume. Search volume is part of Autocomplete's algorithmic criteria, but throughout this chapter, I provide evidence that it is a much more minimal part that is usually assumed and, in some instances, may not feature at all in certain suggestions. Nevertheless, due to the widespread misconception that Google Autocomplete provides a direct reflection of query volume, it has gained a status as a kind of digital oracle that supposedly knows us better than we know ourselves.

Instances of Autocomplete's treatment as a digital oracle can be seen throughout popular culture. For example, board games such as *Weird Things Humans Search For* and *Autocomplete: The Game* and online games such as *Google Feud* and *idiots.win* replicate the structure of the television game show Family Feud in which players attempt to guess the most common responses to a question (see Figure 11). Contestants on the show are tasked with correctly reading the pulse of the wider population and games like *Google Feud* give the impression that Autocomplete suggestions are a way of simply expanding that sample size.

The attitude that Autocomplete suggestions represent the most widespread public opinions sparks great interest, particularly because many top suggestions are often strange. An example of this can be seen in numerous genres of YouTube videos, including *Wired* magazine's ongoing series 'Autocomplete Interviews', which consists of interviews with various celebrities, in which the questions asked are not devised by a human interviewer, instead, they are derived from Autocomplete suggestions associated with their name. The misunderstanding that these suggestions are a direct indication of search volume is perpetuated through their titles, which all follow the same formula such as 'Matt Damon & Julianne Moore Answer the Web's Most Searched Questions' (see Figure 12).[3]

---

[2]I present a number of examples throughout, but for examples of each type see the following: general journalism, Alex Hern's article for *The Guardian* 2016 'Google denies 'Tories are/Labour are' autocomplete 'conspiracy theories''; technology journalism, Sean Hollister 'Google promises to remove search suggestions that might seem political – even if they're true' *Verge* 2020; academic, Wang et al. 'Game of Missuggestions: Semantic Analysis of Search-Autocomplete Manipulations' 2018; industry resources, 'Google Suggest' entry in *Ryte Wiki Digital Marketing Encyclopedia*.

[3]In addition, Wired interviewed Google's Ben Gomes (VP, Search Engineering) and Chris Haire (Product Manager, Autocomplete) in their Autocomplete series in an episode titled: 'Google Search Team Answers the Web's Most Searched Questions.' At no point in the interview do they attempt to debunk the myth in the show's title that Autocomplete suggestions are a representation of the commonly searched questions. Later in this chapter, I argue that Google benefits from this misconception as it allows them to avoid their full ethical responsibility for suggestions. This episode is a perfect example of a situation in which Google could easily clarify how suggestions are generated for a large audience and choose not to do so.

Figure 11 A screenshot of *Google Feud* mid-game, in which the player is asked to guess the correct Autocomplete suggestions for the query [where can i buy human], designed by Justin Hook. Accessed 16 April 2021.

The format is clearly popular; the series has been running for over five years and – as of July 2022 – consists of 238 videos. However, such interest in Autocomplete queries is not simply related to celebrities; another genre of Autocomplete videos consists of vloggers simply reading out and reacting to queries suggested by Autocomplete, from their standard searching or through playing Google Feud or idiots.win. The ten most viewed videos of this type collectively have 98.6 million views on YouTube, as of 16 April 2021. The videos reflect the often bizarre nature of Autocomplete suggestions, with titles that recur around the question, 'what is wrong with humanity?' or 'I CAN'T BELIEVE PEOPLE GOOGLED THIS'.[4] This fascination develops from the misconception that Autocomplete reflects the kinds of questions people ask Google the most. While the direct link between queries and suggestions is unfounded, Autocomplete suggestions *are* an insight into the way that Google collects and organizes language. In this way, studying Autocomplete might not provide information on the queries of users but it

---

[4]Titles of videos by the channels 'DanAndPhilGAMES' and 'Unspeakable,' respectively. For other popular examples of the genre, see Markiplier's 'CAN'T STOP LAUGHING!! | Google Feud' and jacksepticeye's 'WHO SEARCHES THIS STUFF? | Google Feud #3.'

Figure 12 Stills from *Wired*'s 'Autocomplete Interviews'. Accessed 16 April 2021.

can illuminate many of Google's activities, from its Google Books scanning project to its increasing reliance on machine learning neural networks.

Autocomplete's minimal academic attention

Although Autocomplete is one of the most discussed aspects of search engines in public discourse, compared to other aspects of search engines, academic attention is relatively scarce. Autocomplete has been available as an experimental feature since 2004 and as a compulsory component of Google Search since 2008, after which it has become an unavoidable part of search engines. However, the existence of Autocomplete and its effects on how users search is often ignored or simply mentioned in passing. Academic publications that focus on Autocomplete typically fall into one of three distinct categories, each with relative limitations. First, legal scholars have addressed the legal precedents regarding whether or not Google is responsible for the Autocompleted queries and whether or not they are required by law to remove defamatory Autocomplete suggestions.[5] Such

---

[5]For examples, see 'Google's Autocomplete Function – Is Google a Publisher or Mere Technical Distributor? German Federal Supreme Court, Judgment of May 14, 2012 – Case No. Vi Zr 269/12 – Google Autocomplete' (Peifer), 'Search Engine Liability for Autocomplete Suggestions: Personality, Privacy and the Power of the Algorithm' (Karapapa and Borghi), 'Cache-22: The Fine Line Between Information and Defamation in Google's

research draws attention to the inconsistent rulings worldwide and the often anachronistic way that courts conceptualize automated suggestions. However, the focus and discussion are primarily on whether or not Google is liable and if certain Autocomplete suggestions can be removed, rather than the broader cultural and ethical questions raised. Second, scholars such as Safiya Noble, Paul Baker and Amanda Potts, and Alexandra Olteanu et al., have written powerfully about offensive and prejudiced content of Autocomplete suggestions. Their work provides a call-to-arms about the harmful reproduction of stereotypes that have been found within Autocomplete. I discuss their work in more detail later in this chapter, as it has much to add to wider critiques of Silicon Valley. However, much of this work does not attempt to address where these offensive stereotypes come from and often reproduce misconceptions about how Autocomplete suggestions are generated. As I evidence in this chapter, Google have been actively complicit in sustaining the fallacy that suggestions directly reflect popular searches, thus shifting the blame onto their users. Therefore, because Google have been more guarded about how Autocomplete works than other aspects of their search engine, I focus directly on how the tool operates to ground my critique. Finally, the third type of Autocomplete scholarship revolves around speculations regarding the content itself, which often raises important questions but is frequently detached from the technical aspects of its function. Examples of this include two chapters in König and Rasch's 2014 edited collection which address Autocomplete directly: Martina Mahnke and Emma Uprichard's 'Algorithming the Algorithm', and Mary E. Luka and Mél Hogan's 'Polluted and Predictive, in 133 Words'; significantly, both are listed as 'creative reflections'. This designation is important; all four authors listed are professional academics, either professors or graduate students, but they chose to frame their research as a series of creative provocations that shy away from attempting to provide robust or systematic conclusions.

Hogan and Luka, for example, collected Autocomplete suggestions for a list of 133 queries, chosen at random, over a four-year period; they highlight two [daughter is] and [boyfriend is]. In their discussion, they consider the different kinds of suggestions without trying to devise where the suggestions come from, whose voices they represent, and whether or not their examples are actually searched more than other queries. They write that:

> I think the words and the searches they suggest point to things people are searching out in private. Real questions. Real worries. It might show how fucked up we all are. What do you think? Look below at 'daughter is' – while the suggestions change a little over time, the sentiment remains the same. I find that it's the words that denote a relationship – daughter or boyfriend, for example – are the most deranged. People searching out answers about (and maybe on behalf of) others? Can Google suggestions become a way to suss out what others are experiencing? Is it where we go to feel normal, even if that normal is twisted? (242–3, including Table 2)

Autocomplete Function' (Popyer), 'Teaching Fairness to Artificial Intelligence: Existing and Novel Strategies Against Algorithmic Discrimination Under EU Law' (Hacker), and 'Speech Across Borders' (Daskal).

Table 2 Autocomplete suggestions collected by Hogan and Luka between 2010–2013.

2010	*2011*	*2012*	*2013*
daughter is:	**daughter is:**	**daughter is:**	**daughter is:**
overweight	mean	pregnant	pregnant
depressed	pregnant	depressed	calling ringtone
moving away	always cold	cutting herself	spanish
pregnant	constipated	spanish	an atheist
a bully	a bully	pregnant with dads child	sexting
mean	a loner	constipated	getting married
tired all the time	cutting herself	mean	depressed
calling ringtones	tired all the time	out of control	a brat
losing hair	overweight	disrespectful to	taller than me
a prostitute	calling ringtone	mother	a tomboy
		a brat	
boyfriend is:	**boyfriend is:**	**boyfriend is:**	**boyfriend is:**
depressed	distant	distant	depressed
distant	depressed	selfish	immature
ignoring me	selfish	a virgin	a virgin
selfish	sick	boring	a douchebag
insecure	ignoring me	depressed	boring
a virgin	cheap	a jerk	ignoring me
moving away	too big	sick	moving away
a jerk	gay	controlling	selfish
too big	boring	too clingy	distant
	mad at me	insecure	gay

Hogan and Luka's discussion touches on a wide range of issues concerning the relationship of individuals to technology. Their Autocomplete suggestions contain a variety of affects, similar to the kinds of decontextualized snippets of conversations one might overhear in public. However, as intriguing as their longitudinal sample is, their chapter provides no deeper insight into Autocomplete than the YouTube videos of celebrities and vloggers discussed earlier. Their chapter focuses on rhetorical questions regarding why people might search such queries; however, the way in which Autocomplete operates is untouched. Where, for example, is the suggestion '[daughter is pregnant with dads child]' (242) coming from? The authors assume that a large number of users are searching this query more than most other queries beginning [daughter is]. This chapter critiques that deceptively simple explanation; nevertheless, such an example highlights the importance of understanding how such results are generated. Without an understanding of *why* or *how* Autocomplete suggests the queries it does, any amount of collected Autocomplete suggestions can only be of limited value.

Therefore, having established both public use of Autocomplete and academic approaches to understanding it, this chapter represents a drawing together of the available evidence, to present the most probable description of how Autocomplete operates. In doing so, I propose a shift to the kinds of ethical standards that we hold Google to. Throughout, I will discuss the particular methodological challenges that all scholars face, regardless of disciplinary background, and the debates that make Autocomplete suggestions such a crucial area of study. In addition, such discussions emphasize how Google's tool is central to wider contemporary debates around representation and identity, legal freedoms of individuals and the press, normalization of behaviours and stereotypes, personalization, and how social attitudes and inequality can be exacerbated online.

The biases of autocomplete: Stereotypes and discrimination

Safiya Noble, in her 2018 work *Algorithms of Oppression*, is one of the key writers to document the range of offensive stereotypes found within Autocomplete suggestions. She highlights the racist set of suggestions collected in 2013 provided for the query [why are Black people so], including 'loud, lazy, rude' (20) and contrasts the deeply offensive differences between the suggestions for [why are Black women so] and [why are white women so]. These examples have since been quietly removed by Google and are one of the notable exceptions where Autocomplete now does not trigger. However, the importance of these examples goes beyond specific instances. As Noble states,

> What we know about Google's responses to racial stereotyping in its products is that it typically denies responsibility or intent to harm, but then it is able to 'tweak' or 'fix' these aberrations or 'glitches' in its systems. What we need to ask is why and how we get these stereotypes in the first place and what the attendant consequences of racial and gender stereotyping do in terms of public harm for people who are the targets of such misrepresentation. (82)

Building on Noble's important demand, this chapter aims at uncovering the 'why and how' of Autocomplete for exactly that reason. The difficulty is that the popular discourse sees Autocomplete as simply holding up a mirror to societal values. Noble contends that such an attitude takes too much of the blame away from Google. I agree and my later findings regarding Google's RankBrain machine learning provides new evidence that Google are even more responsible for the kinds of racism, sexism, and offensive suggestions of Autocomplete than is usually assumed.

An ethically important aspect is that the Autocomplete function cannot be turned off by individual users. Boaz Miller and Isaac Record describe the consequences of this problem in the following way: 'users' exposure to autosuggestions is involuntary. Users cannot type a search without encountering autosuggestions. Once seen, they cannot "unsee" the results' (1949). Therefore, a key consequence of involuntary exposure is that even 'initially disregarded associations sometimes transform into beliefs because humans are prone to source-monitoring errors: subjects mistake the original information source and may put more or less credence in the information than they would have given the correct source' (1949). It is, therefore, essential to pay serious attention to negative stereotyping and offensive associations presented within Autocomplete suggestions.

This is particularly the case if we feel we are immune to such automatic messaging or deny the potential impact on wider society. Our biases and attitudes towards the world are not simply the product of intentional thinking and evidence-based decision-making. To dismiss discriminatory suggestions as easily ignored or too outlandish to be believed is to wilfully ignore the effects that normalized stereotyping can have on society.

Google have a range of policies it uses to omit certain Autocomplete suggestions, which are listed on their page 'Google Search Help: Autocomplete Policies'. Instances predictably range from 'Violent or gory predictions' to 'Sexually explicit, vulgar, or profane predictions'. For the present context of stereotypes and discrimination, the most important omission policies are 'Hateful predictions against groups' and 'Sensitive and disparaging terms associated with named individuals'. Google Autocomplete's list of omissions, in which no suggestions are listed, are usually the result of public pressure: high-profile campaigns, in the case of groups and defamation court cases, in the case of named individuals. These omission policies might appear to be steps in an ethical direction; however, they represent Google's response of hiding, rather than addressing, the tool's underlying issues of bias and discrimination.

One of the earliest campaigns that focused on Autocomplete's suggestions took place in 2011 and aimed to 'sweeten up the Romanian image' (see Gurp 'Romanians are Smart') through collective action. The campaign was a reaction to the negative Autocomplete results for [Romanians are] (see Figure 13) and in an attempt to change the suggestions, users were urged to repeatedly search [Romanians are smart], with the hope that this would become the primary suggestion. The organization even set up a semi-automated system on their website that would repeatedly search [Romanians are smart] in a variety of languages. Although the campaign did not succeed in changing the suggestions, the publicity that it generated led to Google disabling suggestions for the query [Romanians are].

The most influential example of work that uses Autocomplete to highlight persistent misogynistic attitudes was a 2013 campaign by UN Women in association with Memac Ogilvy and Mather, Dubai, which concerns the Autocomplete suggestions associated with the word 'women'. The UN Women's advertising campaign used 'genuine Google searches to reveal the widespread prevalence of sexism and discrimination against women. Based on searches dated 9 March 2013, the ads expose negative sentiments ranging from stereotyping as well as outright denial of women's rights' (UN Women). The advertisements (see Figure 14) depicted the Autocomplete suggestions for the particular phrases entered: [women cannot], [women shouldn't], [women should], and [women need to] all of which portray highly sexist attitudes.

The UN Women campaign gained wide media attention and spawned a number of copycat campaigns for other issues, including examples relating to race, religion, and nationality that showed negative stereotyping (e.g., see Marc van Gurp's 'Google's Autocomplete' and 'The Shocking Answers'). One of the main issues of these kinds of campaigns is that, because they are focused on general nouns and collective identities, they only relate to the most noticeable instances of Autocomplete suggestions related to discrimination, which I refer to as *first-order stereotyping*. Later on in this chapter, I argue that these *first-order* examples are

Figure 13 Campaign poster for 'Romanians are smart' campaign. Credit: Kandia Dulce.

much less harmful and problematic than what I call *second-order stereotyping. Second-order stereotyping* for Google Autocomplete represent the kinds of biases that only become visible in aggregate, such as the fact that – on average – women's names result in more sexist suggestions than men's names, which on an individual scale may not be as apparent to users as the suggestions for a query stem such as [women are]. Google's approach of disabling suggestions for the specific query stems [women shouldn't] or [Jews are] only relates to a fraction of queries that might embody misogyny or anti-Semitism. In addition, Google's decision to hide rather than address these suggestions is one example of how they avoid taking responsibility. This is compounded by the fact that most of the campaigns perpetuate the misconception that Autocomplete suggestions represent

Figure 14 UN Women Campaign highlighting the Autocomplete suggestions for [Women shouldn't], including [have rights], [vote], [work] and [box] and Autococomplete suggestions for [women should], including [stay at home], [be slaves], [be in the kitchen], and [not speak in church]. See 'UN Women ad series reveals widespread sexism' 21 October 2013. Credit: UN Women and Memac Ogilvy & Mather, Dubai.

a direct reflection of search volume. Noble writes directly about these campaigns in the following way:

> The [UN] campaign suggests that search is a mirror of users' beliefs and that society still holds a variety of sexist ideas about women. What I find troubling is that the campaign also reinforces the idea that it is not the search engine that is the problem but, rather, the users of search engines who are. It suggests that what is most popular is simply what rises to the top of the search pile. While serving as an important and disturbing critique of sexist attitudes, the campaign fails to implicate the algorithms or search engines that drive certain results to the top. (15)

These results are morally outrageous and the question of responsibility is clear-cut: Google should be held accountable. The question of where these attitudes originate is much more complex and has yet to be answered conclusively. As discussed earlier, the main approach towards this question has been from a legal perspective. This stems from lawsuits in which individuals or corporations fight to have negative Autocomplete results removed for their name or company. Rather than focusing on where the sentiments derive or how they are produced, this legal approach explores questions of liability, freedom of speech, and the rights of specific individuals to have suggestions removed.

I do not aim to provide a full survey of the range of legal rulings on Autocomplete court cases as this has been done elsewhere.[6] However, a summary is that, worldwide, the rationale, procedure, and results of each case have been wildly various. This situation is put best by Stavroula Karapapa and Maurizio Borghi in their 2015 review of court cases regarding Autocomplete:

> Besides the fact that courts may reach different conclusions as to the liability of the search engine, the *logic* they follow in reaching a judicial outcome varies substantially to an extent that no solid judicial trend can be assumed. This is not only because laws protecting personality and corporate rights differ from jurisdiction to jurisdiction, and there are also variations on a case-by-case basis, but also because of the ambiguity as to whether algorithmically determined word combinations can actually bear a connotative meaning that could thereinafter result in legal implications. (263, emphasis mine)

The variety of outcomes signals how anachronistic and underdeveloped current conceptions of platforms, data, algorithms, and machine learning are in the eyes of the law. For example, in cases in the United States, Autocomplete suggestions have been successfully defended as protectable under the first amendment as the 'algorithm itself is written by humans and therefore embodies a human editorial judgement' (267). Whereas the French Supreme Court have followed the opposite rationale, dismissing cases regarding defamation because it was deemed that the 'word combinations generated by the Autocomplete function are not an expression of thought or intellectual reasoning, but a technical method to facilitate the search' (278). There is no agreed-upon definition of the kind of object Autocomplete suggestions are; such results are a complex interplay between automated technical systems, human-directed editorial engineering control, and the aggregation of vast numbers of linguistic texts: previous search queries and web content, both born-digital text and digitized language.

One of the most influential distinctions developed from the outcome of a 2014 case between the Spanish Data Protection Agency (AEPD) and Google Spain in the Court of Justice of the European Union (CJEU). The case found that each complaint should be viewed on a case-by-case basis and set the precedent for Google's inclusion of a 'report inappropriate predictions' link, mentioned earlier, that allows individual users to report specific suggestions that they considered inappropriate. In addition, the court extended the 'ground to request for removal to instances where Autocomplete suggestions do not need to convey a defamatory meaning or false factual information' (283). Therefore, since 'May 2014, EU citizens have been able to apply for search engine companies to remove search results [and Autocomplete suggestions containing] their name if the information is deemed to be irrelevant or in other ways inaccurate' (Lindsköld 768). It

---

[6]See Jennifer Daskal (2019), Philipp Hacker (2018), Elena Esposito (2017), Anne S. Y. Cheung (2015) and by Stavroula Karapapa and Maurizio Borghi (2015).

was from this case that the now infamous phrase *right to be forgotten* became a point of academic, legal, and public debate. However, it is up to Google to make decisions relating to 'report inappropriate predictions' requests; I evidence a specific example in the later section on *second-order stereotyping*, whereby multiple 'report . . .' requests for the same example were ignored by Google, which demonstrates why framing complaints around individual suggestions leads to broader ethical issues becoming ignored. In addition, sociologist Elena Esposito, argues that the result of successful *right to be forgotten* complaints use the word 'forgotten' in a misleading way, whereby an individual suggestion might not appear but the information is still being used by Google as 'data for a variety of secondary uses largely independent of the intent or the original context for which they were produced' (7–8). Given this, although Google results or Autocomplete suggestions might not point a user directly to web pages covered by legal rulings, they are far from forgotten and the data are still available for Google to use in other capacities. Therefore, even in successful legal rulings, the broader discriminatory associations presented in Autocomplete have not been addressed or curtailed.

Predicting and shaping user attitudes: The origins of Autocomplete

When addressing the ethical implications of technologies, it is vital to consider that there are always alternatives to our current norms. In this vein, it is important to note that Google Search did not always have a drop-down list of suggestions, nor was Autocomplete designed with the expectation that it would become one of the most central parts of the contemporary search engine experience. Google Search's Autocomplete tool was invented in 2004 by Google engineer Kevin Gibbs originally as an URL predictor to save time when typing a website address. This built on a much older convention of command-line completion that dates back to the 1960s and is still common today, whereby programmers use the tab key to complete coding strings used previously in the program. Rather than drawing from the previous fixed inputs of a single programmer, however, Gibbs' tool aimed to respond to the open-ended Google queries of all users. Gibbs' release statement introduces the new feature, which at that time was an optional tool, by focusing on two ideas, speed and discovery: 'We've found that Google Suggest not only makes it easier to type in your favourite searches (let's face it – we're all a little lazy), but also gives you a playground to explore what others are searching about, and learn about things you haven't dreamt of' (Gibbs). Autocomplete stayed as an optional 'labs' tool until 2008 when it became a compulsory part of Google Search. Autocomplete was originally introduced in a 2004 blog post, which used an anecdote in which one of the engineers working on the project has forgotten the artist of a particular song, which happens to be a song he wants to be played at his wedding. By typing in some of the lyrics [from this], Google's Autocomplete tool suggested [from this moment by shania twain]. Without even needing to finish writing his query, Gibbs' question had been answered. The particular anecdote is well-chosen to minimize fears: there is only one correct answer to the query and the answer required is unambiguous, there are no ethical risks if the answer is wrong, and the emotional example of wedding music allows the article to present the new inclusion of suggestions as an unquestionably positive change.

When Autocomplete was made a compulsory feature in 2008, Google's public statements made appeals to speed: 'Who wants to spend their time typing [san fransisco chronicle] when you can just type in 'san f . . .' and choose the suggestion right away?' (Liu). In addition, examples were included that would help make a user's query more specific, rather than altering its meaning. 'Instead of just typing [hotels in washington] – did you want [hotels in washington dc] or [hotels in washington state]?' (Liu). Making users formulate more specific queries simplifies the search process for Google rather than users. Persuading users to search for [San Francisco Chronicle] articulates their search in terms which can be more easily fulfilled and evaluated from an information retrieval perspective: for example, did this search bring up the newspaper's own website or the website of a competitor, a website describing its history, a Wikipedia page? Users' expectations for specific results are statistically easier to predict and navigational queries are easier to satisfy than more open-ended informational ones. The editorial control, via algorithm maintenance, required for a search such as [San Francisco Chronicle] is easier than a query such as [San Francisco], which has a greater number of different contexts or expectations. As covered in Chapter 1, search engineers evaluate the success of their algorithms by making predictions about queries and measuring if the user was satisfied that the results matched their intended query. How then to evaluate a short unrefined query of a place, for example [San Francisco]? Does the user wish to see an overview of websites relating to San Francisco, or do they have something specific in mind but have not included enough information in their query? Or do they have no specific intention but are simply curious about the kind of websites that would be returned? A more generalized search, such as [San Francisco], places the onus onto Google to make editorial decisions about importance and relevance. What elements should be prioritized: informational pages about its politics, history, geographical location, and culture? Or more practical kinds of results, such as recent news, currently open businesses and weather forecasts? Or perhaps non-linguistic kinds of media, such as photos and videos? The list of results for such an open-ended search will never hope to satisfy every searcher; making queries specific allows Google to treat them as intention-based and, therefore, having clear metrics for success. Doing so promotes an attitude that Google's results are objective, simply by virtue of reducing ambiguity. A key consequence, therefore, of Autocomplete is that in addition to changing users' queries at the time of a search, by offering a selection in the drop-down list, it also moulds the expectations used to formulate future queries. Google's suggested benefit of speed works in combination with this narrowing of topic. Making the average time of query formulation quicker reduces the time users take to contemplate their queries and consider their own aspirations and expectations before being presented with Google's. These reasons intensify how damaging the earlier examples of offensive stereotypes are, not only in the current values that they embody but also their potential effect on users' future searches.

So, how does Autocomplete operate?

Google have always been especially vague about how Autocomplete operates; even though the details of their algorithms are not revealed to the public, the general principles behind most other aspects of Google's search engine are disclosed by the company. An example of this is Google's openness about how their various algorithms are used to rank results. Even though the public does not know the exact details of the PageRank algorithm, it is public knowledge that highly ranked pages are those with significant numbers of incoming hyperlinks and/or hyperlinks from highly ranked pages. An individual without a technical background, or specific knowledge of the PageRank algorithm, can understand that the basic philosophy behind Google's ranking is that it prioritizes widely known sites (sites with a significant number of incoming hyperlinks, e.g., whitehouse .gov) and pages linked to from those highly ranked sites (e.g., any web pages that are hyperlinked from the whitehouse.gov website). Understanding this general principle explains why previously established institutions often rank highly in Google's results, or why the public interest in a Wikipedia page correlates with its ranking.

In comparison, Autocomplete has no such general principles and this is why the misconception that search volume is the main, or only, criterion has dominated in both public and academic discourse. To reveal the extent of Google's deliberate obscurity, I have reproduced excerpts from three versions of their official statement: the first is the earliest version of their statement that could be found (18 April 2013, see Figure 15), the second is from 9 April 2015 (see Figure 16), and the third is their current statement,

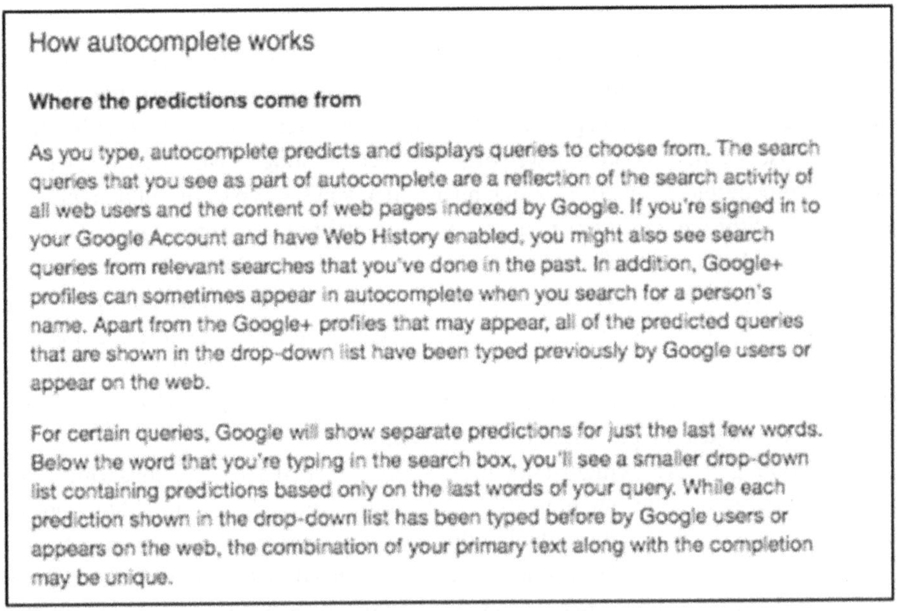

How autocomplete works

Where the predictions come from

As you type, autocomplete predicts and displays queries to choose from. The search queries that you see as part of autocomplete are a reflection of the search activity of all web users and the content of web pages indexed by Google. If you're signed in to your Google Account and have Web History enabled, you might also see search queries from relevant searches that you've done in the past. In addition, Google+ profiles can sometimes appear in autocomplete when you search for a person's name. Apart from the Google+ profiles that may appear, all of the predicted queries that are shown in the drop-down list have been typed previously by Google users or appear on the web.

For certain queries, Google will show separate predictions for just the last few words. Below the word that you're typing in the search box, you'll see a smaller drop-down list containing predictions based only on the last words of your query. While each prediction shown in the drop-down list has been typed before by Google users or appears on the web, the combination of your primary text along with the completion may be unique.

Figure 15 Google's Official Statement regarding Autocomplete 'Google Inside Search: Autocomplete' dated 8 April 2013. Accessed 12 August 2017, via the Wayback Machine.

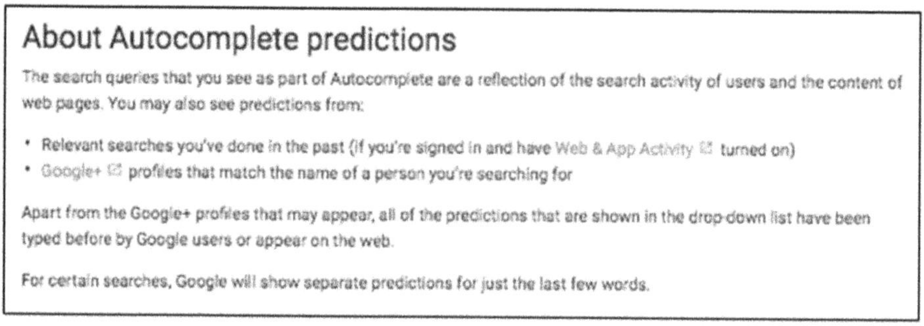

About Autocomplete predictions

The search queries that you see as part of Autocomplete are a reflection of the search activity of users and the content of web pages. You may also see predictions from:

* Relevant searches you've done in the past (if you're signed in and have Web & App Activity ☑ turned on)
* Google+ ☑ profiles that match the name of a person you're searching for

Apart from the Google+ profiles that may appear, all of the predictions that are shown in the drop-down list have been typed before by Google users or appear on the web.

For certain searches, Google will show separate predictions for just the last few words.

Figure 16 Google's Official Statement regarding Autocomplete 'Google Search Help: Autocomplete' captured on 9 April 2015. Accessed 12 August 2017, via the Wayback Machine.

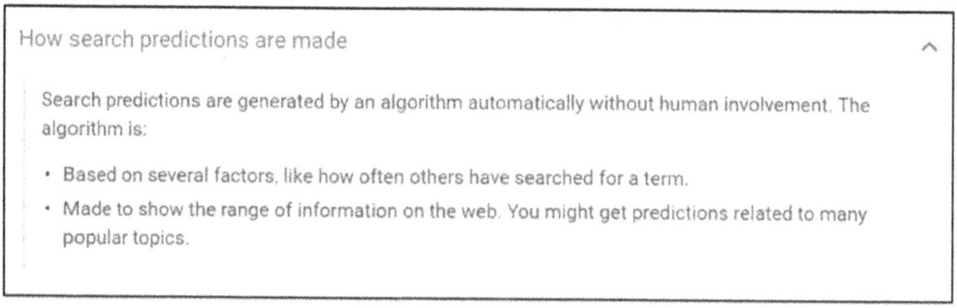

How search predictions are made

Search predictions are generated by an algorithm automatically without human involvement. The algorithm is:

* Based on several factors, like how often others have searched for a term.
* Made to show the range of information on the web. You might get predictions related to many popular topics.

Figure 17 Google's Official Statement regarding Autocomplete 'Google Search Help: How search predictions work on Google'. Accessed 4 May 2021.

as of 4 May 2021, which has remained consistent since 2017 (see Figure 17). The key recurring phrase that is important for this current analysis is the following: in 2013, 'search queries that you see as part of Autocomplete are a reflection of the search activity of all web users and the content of web pages indexed by Google' (Google, 'Google Inside Search: Autocomplete'); in 2015, 'search queries that you see as part of Autocomplete are a reflection of the search activity of users and the content of web pages' (Google, 'Google Search Help: Autocomplete'); and in 2021, 'The algorithm is: Based on several factors, like how often others have searched for a term. Made to show the range of information on the web' (Google, 'Google Search Help: Search Using Autocomplete'). Comparing Figures 15–17 shows that Google have become increasingly evasive. However, there has always been a consistent and central reference to using the content of the web to model suggestions, not just the previous queries of other users.

Due to Google's various digitization projects, in particular, Google Books which, as of their most recent announcement in 2019, had scanned and indexed '40 million books in over 400 languages' (Lee), the content of the web consists of much more than web pages and digitally-born content. In addition, Google have stated that around 15 per cent of all queries are unique and have never been searched before, as Sullivan estimated in 2016: '15 percent of three billion is still a huge number of queries never entered by any human searcher – 450 million per day' (Sullivan, 'FAQ: All about the Google RankBrain'). The figure of 15 per cent unique queries has remained a consistent figure used in Google's technical blogs and public communications as recent as 2021.[7] Apart from specifically removed content, like the examples discussed earlier, Autocomplete is always triggered by a query formulation; Google have outlined that it uses machine learning to produce suggestions for unique queries. We know from Sullivan's 'FAQ' that since 2016 RankBrain, Google's machine learning metric, now triggers for all queries and is the third most important signal for providing results. What remains unconfirmed is the extent to which RankBrain provides Autocomplete suggestions. This chapter hypothesizes that Google's machine learning has a significant influence on Autocomplete suggestions for all queries, not just the 15 per cent of unique queries. The consequence of this, I argue, is that Autocomplete suggestions reflect a broader textual relationship drawn from a much larger corpus of human thought: books scanned by Google Books, the number of which is steadily increasing towards the inclusion of all published texts worldwide. The consequence of this is that Google must address the biases, stereotypes, and problematic content of a body of knowledge vastly more complex than the comparatively discrete inputs of search queries. In the next section, I use various examples to argue that when Autocomplete draws from Google's corpus, the suggestions trigger for individual words and small word grouping patterns, rather than the dominant assumption that Autocomplete suggestions simply reproduce previous search queries verbatim. Therefore, before explaining the mechanics of RankBrain, I will highlight an example of why the *method* used to generate Autocomplete suggestions is vitally important. The actual operation of how suggestions are generated is often ignored in scholarship that only focuses on the content of suggestions, particularly those that present sexist or racist beliefs. The following example shows how the technique of how Google generates suggestions can raise even more critical questions than the suggestions themselves.

Second-order stereotyping: Sexist suggestions for female scientists

On 15 July 2017, the genomics scientist Tuuli Lappalainen (@tuuliel) tweeted the following screenshot (Figure 18) showing the Google Autocomplete suggestions for her name. She continued her statement over five following tweets (Figure 19). Lappalainen's comments reflect the erroneous, but widespread, attitude discussed earlier that Autocomplete suggestions are an exclusive reflection of search volume, that is, an exact reflection of the most commonly searched queries. In the tweet in Figure 18, Lappalainen places the blame for the results on 'fellow scientists' rather than on Google. Wherever the blame lies, Lappalainen's outrage and frustration are more than warranted and reflect the persistent sexism of everyday life. Consequently, Lappalainen's tweets became a site

---

[7]See, Google Fellow and Vice President of Search Pandu Nayak's official blog post 'Understanding searches better than ever before' published on 25 October 2019. For the most up-to-date reference to 15 per cent of unique queries, see Google 'Useful responses take many forms,' accessed 28 June 2021.

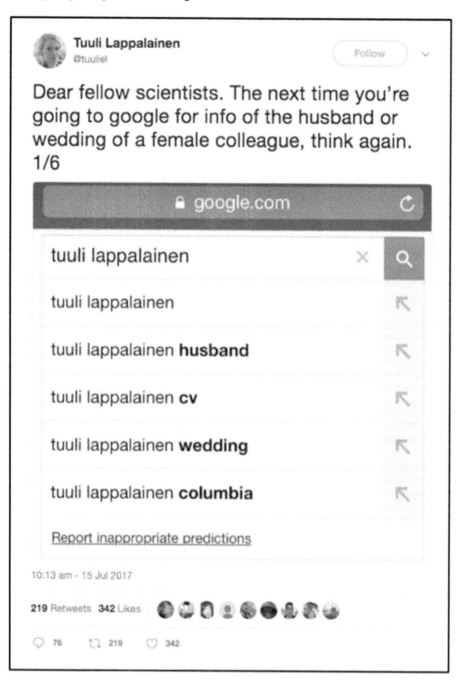

Figure 18 Tweet from Tuuli Lappalainen showing a screenshot of the Google Autocomplete suggestions for her name. Posted to Twitter on 15 July 2017.

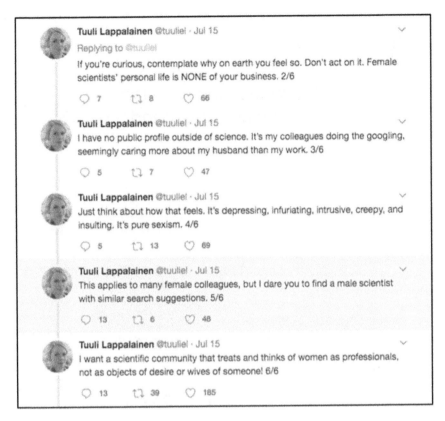

Figure 19 Five further tweets from Tuuli Lappalainen in 'reply' to her original screenshot (see Figure 18). Posted to Twitter on 15 July 2017.

of discussion in which various Twitter users weighed in with a range of comments and examples. Users retweeted previous examples found by neurobiologist Leslie Vosshall in 2016 (see Figure 20).

A year earlier than Lappalainen's discovery, the anecdotal findings of Vosshall in 2016 had led evolutionary ecologist Florence Débarre to collect a sample of Autocomplete suggestions for 1856 contemporary scientists (427 women and 1429 men) and analyse the 'proportions of people for whom "husband" and/or "wife" are suggested; [and] also looked for the word "married"'. Débarre did the same for smaller samples of tennis players and Hollywood actors, with which to compare the results. Débarre's scientists were taken from those listed in the American Academy of Arts & Sciences, Howard Hughes Medical Institute, and TED talk speakers listed under science. The TED talk aspect was highlighted in order to evaluate the impact that relative fame might have; many discussing the issue online argued that scientists with notoriety might be receiving more gendered searches as a result of being a public celebrity, in comparison to lesser-known individuals whose names would only be searched in a professional context.

Débarre's findings were that 'the proportions of "wife" and/or "husband" [suggested by Autocomplete] are higher among Google suggestions for female scientists' (see

Figure 20 Tweet from @pollyp1 (Leslie Vosshall), originally from 20 May 2016. Retweeted by @Scitabanis 15 July 2017.

Figure 21). Female scientists were almost four times more likely to have [wife] and or [husband] suggested by Google Autocomplete than their male colleagues. Débarre also ruled out the hypothesis that relative fame was associated with suggestions of a personal nature, such as 'husband' or 'married'. The data showed no examples of male scientist TED speakers who had 'wife' or 'husband' listed in their Autocomplete suggestions, whereas the number was significant for female scientists, although this number was significantly lower than for female scientists who had not given a TED talk. Therefore, such personal suggestions could not be attributed to the consequences of being in the public eye and being searched for in a non-academic context, as was suggested in the wider Twitter debate.

These results confirm the various anecdotal reports that keywords such as 'wife' or 'husband' occur significantly more often – by a factor of four – in searches for female scientists than for male scientists. Such an instance represents an example of what I term *second-order stereotyping* in Autocomplete suggestions. Previous scholarship into

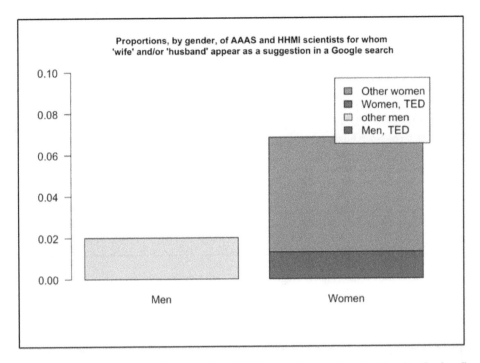

Figure 21 Proportions by gender, of AAAS and HHMI scientists for whom 'wife' and/or 'husband' appear as a suggestion in a Google Search, where 1.0 represents a 100 per cent occurrence of wife or husband search terms. Sample size of 1856 individual scientists (427 women and 1429 men). Taken from Florence Débarre's 'Are Google Suggestions Sexist?', this graph shows that relative fame, as represented by an individual having given a TED talk, does not have a significant impact on the gender distribution of the results.

offensive and discriminatory Autocomplete suggestions has only focused on *first-order stereotyping*, that is, the suggestions for collective identities and general nouns, such as [women shouldn't . . .], [Jews are . . .], [black men should . . .], [romanians are . . .]. Google have disabled suggestions from appearing on many of these instances, which in itself is an attempt to avoid the ethical duty inherent in developing tools of this kind. However, these *first-order* examples are few in number compared to *second-order stereotyping*, that is, the kinds of biases in suggestions for specific instances of those more collective identities. That, collectively, female scientists might all be receiving sexist Autocomplete suggestions for queries containing their names is much more insidious and damaging than *first-order* instances. At the time of Lappalainen's original tweet, there was a lot of vocalized support for the issue and a large number of responses disclosed that they had used the 'report inappropriate predictions' feature. Figure 22, taken one month later, shows the lack of change to the suggestions and Figure 23 documents that almost four years later [husband] features as the second suggestion.

In addition to the specific example of Tuuli Lappalainen, I wanted to see if the sexist trend observed in Débarre's study in 2016 had changed over the last five years. With technical assistance from Greg Tyler, who forked Débarre's code to regenerate the data, I

Figure 22 Google Autocomplete suggestions for Tuuli Lappalainen. Accessed 14 August 2017.

Figure 23 Google Autocomplete suggestions for Tuuli Lappalainen. Accessed 5 May 2021.

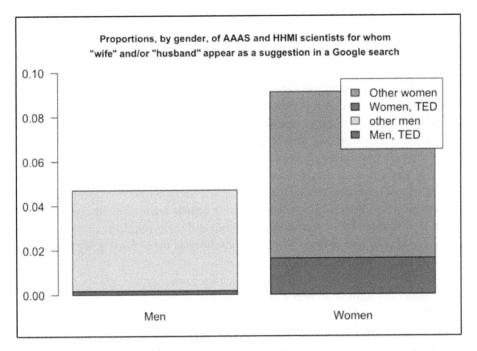

Figure 24 This graph shows my repeat of Débarre's study conducted on 12 May 2021, roughly five years later. This graph is an updated version of Figure 21, which shows results from 2016.

repeated the study and reran the analysis.[8] Figure 24 shows my 2021 updated version of Débarre's 2016 graph pictured in Figure 21.

Comparing my 2021 results with Débarre's 2016 study show that the names of female scientists still generate significantly more instances of [wife] or [husband] as Autocomplete suggestions than their male colleagues. The difference between male and female scientists has reduced: suggestions of [wife] and [husband] for women is now closer to twice as often as men, rather than roughly four times as it was in 2016. However, there is still a significant sexist bias in the suggestions. The other difference is that the suggestions of [wife] and [husband] for all the scientists have increased and more than doubled in the case of male scientists. Therefore, there is also a wider trend in which all of Autocomplete's suggestions for the sample of 1856 scientists have become more intrusive and less professional. Given that sexist Autocomplete suggestions are still an active problem, it is important to understand where they are coming from and what parts of Google's process are most responsible.

---

[8]Tyler's updated version of Débarre's code can be accessed at the following address: https://github.com/gregtyler/GoogleSuggestions

RankBrain and the biases of machine learning

Through an attempt to deduce the part of Google Autocomplete's process that is responsible for the *second-order* sexist results outlined in the previous section, I hypothesize that RankBrain is the source of such suggestions. I outline the reasoning behind this claim next, after explaining what RankBrain is and how machine learning has come to influence almost every part of Google's operations. RankBrain is a machine learning neural network that was originally established to increase the success rates of results provided for unique queries. RankBrain was designed to trigger for all queries that had never been searched before, which represented 15 per cent of all searches submitted to Google, and reword that query into a query that had been searched before. RankBrain would then track whether the user's actions seemed to indicate whether or not this substituted query was successful or not and then record the success or failure as a piece of information about how similar or different the original query was from its replacement. As Sullivan describes:

> Imagine that RankBrain sees a search for [best flower shop in Los Angeles]. It might understand that this is similar to another search that's perhaps more popular, such as [best LA flower shops]. If so, it might then simply translate the first search behind the scenes into the second one. It would do that because for a more popular search, Google has much more user data that helps it feel more confident about the quality of the results. ('Google Uses RankBrain for Every Search')

This system is much more advanced than simply assigning a range of synonyms to each word, as had previously been the case. Due to the success of RankBrain, Google started to employ the machine learning neural network for all queries and as of 2016 became Google's 'third most important signal' after 'content' and 'links': the bedrock of search engine logic (Sullivan 'FAQ: All About . . .'). Considering that Google use around 200 signals broken up into '10,000 variations or sub-signals', RankBrain does not simply represent an issue related to Autocomplete but constitutes a key part of Google's whole system. In addition, Google's competitors also rely on machine learning; Microsoft, for example, has been working on its machine learning system, RankNet, since 2005, employing it as part of Bing's ranking signals. None of the existing research regarding Autocomplete discusses RankBrain, which I argue is critical to understanding how it operates but also the kinds of ethical questions that need to be addressed.

In 2011, Google started training its machine learning software on their Google Books corpus, which at that time was around '6% of all books ever published' (Lin et al.), focusing on books in eight languages from 1800 to the present. Google researchers evidence, in a number of academic papers, their process for using machine learning to syntactically annotate n-grams for those eight languages, that is, automatically assigning words grammatical values based on their use throughout their Google Books. In addition, RankBrain was also able to map the changing usage from 1800 to the present. The kinds of language use found in the Google Books corpus do not necessarily reflect patterns of online language use. In Chapter 1, I highlighted how the distinction between questions and queries gave an insight into how search queries follow patterns, but not necessarily grammatically correct ones. For this reason, Google's RankBrain system is also trained on the language of queries submitted to Google, as well as the born-digital content of the web. Such wildly different sources lead to the most varied linguistic corpus ever complied, although its underpinning philosophy is really no different from Ramon Llull's thirteenth-century attempts or the other historical projects outlined in Chapter 2. Google's aim is to collect as much information as possible to be used as answers to queries but also as data to feed the decision-making process. Importantly, the logic behind RankBrain is that with enough data, we might know the answers to questions yet to be asked.

The machine learning behind RankBrain functions by building vectors from corpora of text. Figure 25, taken from one of Google's academic papers written by Tomas Mikolov, Ilya Sutskever, and Quoc Le 'Learning the Meaning Behind Words', demonstrates these vectors through a principal component analysis (PCA) projection. Using a system called Skip-gram, the machine learning system builds a neural network, which 'can train on more than 100 billion words in one day' (Mikolov et al., 'Distributed Representations' 2). In doing so, the system builds up a series of relationships between words and groups of words (n-grams). Such a system can operate in tandem with Google's Semantic Search methods discussed earlier to assign values to search terms so that they can be tagged as

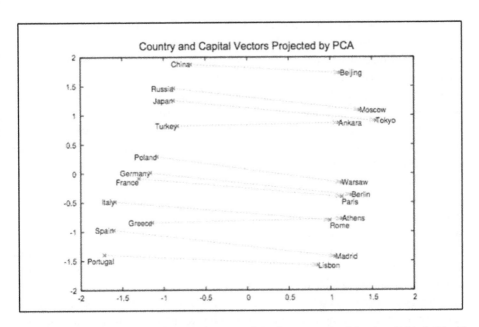

Figure 25 Taken from Mikolov, Sutskever, and Le 'Learning the Meaning Behind Words' 2013 original caption reads: 'Two-dimensional PCA projection of the 1000-dimensional Skip-gram vectors of countries and their capital cities. The figure illustrates the ability of the model to automatically organize concepts and learn implicitly the relationships between them, as during the training we did not provide any supervised information about what a capital city means'.

people or places and be treated differently computationally. Figure 25 shows a simple example of the neural network's organizational capacity to recognize the relationships between capital cities and countries, *and* the different relationship between capital cities and other capital cities, which it plots as vectors. Such a model is useful for idiomatic language or instances where combinations of words are frequently used together to signify a separate concept, Mikolov et al. use the example that '"Boston Globe" is a newspaper, and so it is not a natural combination of the meanings of "Boston" and "Globe". Therefore, using vectors to represent the whole phrases makes the Skip-gram model considerably more expressive' (2). Google's use of machine learning is another nexus in which the disparate parts of Google's company (and the wider projects of Alphabet) become related. Google now use machine learning in all their products, from Google Maps' Street View to YouTube's method of suggesting videos to users. Steven Levy described machine learning as Google's core 'corporate mindset' citing CEO Sundar Pichai's statement in late 2015:

> Machine learning is a core, transformative way by which we're rethinking how we're doing everything. We are thoughtfully applying it across all our products, be it search, ads, YouTube, or Play. And we're in early days, but you will see us – in a systematic way – apply machine learning in all these areas. (qtd. in Levy, 'How Google Is Remaking Itself as a "Machine Learning First" Company')

Although this book is focused on Google's search engine, that technology is part of a much wider narrative: scanning all the books ever published, photographing every street, collecting data on offline behaviours in people's homes, aggregating data of every dynamic pattern it can from influenza epidemics to traffic flow, funding companies such as 23andme, a service for reading the DNA of customers – all of these and more – represent the logic in which Google see the world as data to be collected and put to use. In particular, the collection of data in such large quantities enables and reinforces the use of neural network machine learning. At the start of Google's book-scanning project, which aimed to photograph all pages ever printed, an engineer summed up the project in the following way: 'we are not scanning all those books to be read by people. We are scanning them to be read by an AI' (Uncredited Google Engineer qtd. in Dyson 313). Therefore, when highlighting the ethical problems developed by machine learning in one area, Autocomplete, for example, we should expect to see similar biases in Google's other products and services.

It might seem difficult to survey the linguistic patterns and associations created by Google's systems, but I have developed a number of simple exercises to draw these out and make them readable on an individual scale. One of the ways of making visible Autocomplete's relationship between words, developed from machine learning, can be carried out in the following way. First, use an online random word generator to generate two random words. Then use a random letter generator to find one letter. Second, load up a fresh browser while using a VPN and enter the two random words and letter. Finally, follow the first suggested term, then add a new random letter to provide new Autocomplete suggestions, following the first result in turn. What you find are isolated

Figure 26 A demonstration of how Autocomplete suggests words for very rare queries, for which it will have minimal direct search data to draw from. Formulated 4 May 2021.

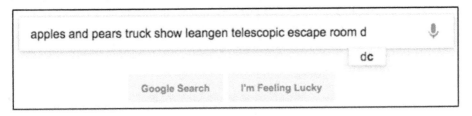

Figure 27 Following Autocomplete suggestions resulting in a nonsensical query in the early days of RankBrain. Formulated 12 August 2017.

pockets of overlapping meanings, which make sense in blocks but not as a whole. For example, Figure 26, in which [pool consultation] [consultation questions] [questions and answers] and [answers nhs] [nhs England] make sense independently but not as a whole.

The reason for using two random words is that there is likely minimal direct data on what to predict after [pool consultation q] so Google uses its machine learning to make its best guess. In the early days of RankBrain, these suggestions were much more variable and strange, see Figure 27 for an example from 2017, which can be compared to more recent examples, see Figures 28–30. In 2021, the suggestions are more repetitive and predictable, like suggesting [pdf] fairly consistently for [p. . .] or [for sale] for [f. . .], regardless of the context.

Why is this important? This shows us what Google does when it does not have much previous information available on a query: it is a glimpse into RankBrain's predictive relationships between words. This is important because when we look at examples of people's names, particularly people who are not famous and whose names do not get searched often, we see that Google is making the *same kinds of predictions about them*. Google uses RankBrain to guess what comes after [pool consultation q] and provides

Figure 28 Further demonstrations of how Autocomplete suggests words for very rare queries, for which it will have minimal direct search data to draw from, formulated 4 May 2021. In comparison with 2017, the examples provide a much more predictable set of suggestions, regardless of the previous words used earlier in the query.

Figure 29 Further demonstrations of how Autocomplete suggests words for very rare queries, for which it will have minimal direct search data to draw from, formulated 4 May 2021. In comparison with 2017, the examples provide a much more predictable set of suggestions, regardless of the previous words used earlier in the query.

[. . . questions] as the suggested search completion, see Figure 26. In the case of Tuuli Lappalainen, RankBrain lacks the prior query data it might have for a popular query, but it can work out that it is a female name and that female names can be related to [husband] and [wedding] regardless of other contexts related to that specific name. Because of

Figure 30 Further demonstrations of how Autocomplete suggests words for very rare queries, for which it will have minimal direct search data to draw from, formulated 4 May 2021. In comparison with 2017, the examples provide a much more predictable set of suggestions, regardless of the previous words used earlier in the query.

RankBrain's logic, people do not need to be searching for [Tuuli Lappalainen wedding] or [Tuuli Lappalainen husband] for these to show up as Autocomplete suggestions. The fact that Google have always been vague about how Autocomplete suggestions are generated plays to their advantage. The persistent myth – that Google do not try to correct – is that Autocomplete suggestions are an exact reflection of search behaviour. Instead, as outlined previously, Google use a much broader corpus, including everything on the web, which means that the kinds of suggestions are the direct result of algorithmic curation and the aims of programmers, not simply the public at large. The misconception that suggestions relate to search volume plays to Google's favour by making it appear that users are simply misogynistic in their search behaviour. This might be the case; however, it might also be that Google's RankBrain is reinscribing misogynistic values found in their wider data, but not necessarily in their bank of previous searches. If this is the case, Google is not holding up a mirror to users of search, but instead creating misogynistic suggestions in entirely new contexts. In doing so, they are not just perpetuating misogyny or racism, but actively creating it. Therefore, I argue that this example of RankBrain allows me to extend the existing critiques of Noble, Baker and Potts, and Olteanu et al., highlighted earlier and suggest an even more damming appraisal of Google's role. Google is not simply facilitating existing racism and sexism, but instead actively recreating and encouraging these behaviours in contexts where they might not have existed previously.

The significant influence of RankBrain also speaks to the important relationship between computational approaches, management structures, and ideological positions. Cade Metz, in a 2016 *Wired* article, discusses the shift in Google's management structure after the retirement of Amit Singhal, then Head of Google Search, and replacement by John Giannandrea. Metz describes the transition as an 'ideal metaphor for a momentous shift in the way things work inside Google – and across the tech world as a whole', that is, from algorithms that followed a strict set of rules coded by engineers to machine learning in the form of neural networks and forms of AI. Metz cites a number of Google's current and ex-employees including software engineer Edmond Lau, who argues that

> Singhal carried a philosophical bias against machine learning. With machine learning, he wrote, the trouble was that 'it's hard to explain and ascertain why a particular search result ranks more highly than another result for a given query'. And, he added: 'It's difficult to directly tweak a machine learning-based system to boost the importance of certain signals over others'. Other ex-Googlers agreed with this characterization. . . . Yes, Google's search engine was always driven by algorithms that automatically generate a response to each query. But these algorithms amounted to a set of definite rules. Google engineers could readily change and refine these rules. And unlike neural nets, these algorithms didn't learn on their own. As Lau put it: 'Rule-based scoring metrics, while still complex, provide a greater opportunity for engineers to directly tweak weights in specific situations'. (qtd. in Metz)

Metz's article was published in February 2016, at this time RankBrain, Google's machine learning neural network was running on 15 per cent of unique queries, as outlined earlier. However, it only took until June 2016 for RankBrain to become Google Search's third most important metric, activating for every search, which continues to be the case today. In Chapter 4, I offer a comparison between search results before this shift, in 2015, and after the shift, 2017, as well as results from 2021. From the small sample of results collected, it was clear that queries submitted in 2017 produced results that were highly consistent across different contexts. In particular, queries that used very different phrasing and even different languages resulted in many commonly occurring results. This suggests that during this time Google was not simply treating each word or phrase as an isolated query, instead, placing the results within a wider structure of presumed function. Such patterns of organization provide evidence that RankBrain's status as the third most important metric had a concrete impact on the nature of search results.[9]

Google have dedicated significant resources towards developing AI and neural network technology in a number of their ventures, since at least 2011, when Google Brain was founded. Andrew Ng, founder and former head of Google Brain, Google's deep learning neural network program, gave a sense of its pervasiveness in a 2012 interview with NPR:

> Machine learning and artificial intelligence is a pervasive technology today, and most of us use it dozens of times a day without knowing it. Artificial intelligence technology is responsible for giving us high-quality Web search engines, practical speech recognition, machine translation, even self-driving cars.

---

[9]This homogenization of contexts and the role of RankBrain is discussed in greater detail in Chapter 4. In particular, I discuss the changes between the 2017 and 2021 results, which suggest changes to RankBrain's influence on consistent ranking between contexts.

Figure 31 A photograph taken by the author.

In the interview, Ng explains how Google Brain gave a neural network of 16,000 computer processors 'three days on 10 million YouTube clips' without explicit instructions or directions. In a conclusion that feeds neatly into the soundbite culture prevalent in technology journalism, after three days were up the neural network 'learned how to recognize a cat'. The nuance of what such a claim really means is often glossed over. A later Google project, DeepDream, developed in 2014, 'was invented to help scientists and engineers to see what a deep neural network is seeing when it is looking in a given image' (Google, 'DeepDream: About'). Figures 31 and 32 demonstrate how DeepDream interprets an image. The result is a useful metaphor for conceptualizing the patterned but often inscrutable phrases within Autocomplete suggestions. DeepDream has interpreted the grass as a mixture of fish and reptiles and parts of the tree trunk as the faces of dogs, visual data that makes some sense in isolated parts of the picture but are clearly inaccurate interpretations in the context of the photograph. Both examples give an illusion of understanding. Autocomplete displaying a vectored relationship, seen in Figure 26, between [pool consultation] [consultation questions] [questions and answers] and [answers nhs] [nhs England] makes just as much sense as DeepDream's interpretation of tree trunks as dogs.

These images give some insight into the kinds of pattern-matching systems developed in neural networks, but do little more than play into the fantasies inherited from science fiction, literarily complete with androids dreaming of electric sheep. However, to return to Metz's survey of current and ex-Google employees, the difference between what it means to *understand* the processes of algorithms versus neural networks is significant:

Figure 32 The photograph of Figure 31 processed by DeepDream via https://deepdreamgenerator .com/

The truth is that even the experts don't completely understand how neural nets work. But they do work. If you feed enough photos of a platypus into a neural net, it can learn to identify a platypus. If you show it enough computer malware code, it can learn to recognize a virus. If you give it enough raw language – words or phrases that people might type into a search engine – it can learn to understand search queries and help respond to them. . . . As Google moves search to this AI model, it's unclear how the move will affect its ability to defend its search results against claims of unfairness or change the results in the face of complaints. (Metz)

Metz argues that even experts cannot fully understand how neural networks work, which is troubling in itself. However, more significant is the binary attitude whereby such techniques can work or fail to work, as if search engines can be described in the same terms as a programme that can recognize, or fail to recognize, a virus. Relying on the word 'work' conflates two aspects of Autocomplete: how Autocomplete *operates*, colloquially what lies under-the-hood, and how Autocomplete *functions*, the social and technological consequences of its implementation. It cannot be emphasized enough that algorithms are never neutral and always codify a set of cultural, social, and philosophical attitudes. The implementation of neural networks, even if their operation is more opaque, does the same. The operational differences between algorithms and neural networks are significant, but their functional outcomes are intertwined. However, knowing that they operate in tandem, but with little evidence concerning their level of influence, means that a critique of either logic is difficult. This exacerbates the problems caused by the hidden nature of Google's ranking criteria and has particular ramifications for Google's accountability for its results and suggestions, both in the legal context of potential libel and in a social context regarding the perpetuation of stereotypes. The following section reflects on the specific kinds of sexism that develop out of neural networks in a more insidious way than with previous algorithmic techniques.

Automated misogyny for every individual

The examples provided by Vosshall and Lappalainen and the study conducted by Débarre, which I reran in 2021, all took place when Google's neural network RankBrain was the third most important ranking signal for all queries. However, the evidence suggests that RankBrain's original logic, based on responding to unique niche queries, has been imported into Autosuggest queries on a large scale. It is clear that Autocomplete suggestions for the names of specific people are gendered en masse, not just suggestions for words such as [woman] or [girl]. The original purpose of RankBrain was designed to make predictions about instances without much data to draw from; in this case, Google's corpus has a large volume of information on the topic of 'research scientist' or 'woman' but not on each individual research scientist. Rankbrain's purpose is to take unique or uncommon queries and substitute information based on other more common queries, based on predictions that the two search terms have something in common. How such commonality is established is an important issue and its consequences bring a number of difficult debates regarding representation. Are such suggestions based on the aggregated data of previous searches, or do they represent the more historical gendered relationships that would be evident in the Google Books corpus? In addition, is the fact that these Autocomplete suggestions continue to occur, even after direct feedback, a sign that such suggestions are deemed useful to a majority of users?[10] The updated tests that I performed in 2021 show that these issues are not simply the growing pains of early implementation of machine learning but their fundamental logic. We must look past the marketing fanfare that celebrates machine learning as incomprehensibly high-tech and see it for what it really is: a method for finding patterns and reinscribing the biases and oversimplifications that perpetuate stereotypes, discrimination, and bigotry.

What makes the findings of Débarre's 2016 study and my 2021 replication of it particularly insidious is that suggestions are directed towards specific individuals, rather than group identities. The most widespread discussion of Autocomplete's reproduction or reification of stereotypes has focused on *first-order* examples such as the campaigns by UN Women or Romanians are Smart, which relate to stereotypes attached to common nouns of gender, nationality, ethnicity or religion rather than the names of individuals, which I term *second-order*. As for the origin of their contents, Autocomplete suggestions

---

[10]The Twitter threads, previously highlighted, contain messages from a number of users stating that they had reported the suggestions using the associated 'report inappropriate predictions' link.

are drawn from the linguistic arrangements of search patterns and the content of the web, which includes the (as of 2019) 40 million volumes of printed text scanned by Google Books. The lack of detail provided by Google regarding how these different sources are weighted makes it impossible to ascertain the source of such attitudes, misogynistic or otherwise. Autocomplete suggestions are the consequence of a wider linguistic network that, for example, has strong associative links between female names and words related to weddings and marriages. In these examples, Autocomplete becomes a tool: not one that helps users to search faster but a tool that clarifies a set of attitudes – attitudes such as white supremacy, heteronormativity, and racism that will already be painfully obvious to those impacted. Google's response to the various campaigns highlighting offensive suggestions for general nouns was to disable Autocomplete suggestions for those and related searches. Such a decision may reduce the extent to which certain attitudes are perpetuated, but it also hides the underlying issues that, given their priority in previous suggestions, still need to be challenged. Most importantly, these attitudes continue to be perpetuated in less explicit examples, whereby bigoted attitudes are attached to personal names or other single instances, which only become clear in aggregate. The action of disabling particular instances, such as [women shouldn't] or [Jews are], does not address the deeper issue that Autocomplete suggestions will always represent and reiterate a set of values.

The findings I have presented show that Google's neural network has learned about gendered discourse and that, in some contexts, these suggestions have been deemed *useful*: users have clicked on them, which perpetuates the problem. Although, given RankBrain's function, the suggestion being clicked on might be for a different topic that has been deemed related by the neural network. For example, users following suggestions for [Queen Elizabeth husband] or [Beyoncé husband] become evidence to provide [husband] as an Autocomplete suggestion for other female names, such as research scientists. These other names, which have been searched for less and have minimal data from which to draw, might then provide [husband] as a suggestion, regardless of the actual search behaviours for that specific name. We can use these conclusions to return to the example of Tuuli Lappalainen's sexist suggestions. Lappalainen has every right to be outraged that [husband] and [wedding] are Autocomplete suggestions for her name but this does not necessarily mean that her fellow scientists are searching these terms. They might be and I am certainly not trying to deny the widespread sexism within academia; however, what I am proposing as the possible reasoning for these suggestions may be a much more systemic problem. It may be the case that Google is not just reflecting existing sexist attitudes and behaviours but actively creating and encouraging them too.

In the essay 'Technology Is Society Made Durable', Bruno Latour writes that 'we might call technology the moment when social assemblages gain stability by aligning actors and observers. Society and technology are not two ontologically distinct entities but more like phases of the same essential action' (129). In the context of Google's machine learning projects, the actors and observers include all online users and every word, idea and sentiment contained within books scanned by Google Books. The discourse around machine learning often asserts that a lack of human guidance leads to neutrality or objectivity. However, the previous examples show that particular values and attitudes are perpetuated and encouraged, or to use Latour's terminology, stabilized and made durable. Even if none of the suggestions are followed, their very presentation to a user influences their outlook on the world. This is particularly important given the widespread misunderstanding that suggestions are simply reflective of actual search volume. It is a misconception that benefits Google by shifting the perceived responsibility and one that they have not tried hard enough to dispel. Google Autocomplete does not simply stabilize or highlight dominant cultural beliefs, but rather it actively expands systemic misogyny into new areas and inflates other offensive discourses.

Here it is relevant to think back to the legal rulings discussed earlier in this chapter, particularly those concerning *the right to be forgotten*. Although courts have come to a variety of conclusions, the only consistent legal gain is the precedent that individuals can report particular suggestions as inappropriate. These associated issues demonstrate why the earlier examples of specific female scientists, whose names Autocomplete suggested terms such as [husband], [wife] and [wedding], represent a particularly important example. The right for removal does not require that the listings present false information or defamatory meanings, which should allow such measures to cover stereotyping. However, removals are considered on a case-by-case basis; many people claimed via Twitter to have submitted removal requests to Google but, as demonstrated earlier, these have clearly had no effect. Although, even if Google did redact these suggestions, on a case-by-case basis, the suggestions without requests would continue to appear and become even more noticeable. The individual women affected are unlikely to take Google to court over their suggestions, considering the cost, risks, and potential publicity involved. The findings of Débarre and my 2021 follow-up study, outlined earlier, demonstrate that Google's Autocomplete perpetuates particular attitudes towards women that can only be viewed in aggregate. These examples may be more indirect than the visible misogyny of the suggestions for [women should . . .], but their impact may be more insidious. This highlights an important issue regarding who should have access to and/or control over information regarding real-life individuals, particularly when this information does not relate to those specific individuals, but instead, represents wider cultural attitudes or beliefs.

Google should be held to account. Given that its enormous revenue is built on the backs of users – our web pages, our hyperlinks, our behaviour – Google have a duty of care towards everyone impacted by their technologies. This should be considered a material duty; Google are capable of hiring thousands of employees to look for patterns in the data and they should be making these findings public.[11] There should be careful scrutinizing of what attitudes become forced upon users on a global scale and the

---

[11]Google do hire people to rate the quality of results through comparing two sets of results side-by-side, but they are not tasked with looking for bias: 'We have more than 10,000 search quality raters, people who collectively perform millions of sample searches and rate the quality of the results according to how well they measure up against what we call E-A-T: Expertise, Authoritativeness and Trustworthiness.' Sullivan 'How Google delivers . . .' Also see, Sullivan 'How insights from people . . .' The guidelines document given to raters is available online, and it should be noted that there is not one instance of the words 'bias', 'stereotype' or 'discrimination' in its 175 pages. See Google 'Search Quality Evaluator Guidelines' and 'Rigorous Testing.'

decisions regarding how to deal with these results should be made collectively. However, scrutiny requires time, patience, and reflection for an individual to even acknowledge an issue, let alone consider how we might deal with it. Google have been actively working against such conditions by making the search process as quick as possible. Speed has been a practical and ideological focus throughout Google's history and its most important influence has been upon Autocomplete.

Speed

In 2009, a year after it had been made a permanent feature of Google Search, engineers made several significant changes to the Autocomplete tool, which at that time was named Google Suggest. These were announced to the public with one main reason given: speed. As with the sentimental wedding music anecdote used to introduce users to Autocomplete, these new 2009 features were introduced by the product managers Effrat et al. using a similar focus, titled 'Faster Is Better on Google Suggest'. The idea that faster is always inherently better is not only a common cliché but one which enables measurable assessment. Other common technology truisms such as easier is better (user-friendly) and beautiful is better (design principles) cannot be *proved* in the same manner that speed can. Therefore, focusing on speed narrows the scope of assessment; Google's blog post begins:

> As we prepared to write this post, we discovered a common childhood passion for fast things: high-speed trains, roller coasters, firetrucks, and more. That may be a key part of why we're so excited to be working on Google Suggest, since it saves time by giving suggestions as we're typing our searches. (Effrat et al.)

The false naivety of this opening links their changes not only to the prelapsarian state of childhood but also configures time, and its compression, in terms of efficiency (trains), excitement (roller coasters), and safety (firetrucks). Google's post regarding the changes focuses on time-saving as an objective measurement of improvement, rather than appeals to quality, which allows them to sidestep the subjective issue of what kinds of behaviours Autocomplete is designed to elicit. However, time acted as a red herring: the major changes made to Autocomplete in 2009 significantly changed the functional role of Autocomplete in a more complex way, making it more personalized, localized, and situational. These changes provide users suggestions based on their previous searches, make different suggestions based on a user's location and alter the suggestions based on the current page from which the user is searching. The changes that were made to Autocomplete in 2009 focus on making Autocompleted suggestions less homogenous, responding more directly to the context of the user. Chapter 4 specifically addresses relevance in the context of Google Search as a whole. Consequently, the remainder of this chapter will establish some of the foundational issues that will be discussed further in the following chapter.

In addition to time-saving, Effrat et al. outline four other changes made in 2009: 'suggestions on the results page', 'personalized suggestions', 'navigational suggestions', and 'sponsored links in suggestions'. These alterations fundamentally changed the function of Autocomplete, away from the generalized list of suggestions and towards a contextual framework that relates to the general shifts of Google's search engine from then onward. These shifts were further enhanced by changes made in response to the growing use of mobile and declining use of desktop devices, with which to search queries.

Beginning with 'suggestions on the results page', this meant that the suggestions provided in Autocomplete corresponded to the page the user might be on at the time. Their example is while searching Google from a Google Search results page concerning roller coasters (notice how their earlier example reinforcing speed and fun recurs) entering [b] into the search field would provide the user with suggestions concerning roller coasters, rather than just the regular suggestions for the letter 'b' (see Figure 33). This provides a personal narrative structure to searching that did not exist previously. Whereas Autocomplete pre-2009 provided a universal list of suggestions, this feature tailored suggestions to the user to act as a directional aid, connecting searches and limiting the user's field of view. This logic continues today, as can be seen in an updated example of suggestions for [b] on a results page for [roller coasters] (see Figure 34). This relates to change number two, referred to as 'personalized searches' (see Figure 35), and promotes repeat search behaviours.

Figure 33 Autocomplete results for [b] while on a Google results page for [roller coasters], taken from Effrat et al. Accessed 5 April 2014.

Figure 34 Autocomplete results for [b] while on a Google results page for [roller coasters], searched on 6 May 2021.

Figure 35 Demonstration of personalized search, taken from Effrat et al.

This tool does not differentiate between search queries from the past which were helpful or unhelpful for the user, a difficult quality to measure. Neither does this feature base the reminder of previous searches around topic or theme, instead, it simply follows the letters or words beginning a search query. In some situations, it might be argued that this addition makes searching faster, in particular when the user is aiming for a specific page they have visited before or visit regularly. It is less useful for searches that require multiple queries over a period of time, news for instance, where a more accurate search which would outline a developing situation, for example, a search for [Ukraine] might have been useful in the early stages of the 2014 Ukrainian revolution, to get an overview of which websites had stories pertaining to the country. However, to keep up with the revolution and its aftermath as it unfolded varying searches such as [Ukraine Russia], [Ukraine Crimea], and [Ukraine US reaction] would be more useful than a repeated search of [Ukraine]. In addition, these previously searched 2014 queries would be suggested to users searching queries relating to Ukraine at future points in time, such as the events of 2022, currently unfolding as I write this book. Therefore, automatically suggesting verbatim repetitions of previous searches does not aid a user to look at a situation in multiple ways, build on their knowledge, or come across new sources. Even minor variations in the wording of a query can change the kinds of results significantly, as will be outlined in the following chapter. In 'Querying the Internet as a mnemonic practice', Andrei Zavadski and Florian Toepfl demonstrate that the 'outcomes of the queries "Annexation of Crimea" and "Incorporation of Crimea", . . . – despite referring to the same historical event – produced fundamentally different results [with] opposing memories of the event' (33). This finding was true for both Google and Yandex, the main competing search engine in Russia. Therefore, this aspect of Autocomplete works to push users towards searching queries exactly as before, which is less likely to provide different kinds of viewpoints and may present a biased outlook on events.

The last two main feature additions of 2009 relate to the conceptual merging of search and web address functions. 'Navigational suggestions' enabled specific websites to be included in Autocomplete suggestions meaning that, for some websites, users could travel directly to suggested sites without even searching. Finally, the inclusion of 'sponsored links in suggestions', a feature which has now been removed, allowed paid advertising to be included in the drop-down list of suggested terms. The exact reasons for why this particular feature was decommissioned are unknown but decisions were made that we might assume have to do with the perceived neutrality of Google Search and the perception of Autocomplete as a functional part of Google Search rather than as a moneymaking venture.

An additional change made in 2009 represents the further direction, discussed earlier, regarding localizations. Originally Autocomplete was simply divided by language, showing the same suggestions wherever the user was based. Google changed Autocomplete in 2009 to reflect localizations, which they explained on their developer blog with the example that 'If you type [liver] in the U.K., you're probably a Liverpool fan (but in the U.S. you'll get more suggestions about liver diseases)' (Kadouch). This logic behind making suggestions more specific and culturally situated came to reflect the future iterations of Autocomplete and particularly its link to Google Now, 'the feed' and Google Discover. The phrasing of the previous quotation, stressing probability of intentions, contextualizes changes to Autocomplete as *functional* rather than outwardly editorial, in regard to wider epistemological and cultural questions. Moreover, the way that the developers framed this change was as an alteration that should not be noticeable by a user: a US-based user should not come across Liverpool FC suggestions or results, even if this is a highly popular search elsewhere. By the same token, a UK Liverpool supporter should be disturbed by suggestions unrelated to football, even if those suggestions for [liver] are more appropriate to most other users worldwide.

Google did not make these localization changes clear to the average user or alterable in any way. Only with the use of a VPN or other technical means is it possible to see the suggestions for the same query in a different part of the world. Making this diversity visible would show users that there are alternatives to what they are being given by Google, which in turn would provide the means to critique the search engine for the sources and viewpoints it amplifies, as well as those that it buries. This aim, to make the tailoring of suggestions and results go unnoticed by users, fits within Google's wider criterion of relevance and serves to underpin the broader aspirations of the company, which go beyond the specific instance of the Autocomplete tool. As will be demonstrated in Chapter 4, Google's main goal is to provide results that are relevant to each user, but through alterations that are hard to spot and make each individual's unique search landscape *appear* to be universal. One of Google's most effective ways to prevent users from noticing variations and considering their conditional nature is quite simple: speed up the process so that users lack the time to reflect.

Speed and judgement: Time to reflect

One of the main trajectories of Autocomplete is its role in speeding up searches. From early descriptions that users would spend less time typing queries to later descriptions that Autocomplete suggestions would make users' queries more specific and thus shorten the entire information retrieval process. The two most significant time-related milestones were the implementation of Google Instant (functional between 2010 and 2017) and Google Discover (established as Google Now in 2012, rebranded as 'the feed' in 2016, and renamed Google Discover in 2018). These two technologies provide an insight not only into the centrality of speed and its relation to relevance but also to the shifting nature of Search more generally, as it moves from a desktop-situated activity to a mobile one. Such a shift is important in order to understand the rise in contextualizing and personalizing results described in the following chapter.

Google Instant was a direct evolution of Autocomplete and its accompanying logic. Released in 2010 and active for seven years, Google Instant was a feature that began searching and presenting results before a user had completed their query, using the top Autocomplete suggestion as its full presumed query. On its release, Google Instant was made the default mode of accessing Google Search for all users. At the press conference announcement detailing its release, Marissa Mayer, then Google's vice president, focused on speed and on the way that search time could be shaved down by minuscule increments. Mayer detailed the average speeds of each part of searching for a query (see Figure 36 for her accompanying slide) and took issue with the average time, 9 seconds, users took to type a query, underlining her point with the nonsensical fragment: 'never

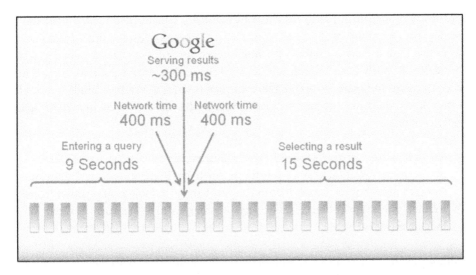

Figure 36 Presentation slide at 13:03 from Marissa Mayer's 'Google Instant Launch Event' detailing the average time taken for the three portions of searching for a query.

underestimate fast' (13:03). Mayer went on to argue that through Google Instant, by combining the total time saved globally, 'you actually will be able to save eleven hours for every passing second' (22:10), the phrasing of which was directed not at the aggregate but to an individual 'you' and your 'passing' seconds. What the global community might choose to do with this time was not addressed.

Google Instant relied on Google Autocomplete's suggestions being accurate for the majority of users in order for the automatic search to be considered a benefit rather than a distraction. Mayer addressed the confidence Google had in the Autocomplete suggestions:

> a lot of people think Google Instant is search-as-you-type, but it's actually search-*before*-you-type. . . . We're actually predicting what query you're likely to do and giving you results for that. . . . There's even a psychic element of it, in that, we can actually predict what you're likely to type and bring you those results, in real time. (18:33)

The argument was not made that Google Instant would change or direct the queries of users, but that the aggregation of information held in Autocomplete's suggestions would be powerful enough to produce a 'psychic' meshing between user and interface. It is this kind of speed-consequential effect that Ken Hillis, Kylie Jarrett, and Michael Petit focus on in their 2013 critique of Autocomplete and Google Instant, a critique that also informs the later discussion regarding relevance. In particular, Hillis et al. draw on the work of Scott Lash, arguing that Google's attempts to speed up interactions between users and the search engine constitute the conditions for play. As Lash argues in *Critique of Information*, 'To play is to be *so* interested, *so* involved immediately as to rule out the possibility of judgement. Judgement involves always a separate and neutral instance. It presupposes a culture of representation. Play . . . does not involve this' (160). Play, a form that Lash usually considers with ambivalence, for Hillis et al. takes on a decidedly negative role. Such a characterization fits Mayer's position, as she gestured towards her slide (pictured in Figure 36) arguing that the total time for a search, around 24 seconds, is too slow and is time that must be saved. Hillis et al. argue that when immersed in the activity of play,

> She or he cannot generate the objective, reflective, reflexive distanced judgement of the transcendental ego variously set forth by Kant, Hegel, and Husserl. Google's model of relevance does not support an epistemological position from whence one might observe reflexively in order to make aesthetic or critical judgements. (74)

Although I am wary of such an absolutist appeal to unmediated objective attention – the previous chapters aimed to demonstrate that attention and thought are always enmeshed, both socially and technologically – reflexivity and critical judgements are evidently the victims of Mayer's 'psychic' 'search-*before*-you-type' (18:33). The heterogeneous vantage point that Autocomplete *could* offer is sidelined; although still visible, other suggestions are dominated by the top suggestion, the result of which fills the entire screen. Although this notion of play is partly useful, both Mayer and Hillis et al. seem to have a rather singular vision of who the average user of Google might be, and the expertise required to rely on Google Instant in the way originally intended.

Google Instant had its detractors; in an article covering its discontinuation, titled 'RIP Google Instant Search, You Were Never Necessary', journalist Rhett Jones referred directly to Mayer's original claims regarding Google Instant's psychic abilities, arguing, 'Yes, it had a psychic element, in the way that someone who constantly interrupts you thinking they know what you're going to say next has a psychic element'. Although Google did not cite a lack of popularity as their reasoning for discontinuing Google Instant, we can never know what impact the potentially disruptive loading and reloading that caused the whole screen to flash and stutter had on different users. For this reason, I argue that play might be a useful model for how it altered the search experience for *some* users, but that this might be limited to specific demographics with particular technical familiarity. For others, Google Instant must have been the complete opposite of immersed play. Assigning play central conceptual importance, in regard to Autocomplete, prioritizes speed and high levels of expertise. In doing so, play emphasizes the capacity for Autocomplete to assist searchers by accelerating, rather than changing, their search queries. As discussed in Chapter 1, it is impossible to fully know the intentions of users; therefore, it is hard to classify whether following an Autocomplete suggestion represents a deviation from a user's original intended query or not. Consequently, this tension, between acceleration and change, is at the heart of every Autocomplete suggestion. However, this is only the case if the Autocomplete suggestions align with the attitude of a user. Autocomplete is designed to function unobtrusively but, as has been demonstrated throughout this chapter, Autocomplete becomes an object of attention in the moments when the tool fails to match the expectations of users.

When the Autocomplete suggestions for a query match the outlook of a user, they can be easily ignored as unremarkable or transparent. However, any Autocomplete suggestion that differs from a user's intended query acts as a moment of failure: Autocomplete has not *broken* in the sense of a shattering wine glass but instead provides a moment of rupture. Suggestions only register as biased or ideological when they fail to match the predicted outlook of a user and become the object of that user's attention. Google Instant enhances such a rupture by filling the user's whole screen with the result that they consider unrelated to their search; the less innocuous the suggested query the more disputable the tool becomes. A pertinent example to consider in the context of Google Instant is one of the stereotypical Autocomplete suggestions provided by Baker and Potts:

> if someone wanted to use the Internet to find the answer to the question 'Why do black holes exist' when they start typing the question into Google, after the first three words, they would be presented with a number of auto-complete suggestions including 'Why do black people have big lips' and 'Why do black people like chicken'. (201)

Their observation was from 2013 and [why do black people like fried chicken] continued to be the number one Autocomplete suggestion for [why do bla] throughout the following years, including 2017: the year that Google Instant was permanently discontinued (see Figure 37).

Baker and Potts do not reference Google Instant; they focus on the aggregation of stereotypes rather than the phenomenological aspects of the search experience on an

Figure 37 Autocomplete suggestions for [why do bla]. Accessed 15 August 2017.

individual basis. However, in the context of Google Instant, such a result being the first suggestion has significant consequences. For the seven years in which Google Instant was the default setting of Google Search, a user typing their search for [why do black holes exist] would be looking at a full page of results for [why do black people like fried chicken] as soon as they had entered [why do bla]. This kind of full-page rupture would have been relatively common, as evidenced by the many offensive examples highlighted earlier.

The popular vlogger genre outlined at the start of this chapter is, after all, all about the shock, strangeness, and humour that top Autocomplete suggestions provide. These are moments of reflection about how Google works, how language functions both on- and offline, and how institutions of power permit or curtail the perpetuation of various attitudes. I want to move away from the rigid dichotomy of success and failure, terms that present the reception of Autocomplete suggestions from Google's point of view. The default nature of Google Instant represented a judgement that Autocomplete suggestions were, most of the time, a successful match for users. The occasions in which Google Instant provided jarring results are not simply moments of user dissatisfaction or failures of the system, but instead opportunities for critique and reflection about the whole of Google's discursive regime. This consequence is a likely part of why Google Instant was discontinued in 2017, although this line of reasoning is unlikely to be included in any official press statements.

Google addressed the reasoning behind discontinuing Google Instant in a statement to the site *Search Engine Land*:

> We launched Google Instant back in 2010 with the goal to provide users with the information they need as quickly as possible, even as they typed their searches on desktop devices. Since then, many more of our searches happen on mobile, with very different input and interaction and screen constraints. With this in mind, we have decided to remove Google Instant, so we can focus on ways to make Search even faster and more fluid on all devices. (qtd. in Schwartz 'Google Has Dropped Google Instant Search')

In the *Search Engine Land* article that contained Google's statement, Barry Schwartz referred to Google's reports, mentioned already in previous chapters, that the majority of Google searches now take place on mobile and tablet devices. As journalist Nick Statt described, given the size of mobile screens 'Instant Search doesn't make as much sense given we use our fingers and virtual buttons to interact with software, and trying to load a results page on top of the onscreen keyboard isn't exactly good user experience design'. In addition to hardware constraints, Google's decision was based on how users search using mobile devices. This leads to the second descendant of Autocomplete predictions, Google Discover.

Originally launched as Google Now in 2012, rebranded as 'the feed' in 2016, and renamed in 2018, Google Discover is both an extension of the logic of Autocomplete and its 'psychic' aspects, as well as a spiritual successor to the kinds of changes made to Autocomplete in 2009 discussed earlier. Google Discover represents the step beyond Mayer's 'search-*before*-you-type' using data collected on individuals to provide users with a personally curated list of news or articles that reflect their interests, but also contextual information based on location, time, and other metrics. For example, the 'Inspiration for your next meal out' feature automatically shows a selection of suggested restaurants around mealtimes, based on the time of day, location of the user, and other data. In addition, Google Discover might decide to display information about upcoming buses and where to catch them around the time a user usually commutes to work, as well as articles to read or videos to watch on the way. The release statement accompanying Google Now's rebranding as 'the feed' charts a course between the Scylla and Charybdis of irrelevance and dystopia:

> People have long turned to Google to get answers, learn about the world, and dig deeper on topics they're passionate about. Today, we are announcing a new feed experience in the Google app, making it easier than ever to discover, explore and stay connected to what matters to you – even when you don't have a query in mind.
>
> Since introducing the feed in December, we've advanced our machine learning algorithms to better anticipate what's interesting and important to you. You'll see cards with things like sports highlights, top news, engaging videos, new music, stories to read and more. And now, your feed will not only be based on your interactions with Google, but also factor in what's trending in your area and around the world. The more you use Google, the better your feed will be. . . . As the world and your interests change, your feed will continue to grow and evolve along with you. (Thakur)

Such a statement represents an overall shift to personalizing information, using contextual signals to deliver information to individuals deemed to be affected. Using machine learning to 'anticipate what's interesting and important to you' carries significant philosophical and social weight. It represents a fine-tuned version of Autocomplete as it originally existed, using data for predicting queries; the approach of 'Google Discover' is that predictions can be more precise and potentially more accurate if they are tailored to specific individuals. Whereas Autocomplete's strange suggestions might provide a vantage point for reflection in highlighting some wider linguistic arrangement, the logic of Discover relies upon machine learning to tighten the informational loop between users and their devices and provide content in a way that appears neutral because of prioritizing personalization over generalization.

It is impossible to know whether applications like Google Discover, that rely exclusively on user data, will become as or more dominant than search engines are today. But it certainly represents the ideological direction and aspirations of Google and other dominant technology companies. Google Project Manager Karen Corby described this shift in the official blog post accompanying the 2018 rebranding from 'the feed' to Discover, in the following way: 'Discover is unique because it's one step ahead: it helps you come across the things you haven't even started looking for' (Corby). The central goal of which is that any personalization of a user's informational landscape is so well predicted that it appears neutral and transparent, or, that they do not even notice at all. The previous Figures 33 and 34 showed an example of a user beginning to search [b . . .] on an existing results page for the query [roller coasters]; in that example, rather than more general suggestions for the query stem [b], the primary suggestions provided relate directly to roller coasters. The user is not notified about this alteration of suggestions, nor is there any way to opt out. Instead, it is intended not to be noticed, which prevents the suggestions from becoming the object of scrutiny. For Google, the bigoted Autocomplete examples highlighted by Noble, Baker and Potts, and others, are not failures because they are untrue or offensive, but because they have become conspicuous. Google's dominant logic and design principles would see racist and misogynistic suggestions as successful if served to racist and misogynistic users, as long as they did not lead to lawsuits. This is why the earlier example of [husband], [wife], and [wedding] being suggested much more frequently for women's names than men's is so important. The suggestions aim to reflect a misogynistic culture to the degree that they are unnoticeable. The main argument of this chapter is that the existing critical discourse that focuses on specific instances of offensive suggestions, such as [Jews should . . .] or [Women shouldn't . . .] simplifies the ethical dimensions of Google Autosuggest. These searches are easily spotted, reported, and (if the press coverage is bad enough) removed. The public conversation that we need to be having is about the values and attitudes that are only apparent in aggregate. At present, Google's metric of relevance, which is the focus of the following chapter, means that Google actively tries to match values with users in insidious ways that are intentionally hard to spot and even harder to escape.

Conclusion

Despite the widespread public interest, there has been minimal academic study of Google Autocomplete. This has caused a variety of misconceptions as to how Autocomplete functions to circulate within academic discourse and the press. This chapter has challenged many of the most widespread fallacies, in particular the idea that Autocomplete represents overall search volume that gives a direct insight into the most searched queries. In addition, I have sought to reframe the existing discourse regarding discriminatory and stereotypical suggestions provided by Autocomplete. Although there is academic work that highlights *first-order* biases and discrimination, in the suggestions for queries such as [women shouldn't] or [Jews are], I argue there has not been enough attention on the *second-order* biases of Autocomplete. In focusing on the example of Autocomplete suggestions for the names of female scientists, highlighting the public debate sparked by Tuuli Lappalainen and Leslie Vosshall, and rerunning the study originally conducted by Florence Débarre, I argue that these *second-order* instances are a much more problematic instance of bias. Moreover, I contend that Google's machine learning neural network initiatives, in particular RankBrain, are not simply facilitating existing sexism but potentially creating these discriminatory suggestions from scratch for contexts with smaller amounts of data to draw from. I tied the rising importance of machine learning from around 2016 to the ideological and management changes within Google. When placed in the context of Google's conceptual dedication to speed and relevance, the question of how search engines should be directing our enquiry and providing us time to reflect becomes even more vital. In the following chapter, I take these ethical issues and relate them to the kinds of search results Google provides to different users around the world. In doing so, I build on the focus of this chapter regarding bias, user agency, and automated representation, while placing these ideas in a cross-cultural and longitudinal context.

CHAPTER 4
GOOGLE'S SEARCH ENGINE RESULTS
WHAT IS A RELEVANT RESULT?

Introduction

Consider the following search queries: [is being gay wrong?], [arranged marriage], [should sex work be legal?], [gun law], [does Hong Kong belong to China?], [fracking], [what is free speech?], [socialism], [are drugs bad?], [should I be vegan?], [abortion], [women should stay at home], [did the Holocaust happen?]. Many of these queries have been discussed directly in previous chapters as real examples that have been used to hold Google to account on moral or legal grounds. Due to Google's global hegemony, each results page consolidates a particular set of values, which can appear neutral or unchallenged due to a lack of alternative ways to search the web. If we searched these queries, should the results be the same for all users around the world? Should some topics present users with context-dependent results? Does Google have a responsibility to dictate moral norms? Should queries related to historical, medical, or scientific topics be treated differently to those that explore social, moral, or subjective areas? Is it even possible to draw such distinctions at all? Given Google's global dominance, what is at stake in these debates is nothing less than the way that human societies gather information, establish ethical norms, treat others, and influence future change.

The questions at the heart of this chapter relate to the kinds of results that search engines should aim to provide. Google's answer and the response from most other technologists, engineers, and critics has always been consistent: search results should be *relevant*. The metric of relevance has been used as the principal goal throughout the search engine industry. However, relevance is used to justify a variety of different kinds of goals; in exploring these various positions and the relationship they have to personalization, this chapter highlights how attitudes towards relevance have real-world ethical implications on users around the world.

The chapter outline is as follows: first, I address a selection of Google's claims about how they see the globalizing reach and epistemological mission of their search engine. Second, I analyse the evaluative frameworks that are used to judge search engine results, both internally by engineers as well as externally by academics and critics. Doing so provides examples of the kinds of implicit normative positions adopted regarding what search engine results *should* be. In doing so, I argue that attitudes towards search results sit on a spectrum between two mutually exclusive perspectives, which I describe as *Idealist* relevance and *Contextualist* relevance. *Idealist* relevance considers search engines as fundamentally either objective, neutral, or democratic. Therefore, the *Idealist* position is that search engines should be built and maintained to enhance their democratic dimension or aim to provide a universal outlook on the world. Conversely, at its most extreme formulation, the *Contextualist* position describes the search engine paradigm as one that provides relativistic truths, which require personalization and the alignment of results to an individual and their particular context. The contemporary contrast, between the *Idealists* and the *Contextualists*, speaks back to the long history of memory technologies outlined in Chapter 2. To ground these discussions in the present day, I explore two key kinds of personalization used online to evidence how and why search results might differ between users.

In order to provide a practical focus for the critical and moral questions raised, the second half of this chapter provides a global and longitudinal study of a set of search results. Although the academic consensus is that search engine results are different for each individual, there is little evidence as to what this looks like in practice. Therefore, my longitudinal study, conducted in 2015, 2017, and 2021, collected search results for a set of related queries while changing certain criteria: the location that the query was sent from, the language used, and the kinds of phrasing and terminology deployed. The range of differences found between contexts demonstrates how search results can differ, from person to person and place to place. The queries used all related to same-sex sexual orientation, which I searched in English, French, and Arabic in the UK, France, and Morocco over a period of six years. I analysed the results in terms of whether they were Pro- or Anti-gay and whether their claims were framed as personal opinions or as statements of fact. My results show how, across the world, the same search queries lead to radically different search experiences and even small alterations to the wording of a query can substantially change the kinds of results Google provides. Consequently, one user might receive overwhelmingly homophobic results framed as statements of fact, while another user may receive opinion-based blogposts and articles supporting gay rights. Such evidence enables the consideration of specific ethical questions regarding how universal or culturally specific search results should be. Should Google's results about same-sex sexual orientation in a country like Morocco, where LGBTQ+ lives are defined as criminal, condemn being gay, or provide alternative viewpoints? Should the search results of a homophobically phrased query be the same as one phrased positively? Should Google try to personalize such results, by either matching the predicted attitudes of users with similar results or by presenting a range of alternative viewpoints? Or should Google provide the same kinds of results for everyone? My results show that Google's algorithmic answers to these questions have changed significantly over time and in quite complex ways. Google's algorithms are always changing and so are the public expectations of its technology. Therefore, this chapter aims to provide the conceptual tools to enter into these important ethical debates so that we can collectively debate the kind of influence ubiquitous information technologies should be having on the world.

'Quantifiable signals' and Malawian witch doctors

Google have a history of saying one thing and doing another. This is why this chapter focuses on the metrics used to evaluate search results and on specific examples of results, rather than on Google's public relations and marketing claims. However, to set the scene, it is useful to get a sense of what the directors of Google's project think their search engine is doing in the world. Their current explanation of how results are ranked is as follows:

> For a typical query, there are thousands, even millions, of web pages with potentially relevant information. So to help rank the best pages first, we also write algorithms to evaluate how useful these web pages are. These algorithms analyse hundreds of different factors to try to surface the best information the web can offer. . . . It's important to note that, while our systems do look for these kind of quantifiable signals to assess relevance, they are not designed to analyse subjective concepts such as the viewpoint or political leaning of a page's content. (Google, 'How Search Algorithms Work')

Google's main criteria is relevance, a term which is fully explored later in this chapter. Here, they use relevance to mean a metric based on objective and quantifiable signals to judge how relevant a page is. However, such a description runs counter to the other claims they make on the same part of the website. In terms of making results useful, the company state that 'Larry Page once described the perfect search engine as understanding exactly what you mean and giving you back exactly what you want' (Google Search: Responses). Such a framing places the usefulness of answers as to how well they fit your cultural niche. In a culture that overwhelming believes in something, to what extent would it be useful to receive results to the contrary? When is the answer to giving 'you back exactly what you want' something aimed to change your mind? Such statements do not necessarily fit with the wider aims of those running Google.

For example, in their 2013 book *The New Digital Age: Reshaping the Future of People, Nations and Business*, Eric Schmidt (CEO of Google from 2001 to 2011 and Executive Chairman for Google in 2013) and Jared Cohen (Director of Google Ideas) present their vision for a global digital future. They share their utopic optimism that 'We will increasingly reach, and relate to, people far beyond our own borders and language groups, sharing ideas, doing business and building genuine relationships' (6). They argue that this new digital age (by which they primarily mean Google) 'will usher in an era of critical thinking in societies around the world that before had been culturally isolated' (34). New technology, they say, will break down barriers and help us to live better lives as more informed world citizens:

> People who try to perpetuate myths about religion, culture, ethnicity or anything else will struggle to keep their narratives afloat amid a sea of newly informed listeners. With more data, everyone gains a better frame of reference. A Malawian

witch doctor might find his community suddenly hostile if enough people find and believe information online that contradicts his authority. Young people in Yemen might confront their tribal elders over the traditional practice of child brides if they determine that the broad consensus of online voices is against it, and thus it reflects poorly upon them personally. Or followers of an Indian holy man might find a way to cross-reference his credentials on the Internet, abandoning him if it is revealed that he misled them. (35)

It is easy to dismiss the way these arguments are made and the tone that the authors use. They talk brazenly with their biases on their sleeves as if all knowledge works unilaterally from total ignorance to wholly developed and objective thinking. This attitude aligns them with the more extreme version of *Idealist* thought that I will outline shortly. They choose their examples carefully to play to their audience and assert that pre-internet, most cultural niches are simply instances of brainwashing, which technology will erase once it inevitably brings the truth. As a counterpoint that undermines this techno-deterministic optimism, their text is strewn with moments of doubt, fifty pages after the previous idealistic quotation, they state that 'Evidence shows that most internet users tend to stay within their own cultural spheres when online, less for reasons of censorship than because of shared language, common interest and convenience' (85). They do not indicate what evidence they have in mind, but given they have more data on how people use the web than any other institution on the planet, we should take note of such a claim. Google – and, in particular, executives and directors like Schmidt and Cohen – have the power to shape their algorithms in ways that enable users to stay within their existing cultural spheres or to rank results to challenge these contexts.

The results of my six-year study demonstrate how at times Google results have been rather consistent across contexts, while at other times, variations in contextual characteristics, such as location, create subcommunities, or niches that experience the web differently. Even if Google were a company devoted to producing world citizens, rather than capital, the question of whether results should be universal or vary between contexts is challenging. The difficulty is that, because of Google's opacity, it is not clear to users what kind of results they have received, how similar or different they might be to other users around the world. Without this clarity, it is impossible for the wider public to debate the ethics of search results. The changes identified in my cross-context longitudinal study demonstrate that search results are not inevitable or immutable. The questions of whether different cultural value systems should be respected or challenged in an increasingly globalized world should not be dictated by a single company. As global citizens, we should not accept a lack of transparency as a justification of moral responsibility and we must hold Google to account.

What *should* search engine results be?

Evaluating search engine results depends on particular perspectives regarding what search engines are or what they ought to be. For example, numerous researchers from the discipline of information retrieval measure the 'performance' of search engine results numerically by 'making judgement[s] about the value, importance and quality' (Goel and Yadav 7) using statistical models. Many legal theorists judge search engine results in terms of whether they are 'fair and diverse' (Diaz 15) and without clear economic biases that relate to competition laws. Various cultural theorists argue that search engines should 'give voice to diverse social, economic, and cultural groups, to members of society not frequently heard in the public sphere' (Introna and Nissenbaum 169) and rate search engine providers and specific results accordingly. Software developers, both Google employees and those outside the company, have a range of user-focused metrics that dictate whether or not new algorithms or ranking systems offer 'better performance . . . and can improve on Web search' (Teevan et al. 449) through measurements of click-rates and post-experiment interviews. This is to say nothing of the large media interest and wealth of journalism that regularly reports on what search engines should and should not be providing for queries.[1] Because search engines are used for such a wide range of purposes that cover various subject areas, researchers, journalists, and the public often talk at crossed purposes as a result of assumptions regarding what search engines are for and what constitutes a good search result.

This section unpacks the more explicit claims regarding the fundamental nature and function of search engines made by technologists, academic researchers, and journalists. Such claims fall on a spectrum between two camps: the first argues that search engines are fundamentally either objective, neutral, or democratic, which I refer to as *Idealist* positions. The second camp, which I have named the *Contextualists*, envisions 'perfect search' (Battelle 252) as personalized, subjective, or contextual. These positions are not simply claims of preference but rather, as the authors see it, descriptions of the inherent nature of search engines, as determined by their technological character. Although both sides agree on the technologies that underpin search – web crawling spiders, indexing and caching, algorithms such as PageRank, Markov Chains, keyword search – their conclusions regarding what a search engine *does* and how such actions are to be *judged* vary greatly. This difference is important because any kind of judgement about search engine results relies on a conception of what search engines are designed to do. These two distinct positions regarding search engines, which I refer to as *Idealist* and *Contextualist*, can also be approximately mapped onto the Platonic and Aristotelean positions, respectively, which were outlined in Chapter 2. Although the rhetoric of some technologists and engineers suggests that they would like to have their Platonic cake and eat it with Aristotelian bites, such epistemological viewpoints are incompatible. Problems emerge due to the two groups using the same terminology but defined in

---

[1] An example that frequently recurs in the news cycle is whether or not sites that promote Holocaust denial should be listed as Google results. For an example, see Frank Pasquale's article 'From Holocaust Denial to Hitler Admiration, Google's Algorithm Is Dangerous,' in which he lists five steps that Google and Facebook 'should take to move toward more transparency and accountability,' a statement which demonstrates a number of implicitly held beliefs regarding how search quality ought to be defined.

incompatible ways, in particular, the terms 'relevance', 'democracy' and 'bias'. By focusing on the underlying argumentation, this section provides clarity regarding current search technology and problematizes the teleological attitude that in the future search engines will simply be *better*.

The Idealists: Search is democratic, relevance can be measured objectively, and answers can exist independently of bias

The notion that Google is inherently democratic is a pervasive argument, one used by Google's marketing department as well as a range of technologists, and one that has been used to defend Google as neutral or blameless in various situations. Computer scientist Ed Felten's description sums up a much larger discourse. He says that 'Google is a voting scheme . . . not a mysterious Oracle of Truth. . . . It's a form of democracy – call it Googlocracy. Web authors vote by creating hyperlinks, and Google counts the votes. If we want to understand Google we need to see democracy as Google's very nature, and not as an aberration'. In the comments section of Felten's piece, he engages with various criticisms, arguing explicitly that web pages that are given a low rank 'can't be Google's fault'. Google used to provide the democratic metaphor as a central part of their self-description, in 2007, their 'Google: Technology' page was given over to describing their PageRank algorithm in the following terms:

> PageRank relies on the uniquely democratic nature of the web by using its vast link structure as an indicator of an individual page's value. In essence, Google interprets a link from page A to page B as a vote, by page A, for page B. But, Google looks at considerably more than the sheer volume of votes, or links a page receives; for example, it also analyzes the page that casts the vote. Votes cast by pages that are themselves 'important' weigh more heavily and help to make other pages 'important'. Using these and other factors, Google provides its views on pages' relative importance.

This metaphor is deeply problematic as it suggests that Google's role is simply to facilitate elections, over which they have no power and responsibility. Although Google's use of the metaphor of voting is an attempt to sidestep criticism, others have emphasized this aspect to hold Google to account. For example, one of the foundational essays in search engine studies, Introna and Nissenbaum's 'Shaping the Web: Why the Politics of Search Engines Matters', argued that search engines should be considered a 'democratizing force' of the web. They describe search engine technology as a way of preventing the economic market from dominating the web, allowing it to 'empower the traditionally disempowered, giving them access both to typically unreachable nodes of power and to previously inaccessible troves of information' (169). For communications theorist Alejandro Diaz, emphasizing the participation of users as fundamental enables us to make certain demands of Google as a global public:

we expect search engines to present the available information in a fair and diverse manner; we expect them, in other words, to be 'democratic'. We should ask about search engines like Google the same questions scholars have asked about traditional media: *Can underrepresented voices and diverse viewpoints be heard through the filter of search engines? What role does advertising play in the returned results? Do a few players dominate the industry?* (15, emphasis in original)

Such questions are used to demand that search engines prioritize the ideas of societies, not just those of companies or individuals treated solely as customers. Data collection is not a voting system and is not inherently democratic.

Even before Google established a monopoly, many voices dissented from the optimistic perspective that the web was inherently democratic. Douglas Schuler's 1998 aptly titled conference paper 'Reports of the Close Relationship Between Democracy and the Internet May Have Been Exaggerated' develops the argument that the web, even before the influence of search engines, is constrained by established institutions and a nexus of opaque power relations. These institutions often use the word 'democracy' as a smokescreen to cover their explicitly antidemocratic actions:

democracy requires a deliberative public process. This point contains three critical ideas: *deliberative* – adequate time must be allotted for hearing and considering multiple points of view; *public* – the discussion takes place in the daylight where it can be observed by all; and *process* – the procedures through which concerns are brought up, discussed and acted upon are clear and widely known.

Although Schuler is not directly referring to search engines, these aspects of democracy are crucial to assessing the claims arguing that search engines are fundamentally democratic. Considering these characteristics demonstrates that to compare Google to a form of voting would appear at best naïve and at worst intentionally misleading. A fundamental characteristic of search engines is that they reply on hidden criteria of judgement. Ranking search results is not like an election, where the fairness depends on the public understanding of how a decision will be made.

In their most distilled form, particular idealistic positions have even been the basis for manifestos; Hiroki Azuma's *General Will 2.0: Rousseau, Freud, Google* argues that Google's monitoring, accumulation, and analysis of data provides an opportunity to 'update the principles of democracy' (xii). For Azuma, the wealth of data collected and processed by search engines provides unprecedented access to the most intimate attitudes of a particular society. Written in 2011, before the Cambridge Analytica scandal, the intensification of the influence of digital platforms on elections, and the rise of disinformation, Azuma's vision of Google's future influence now reads as a chilling account of our present moment. He describes that

in the world of general will 2.0, the private, animal behaviour of the masses (database) will be aggregated and visualized through information technology and will place limits on politicians and experts' public consensus formation (deliberation). The accumulation of animal behaviour will constrain human judgement. (158–9)

Such a quotation reminds us that the mass accumulation of individual behaviours and attitudes is not the same as democracy and carries very different consequences. The difficulty that Azuma highlights is that there are multiple kinds of relevance: personal relevance, contextual relevance, relevance of truth claims, relevance to individual aspirations, or relevance to actual behaviours. Search engines cannot fulfil all of these considerations at once. Search engine scholars Jutta Haider and Olof Sundin describe these tensions and breakdown between different ways of considering relevance as 'frictions of relevance' (78), which they describe in the following way:

> for most intents and purposes, the search engine does not care about society as long as the search result satisfies a 'need', that is, something the individual user experiences as relevant (or pertinent). . . . The notion of frictions of relevance in the case of general purpose search engines describes the dissonance of different individual needs, societal interests, and the vested interests of the stakeholders catered to by the business model of the multisided platform structure. (77–8)

This conceptualization allows us to consider relevance as multiple competing sets of interest, each intersecting with economics, power relations, and politics. Relevance is not simply an abstract measure but an articulation of whose needs get met and the consequences of that prioritization.

The difficulty with measuring relevance

The academic study of relevance is far from new, developing throughout the twentieth century within information retrieval (IR), bibliometrics, Library and Information Science (LIS), Documentation Science, which have their roots in the rise of scientific journals of the seventeenth century and even earlier concerns of epistemology and organization. Stefano Mizzaro's extensive study 'Relevance: The Whole History' represents a literature review of 160 papers, tracing the term's historical development, while speculating on its future influence. Mizzaro's survey and analysis were published in September 1997, the same month that Brin and Page registered the domain google.com. Mizzaro's history outlines the centrality of the term 'relevance' and demonstrates that although the term has been adopted as the main metric for the discipline of IR, there is little agreement on what it represents. Mizzaro's opening epigraph borrows from an earlier literature review by Linda Schamber, Michael B. Eisenberg, and Michael S. Nilan that reached the same conclusion. Schamber et al. argue that,

> Since information science first began to coalesce into a distinct discipline in the forties and early fifties, relevance has been identified as its fundamental and

central concept . . . an enormous body of information science literature is based on work that *uses* relevance, without thoroughly understanding what it *means*. (qtd. in Mizzaro 810, emphasis in original)

The term 'relevance' has come to stand in for a multitude of different measurements. Mizzaro places great importance on a 'widely recognized . . . landmark in relevance history' (815), that of Brian Campbell Vickery's presentation of two papers at the 1959 International Conference for Scientific Information (ICSI). In these two papers, Vickery established a 'distinction between "relevance to a subject" (the relevance of a document to a query for what concerns the topical component) and "user relevance" (that refers to what the user needs)' (816). This description maps onto my distinction between *Idealist* and *Contextualist* thinkers, respectively. Vickery favoured the first metric, which became dominant in IR. By focusing on the relationship between subjects and queries, rather than subjects and users, mathematical models could be instituted with which to measure the effectiveness of retrieval systems, regardless of who was using them and why. This centred the wider discourse of relevance around a pursuit of modelling objective relations. Essentially, calculating relevance in this way led to more repeatable and static values, which were easier to write in code. In gaining such traction, this arbitrary value of *relevance* came to be taken as an objective quality that had been discovered in the universe, rather than manufactured through research.

Søren Brier's *Cybersemiotics: Why Information is Not Enough!* details the influence of such an attitude, in reference to Vickery's 1987 work *Information Science in Theory and Practice*, coauthored with Alina Vickery, which became one of the main textbooks for IR and its related disciplines. Brier articulates the position of Vickery and Vickery in a manner that usefully connects the conception of relevance I have described as *Idealist*:

Vickery and Vickery contend that their concept of information encompasses all types of communication and causal connections and that information is as fundamental to reality as matter and energy. . . . Information is more fundamental than either observers or interpreters. Accepting information as an objective, universal, law-determined thing that humans and machines absorb from nature, change, and multiply by thinking and by bringing it into society through languages, suggests that it must be possible to establish a unifying science of information. (418–19)

This conception of information and relevance as more fundamental than social relations has led to our contemporary discourse that demands that search engine results should avoid bias by providing the most relevant results possible. For example, technologist Adam Raff, in a 2009 *New York Times* op-ed, used the ongoing discussions regarding Net Neutrality, to highlight the increasing influence of search engines:

Today, search engines like Google, Yahoo and Microsoft's new Bing have become the Internet's gatekeepers, and the crucial role they play in directing users to Web sites means they are now as essential a component of its infrastructure as the physical network itself. The F.C.C. [Federal Communications Commission] needs to look beyond network neutrality and include 'search neutrality': the principle that search engines should have no editorial policies other than that their results be comprehensive, impartial and based solely on relevance.

Many would agree with the sentiments underpinning Raff's statement, however, defining relevance in this way, along the lines of *Idealist* objectivity, relies on two key measurements in IR studies: precision and relative recall. These two metrics allow relevance to be measured independent of a particular user's need. To do so, a researcher needs to know the full extent of a particular corpus, to know what kinds of resources have not been ranked highly, as well as alternative ways of searching a repository, in order to make comparisons to other ways of searching. Given the expansive nature of the web and the lack of alternative to Google's search engine, these metrics – fundamental for measuring *Idealist* relevance – do not translate well into evaluating search engines. Not only have Google's competitors been shrinking in number, but those that are still active do not necessarily produce an alternative set of results. Outside of countries such as China that have their own language-specific or country-specific search engines, the two main alternatives, in terms of global market share, are Bing and Yahoo!, with 2.38 per cent and 1.79 per cent, respectively. However, although it is not necessarily widely known, Yahoo!'s search engine is powered exclusively by Bing, the only difference between the two sites being that Yahoo! still acts as a portal for other curated sites. Additionally, investigations have shown that there have been examples where Bing has copied Google's results wholesale, rather than using their own metrics to provide search results. For example, in 2011, Google ran several tests in which they took a range of unique queries, such as [delhipublicschool40 chdjob] and [hiybbprqag], and linked them to specially chosen unrelated web page results. In doing so, they created a system in which copied results could be easily detected; such a system is similar to older methods to detect plagiarism used in cartography, such as the insertion of fake or paper towns, and fictitious entries into encyclopaedias. The tests were outlined in Sullivan's 2011 article 'Google: Bing Is Cheating, Copying Our Search Results' and Amit Singhal's official Google blog post 'Microsoft's Bing uses Google search results – and denies it'. Putting aside the numerous legal issues that the incident raised, this example demonstrates how Google's results represent a gold standard to such an extent that its competitors want their results to replicate Google's, rather than offer an alternative. Such a situation means that traditional metrics for calculating relevance, in a nonpersonalized sense, cannot be applicable. Therefore, the rhetoric that – mathematically speaking – search engines could be measurably neutral, objective, or unbiased is unfortunately impossible with our current metrics. The metrics and rhetoric of *Idealists* thought have gained significant dominance over the way that search engines are evaluated by engineers and have become a familiar defence against the scrutiny of lawmakers, the press, and the wider public. But there are other ways we might conceptualize relevance; these different approaches can be described as sharing a *Contextualist* viewpoint.

The Contextualists*: Search is undemocratic, relevance is a measure of personalization, and all answers are inherently biased*

John Battelle's 2005 landmark study *The Search* closes with a chapter devoted to what Battelle terms 'perfect search' (251–80). In doing so, Battelle outlines what he considered to be the fundamental characteristics of search engines, compared with other ways we have organized knowledge throughout history, and what a fully realized implementation of their logic would look like. Battelle describes 'perfect search' in the following way:

> Imagine the ability to ask any question and get not just an accurate answer, but your perfect answer – an answer that suits the context and intent of your question, an answer that is informed by who you are and why you might be asking. . . . While it's true that most questions don't have an objectively perfect answer, perfect search would provide *your* perfect answer, as you determine it – in a report form, perhaps, or by summarizing key points of view and trends. This perfect search also has perfect recall – it knows what you've seen, and can discern between a journey of discovery – where you want to find something new – and recovery – where you want to find something you've seen before. . . . [T]he search engine of the future [is] more like an intelligent agent – or as Larry Page told me, a reference librarian with complete mastery of the entire corpus of human knowledge. (252)

Battelle's description of '*your* perfect answer' neatly describes the perspective of the *Contextualists*, which has been highly influential in search engine design and evaluation throughout their development. Such attitudes have been used to justify and normalize data collection, for example, recording a user's location so that if they searched [weather], [cafes], or [news], the results could be contextually relevant, rather than pages that would be somewhat relevant to all users in every location at all times. However, the 'why you might be asking' is a complex and political question but one that is nullified by treating users as consumers whose personal desires must not be challenged. Current search engine expectations might consider the 'perfect answer' to the query [weather] to be an indication of the chance of rain, what kind of coat we should wear, or if we should order an Uber. But from a different point of view, the 'perfect answer' to the query [weather] could provide an overview of average temperatures in the last ten years to show that today's bad weather is a direct effect of our climate emergency, or weather reports from other parts of the globe that feel the impacts even more acutely. Such results could even show the comparative carbon cost between ordering an Uber, catching the bus, or walking to work with an umbrella. Such results might not be considered useful or tailored to 'the intent of your question', but they would still be highly contextually relevant for an individual who has the agency and resources to meaningfully change their behaviour. This example should show that there is no single way to determine *Contextualist* relevance and every attempt represents a particular set of ideological assumptions about the purposes of technology.

An example of *Contextualist* design within early search engine development is evidenced in the publications of a Palo Alto research team led by James Pitkow, which foreground personalization as central to the definition of relevance. Published in 2002, 'Personalized Search' documents a series of search engine comparison tests, carried out two years prior, between existing search engines and the team's system of modifying Google's results: Outride. Their Outride technology used various pieces of information, such as the 'last 1,000 unique clicks of each user' (53), to re-rank Google's results for each user in a personalized manner. Pitkow et al. describe the attitude embodied by Outride, in the following way:

> Focusing on the user enables a shift from what we call 'consensus relevancy' where the computed relevancy for the entire population is presumed relevant for each user, toward personal relevancy where relevancy is computed based on each individual within the context of their interactions. The benefits of personalized search can be significant, appreciably decreasing the time it takes people – novices and experts alike – to find information. (50)

Their experiments tested participants in laboratory conditions by giving individuals an information retrieval task, asking them to use various search engines as well as a test condition in which Outride had re-ranked results, to be personalized around each user. Pitkow et al. measured the time it took for users to find the pieces of information and found that their re-ranking sped up the information retrieval. However, focusing on retrieving specific pieces of information, rather than more qualitative or open-ended tasks means that their study did not reflect on the ethics of personalized search. Although we might question the value of speeding up simple searches, Google were impressed with the findings and consequently acquired the 'intellectual property, including patent rights, source code, trademarks, and associated domain names, from Outride Inc'. (Google, 'Google Acquires Technology') in 2001, a year before Pitkow et al. published their results. This acquisition means that Google were interested in incorporating this notion of personalized relevance in their search engine from at least 2001.

A key part of discussions around personalized relevance centres on privacy and surveillance. Michael Zimmer's 2008 article 'The Gaze of the Perfect Search Engine: Google as an Infrastructure of Dataveillance', published in the influential edited collection *Web Search* that he co-edited with Amanda Spink, discusses the extent to which search engines require personal data to function. Zimmer builds on Battelle's notion of *perfect search* to argue that relevant results require 'the collection of personal information [as] a prerequisite of participation' (93). Dataveillance is, for Zimmer, a necessary part of the deal that users strike upon using Google's search engine, which he characterizes in the following way:

> a Faustian bargain emerges with the quest for the perfect search engine: The perfect search engine promises breadth, depth, efficiency, and relevancy, but enables the widespread collection of personal and intellectual information in the name of its

perfect recall [. . . However,] viable and constitutional solutions are difficult to conceive, let alone agree upon. (93–4)

Zimmer's perspective is that for search engines to become 'perfect', data collection and surveillance are necessary. Specifically, Zimmer calls for greater transparency into the metrics of the search process. In June 2016, Google added a feature called 'My Activity', which shows users all the information stored about them. Although a useful step in the direction of transparency, such a tool does not show how this information is used or what other assumptions are made about specific user behaviours. Nor does it challenge the more vital question of *how* search engines should provide results. Whether search engines should personalize or aim for a general relevance is a much bigger issue than each user's privacy. If all users received exactly the same results, how could these be chosen to benefit everyone equally, without discriminating, and not to prioritize some needs over others? Conversely, if Google's results were designed to be entirely specific to each user and their present context, at what point does public discourse start to break down or existing inequalities become exacerbated?

Are search results personalized?

The answer to the question 'are search results personalized?' is not simple and relies on understanding personalization as a heading for a number of different kinds of practices, rather than a distinct activity. To understand personalization in relation to Google's search results, it is helpful to consider two distinct personalization practices: profiling and pattern recognition. Profiling is the activity of assigning individuals with unique identifiers, based on a phone number or email address, which consolidate widespread data collection. These profiles can then be sold and traded so that they follow us into many aspects of our lives. In a report on corporate surveillance and digital tracking, Wolfie Christl and Sarah Spiekermann, write that

> Many companies co-operate at a large scale to complete their profiles about us through various networks they have built up. The profiles they trade are filled with thousands of attributes per person. These networked databases are not only abused to discriminate against people with specific profile attributes, but also attempt to make us change our behavior at scale. (7)

This kind of profiling cross-references different databases to build up characteristics for a user, for example, their assumed gender, political attitudes, income, and credit status. These profiles are used widely for predictive advertising, including Google's personalized advertising, which is discussed directly in this book's final chapter. These categories are also used for what Safiya Umoja Noble refers to as 'technological redlining' whereby profiles are used to 'reinforce oppressive social relations' in a digital equivalent of how redlining by banks and real estate agencies caused people of colour to 'pay higher interest rates or premiums just because they are Black or Latino, especially if they live in low-income neighbourhoods' (1). Ruha Benjamin states that this kind of discriminatory profiling is often defended by the companies carrying out the profiling under the guise of inclusivity and that by 'fixing group identities as stable features of the social landscape, these technical fixes offer a kind of remedy for the shortcomings of a mass-marketing approach to consumer life' (147). Such profiles can be used to produce hyper-targeted advertising in which populations are segregated by income, race, or gender or any of the thousands of identity markers assigned to individuals. The ethical implications of this kind of personalization are significant and wide-reaching, for example, preventing a job advert from being listed to people with a particular marital status, those living in certain neighbourhoods, or nonbinary and gender nonconforming people.

So, if Google relies upon profile-based personalization to generate its advertising revenue, does this mean search engine results are also determined by the same profile-based personalization tactics? The current academic consensus is that, no, profile-based personalization does not play a major role in search engine results in the way that it does Google's advertising programmes. Haider and Sundin explain this in the following way:

> searches are definitely personalised in terms of geo-location of the searcher (Kilman-Silver et al. 2015) and while this makes a lot of sense if we consider the billions of results a simple search for pizza generates, this can potentially also be highly problematic [as] there are always assumptions about what type of people are residents of a certain town or area, and data to describe a location often includes average income, political leanings and so on. There are of course also other personalisations involved, depending on the topic and type of search, such as someone's search history. Yet these personalisations seem to have little impact on the organic search results (compare Hannak et al. 2013; Dutton et al. 2017). . . . Having said that, adverts are clearly heavily personalised and here various types of demographic data is processed to infer information about the individual user. (65–6)

However, this does not mean that Google's results are the same for everyone and to appreciate how this takes place it is important to understand a second type of digital personalization: pattern recognition. Göran Bolin and Jonas Andersson Schwarz explain pattern recognition personalization in the following way:

> The explanatory dimension of representational statistics (e.g. 'this group of people behave like this due to their social composition and their habitus privileging certain kinds of action over others') becomes less important than the establishment of correlations between (probable) behavioural patterns. The socially explainable 'who' behind this pattern is less important than the algorithmically predictable behavioural 'how'. (5)

Rather than building up a list of attributes for specific individuals, this mode of personalization focuses on large-scale behaviour tracking in order to identify relationships between different kinds of behaviours. In using Big Data in this way, algorithmic systems can still personalize the online experience of anonymous individuals or users who cannot be tied to a specific profile. This method certainly still carries biases and can be used as a tool of discrimination, but is much harder to understand, given its predictions do not directly relate to specific demographic categories used in other kinds of personalization. Digital media scholar Tanya Kant describes this complex situation in the following way:

> in order to identify and anticipate individuals for the sake of personalization, the 'person' being tracked is essentially disassembled into a selection of data points. As Cheney-Lippold (2017) considers, we are no longer 'individuals' within the system, but abstract and algorithmically manageable constellations of data. . . . Thus, to speak of Google and Facebook tracking 'you', as privacy advocates often speak of, becomes largely redundant. (50–1)

This kind of pattern recognition means that Google does not need to profile specific individuals to personalize the kinds of results it gives particular users. This concept of pattern recognition provides a way of describing Google's method of providing different results to different users as a form of personalization, even if the search were to be done completely anonymously and, therefore, had no profile to personalize from. Tailoring results in this way produces *Contextualist* relevance, whereby context represents any part of the pattern recognition process and is not limited by the categorizations of user and environment. With this in mind, the following study aims to investigate what kinds of personalization occurs within Google's organic search results. Doing so highlights the kinds of ethical challenges raised by providing different results to users in different contexts, particularly where it is not clear that the results have been personalized at all. However, because these differences are not a filter that can be removed, but rather an intrinsic part of the process, this kind of personalized relevance becomes more difficult to critique than more explicit kinds of personalization.

Methodological challenges of studying search engines

The previous section focused on the question of *what should search results aim to be*. In doing so, I highlighted the two contrasting positions as *Idealist* relevance and *Contextualist* relevance that showed that even when using the same terminology, expectations of search engine technology can vary tremendously. In exploring *Contextualist* relevance, I showed that there are many different ways of tailoring results, some that represent personalization through individual profiling and others, such as pattern recognition, the effects of which are more diffuse, dynamic, and harder to critique directly. The following section aims to capture some of these differences between search contexts to directly explore how Google search results present different kinds of attitudes across various contexts. Cathy O'Neil provides an account of the situation in which researchers find themselves:

Auditors face resistance, however, often from the web giants, which are the closest thing we have to information utilities. Google, for example, has prohibited researchers from creating scores of fake profiles in order to map the biases of the search engine. If the company does in fact carry out bias audits, its preference is to keep them internal. That way they shield the algorithm's inner workings, and its prejudices, from outsiders. But insiders, suffering as we all do from confirmation bias, are more likely to see what they expect to find. They might not ask the most probing questions. And if they find injustices that appear to boost Google's bottom line ... well, that could lead to uncomfortable decisions, ones they'd certainly want to keep out of the public light. (211–12)

Google works to keep researchers from creating multiple user profiles that could be used to show different kinds of profile-based personalization in search results. However, as already detailed, although existing research has found that profile-based personalization, for example, browser cookies or information gained from a signed-in Google account, impacts Google's advertising, it has not been shown to significantly impact Google's non-sponsored search results. But there are other ways of conceiving of 'bias audits' (211). The remainder of this chapter consists of an approach to identify the kind of pattern recognition personalization that I describe as *Contextualist* relevance. In doing so, I analyse a selection of results in order to provide tangible examples to the question, 'what kind of results do we want Google to provide?' In addition, the longitudinal aspect of the study shows the ways that Google's results have changed throughout time, which I hope can enable the kind of public conversation where public citizens can consider the future of search engines and the ethical issues that should be considered.

Particular considerations for collecting search engine results

Researching search engine results presents numerous methodological challenges. First, the data and the specific algorithms are proprietary. As Frank Pasquale puts it: 'Deconstructing the black boxes of Big Data isn't easy. Even if they were willing to expose their methods to the public, [. . . the] conclusions they come to – are determined by complex formulas devised by legions of engineers and guarded by a phalanx of lawyers' (*The Black Box Society* 6). Not only is their secrecy because of market competitiveness, privacy concerns, and legal constraints but also the scale of the teams working on the algorithms mean that even if they were available their size and complexity prevents straightforward analysis.

Second, Rob Kitchin in his influential essay 'Thinking Critically about and Researching Algorithms' (2017), highlights that:

As well as being heterogeneous and embedded, algorithms are rarely fixed in form and their work in practice unfolds in multifarious ways. . . . Companies such as Google and Facebook might be live running dozens of different versions of an algorithm to assess their relative merits, with no guarantee that the version a user interacts with at one moment in time is the same as five seconds later. (21)

In fact, Google run a significantly larger number of tests than this, which they call live experiments. For example, in 2019, Google 'ran more than 17,000 live traffic experiments' in which results are altered at random and user behaviour is used to evaluate and change future results.[2] The result of these experiments is a huge number of changes; for example, in 2018, Google made '3,234', which equates to '8.86' a day (Meyers). The Internet Archive's Wayback Machine can archive snapshots of pages throughout time, but there is no way to return to historical Google search states. If a researcher claims a particular search resulted in a set of results, there is no way to check or repeat their search.

Third, there is no independent index to compare results found with the pages that do not get covered by search engines, what Lewandowski and Sünkler refer to as 'a missing baseline for comparing the results of a search engine to a "gold standard", as favoured in computer science research. It is questionable whether such a baseline can at all be established' (12). Commonly used methods in IR rate algorithms or ranking systems by comparing the retrieved results with a wider corpus or dataset. Therefore, when judging the quality of a set of search engine results, users and researchers can only compare results to other results *also* found using a search engine, mostly a rephrased query submitted to the same engine or an alternative search engine. Not only is the size of the deep web – those pages unfindable by web crawling spiders – unknown, but the vast majority of the surface web's content is also a mystery. Take a simple search, for example, a search for [algorithms] which returns 'about 356,000,000 results'. These results have been indexed by a search engine and returned as results but never prominently enough to be found by users or sufficiently analysed by researchers. Without the resources of a company such as Google, researchers are not able to properly compare the first page of results to the roughly 355,999,990 others to analyse what kinds of results Google might be hiding in plain sight.

Finally, all results are based on hundreds of contextually dependent signals specific to each search. Even the most rigorously organized research conditions cannot avoid providing Google with a range of information, such as location, which means there is no kind of neutral search. As Eszter Hargittai's frames the issue

> results change by user and user location, so a study conducted on one machine in one location by a particular user may not be possible to replicate on another machine under different circumstances, even soon after the initial query. This poses significant challenges for the replication of search results, which is a basic tenet of scientific investigation. ('The Social, Political' 772)

---

[2]For more information see, Google 'Search: How the insights of people . . .' and Google 'Search: Rigorous Testing.'

Search engine results cannot be thought of as universal or generalizable. It is widely agreed by researchers that results differ due to a range of factors. However, there are no studies that try to foreground these differences by collecting and evaluating search results, while changing the signals sent to Google. The existing methodological challenges make it impossible to conduct traditional quantitative experiments and draw definitive conclusions that fit within the 'basic tenet[s] of scientific investigation' (772). However, if we let go of the unrealistic aim of all-encompassing conclusions, rigorous experiments *can* teach us much about what signals are important within particular contexts and in doing so, highlight some of the ethical questions that search results raise. The following sections of this chapter detail an experimental response to this situation that shows an example of how to work productively within these methodological constraints.

Variables that matter: Search experiments in 2015, 2017, and 2021

On 24 November 2015, 22 November 2017, and 17 May 2021, I conducted a series of experiments in which I searched a set of queries related to same-sex sexual orientation under different conditions and evaluated each result listed on Google's first page of results. Six queries written in English were translated into French and Arabic and the eighteen queries were searched with the locations of the UK, France, and Morocco. This led to fifty-four searches, which were evaluated and compared to highlight the different kinds of results produced for each instance. Before presenting the results, I will outline the rationale behind using queries about gay lives, the specific queries used, evaluation method, and Google's public position on providing contextually-specific results.

The rationale behind focusing on same-sex sexual orientation

The topic of same-sex relationships is a useful example for two main reasons. First, gay relationships are treated very differently in various countries, fully accepted and celebrated in some locations, while in others considered legally and morally controversial and subject to significant punishments. Therefore, in many cases around the world, queries about being gay are literally a life-or-death matter. Google's search results provide information on how people should think of themselves and how they should act towards others. The second reason is that the kinds of search results on the topic of same-sex relationships can consist of many different discourses that appeal to various kinds of evidence and argument. The majority of web pages returned by Google for queries related to same-sex sexual orientation aim to be persuasive and are written with an appeal to different kinds of authority, including legal, moral, religious, medical, and anecdotal perspectives. When analysing the differences between search results, it is not only important to highlight whether web pages present positive or negative attitudes towards being gay, but also the form that these arguments take. For example, the basis of their belief and whether the pages are framed as personal opinions or statements of fact. The question of relevance is key here, should an Arabic search in Morocco reflect views that might be highly relevant for that context, that is, a country in which being gay is illegal? Or should results be relevant in terms of a wider international consensus and highlight the voices of legal and medical institutions or LGBTQ+ activists and celebrities? When comparing the effects of terminology, for example, should the kinds of results for a query using the word [gay] be different to those that used the word [homosexual]? The words 'gay' and 'homosexual' represent very different kinds of language use and many institutions have formally designated 'homosexual' as offensive and recommend that it should not be used. For example, the Gay and Lesbian Alliance Against Defamation (GLAAD) publishes a guide that collates various media and industry standards explicitly against the use of the word 'homosexual'. The Associated Press, *The New York Times*, and *The Washington Post* restrict the use of the term 'homosexual' for the following reason:

> Because of the clinical history of the word 'homosexual', it is aggressively used by anti-gay extremists to suggest that gay people are somehow diseased or psychologically/emotionally disordered – notions discredited by the American Psychological Association and the American Psychiatric Association in the 1970s. (GLAAD Media Reference Guide – Terms to Avoid)

Given that these two linguistic registers signify very different things, should a query using the word [homosexual] present more material that is explicitly Anti-gay, or should the results be similar to queries that use the word [gay]? Google uses synonyms for search queries by default so all web pages using the word 'gay' or 'homosexual' will be returned for either search, however, the potential difference lies in how these results are ranked. If 'homosexual' is predominantly used by 'Anti-gay extremists' then are homophobic results the most relevant kind of results for that query? If so, should homophobic pages be ranked higher for queries using [homosexual] than those using [gay]? Such a question lies at the heart of why distinguishing what is meant by *relevance* is so crucial to debates around search results. In their discussion on the ethics of data science, Solon Barocas and Danah Boyd state that 'Unfortunately, certain problems may stem from genuine value conflicts, not simply a lack of attention to the values at stake' (24). In this case, it is not simply a case of researchers pointing out that some Google results are more homophobic than others, but that, if Google's algorithms are designed to give users the results that best fit that user – that is, *Contextualist* relevance – homophobic results may be the outcome of those algorithms working successfully. One of the biggest trends first discovered in 2015 was that queries using the word [homosexual] resulted in overwhelmingly homophobic results framed as 'factual' pages, which cited religious passages and outdated science, while using the word [gay] in queries produced a majority of Pro-gay pages framed as 'opinions', such as first-person accounts of coming out. This trend has changed throughout the study's six-year period but was still visible on a much smaller scale in 2021. There were a number of other findings, which will be discussed in more detail later in this chapter; however, I wanted to highlight this specific example now, to demonstrate that even subtle changes to search queries have important ethical consequences. Now that I have outlined the overall rationale for the study, as well as what is at stake in these debates, I will describe the process of selecting the search queries used and how the search results were evaluated.

Queries used

The six queries for each language were generated in the following way. To show potential differences in terminology, each query was either formulated using the word [homosexual] or [gay]. These two words have very different histories and contemporary usages, so although Google uses synonyms for its search, I wanted to see if this difference would be expressed in the results. To compare general to specific queries, these two words were searched in their singular noun form and also in the context of a question. To test the effects of value-laden phrasing, half the questions were phrased positively and the other half negatively; i.e. [Is being homosexual/gay wrong?] and [Is being homosexual/ gay good?]. These specific questions were taken from the highest-ranking Autocomplete suggestions that clearly presented a positive or negative phrasing at the time of the first study in 2015. These parameters led to the following six queries:

- [homosexuality]
- [gay]
- [Is being homosexual wrong?]
- [Is being gay wrong?]
- [Is being homosexual good?]
- [Is being gay good?]

This list of six queries was then translated using Google Translate into French and Arabic. The reason behind using Google Translate, rather than asking a native speaker, was to get queries that most reflected what Google's algorithms saw as the most comparable in other languages. Each of these queries was searched from the locations of the UK, France, and Morocco using a VPN.[3] This led to a total of fifty-four searches, from which I could compare single word versus sentence query, terminology (i.e., [homosexual] versus [gay]), positive versus negative phrasing (i.e., [wrong] versus [good]), search location, and query language. I searched, recorded, and qualitatively evaluated every search result from the first page for each query in 2015, 2017, and 2021. An example of the fifty-four queries and their evaluation for 2015 is shown in Table 3.

---

[3]A Virtual Private Network (VPN) was used to send queries from servers in UK, Morocco, and France, on a fresh browser, which also served to anonymize the signals. Specific locations were also selected in Google's search settings and the browser history, data, and cookies were wiped after each search so that each query was conducted on a fresh browser. The success of this method was double-checked by running the experiment with a second VPN and using Tor to make sure my real location or any other identifiable information was being picked up by Google and used to serve results for the experiment.

Table 3 This table shows the complete list of the fifty-four search queries tested and the ratings of the first page of results for each, for the 2015 results. French and Arabic queries were translated using Google Translate so that the query would represent what *Google considers to be the most equivalent.*

Country	Language	Term	Opinion Pro-gay	"Factual" Pro-gay	Opinion Neutral	"Factual" Neutral	Opinion Anti-gay	"Factual" Anti-gay
UK	English	Homosexuality	4	1	0	5	1	3
France	English	Homosexuality	2	2	0	4	0	2
Morocco	English	Homosexuality	1	2	0	3	0	7
UK	English	Gay	7	3	0	1	0	0
France	English	Gay	2	6	0	1	0	0
Morocco	English	Gay	3	2	0	3	0	0
UK	French	Homosexualité	1	6	0	2	0	0
France	French	Homosexualité	1	6	0	2	0	0
Morocco	French	Homosexualité	1	6	0	2	0	0
UK	French	Gay	0	0	0	0	0	0
France	French	Gay	0	1	0	6	0	0
Morocco	French	Gay	0	1	0	6	0	0
UK	Arabic	الشذوذ الجنسي	0	0	0	3	3	4
France	Arabic	الشذوذ الجنسي	0	0	0	4	2	4
Morocco	Arabic	الشذوذ الجنسي	0	0	0	4	1	4
UK	Arabic	مثلي الجنس	3	2	0	4	1	0
France	Arabic	مثلي الجنس	4	2	0	2	1	0
Morocco	Arabic	مثلي الجنس	3	3	0	2	1	1
UK	English	Is being homosexual wrong?	1	0	3	1	0	5
France	English	Is being homosexual wrong?	2	0	1	0	0	7
Morocco	English	Is being homosexual wrong?	1	0	2	0	0	7
UK	English	Is being gay wrong?	3	0	2	0	0	5
France	English	Is being gay wrong?	4	0	2	0	0	4
Morocco	English	Is being gay wrong?	3	0	2	0	0	5
UK	French	Est-ce qu'être homosexuel mal?	4	5	0	1	0	0
France	French	Est-ce qu'être homosexuel mal?	4	3	2	1	0	0
Morocco	French	Est-ce qu'être homosexuel mal?	4	3	1	2	0	0
UK	French	Est-ce qu'être mauvais gay?	5	4	1	0	0	0
France	French	Est-ce qu'être mauvais gay?	5	2	2	1	0	0
Morocco	French	Est-ce qu'être mauvais gay?	4	3	2	1	0	0
UK	Arabic	هل كونك شاذ جنسيا خطأ؟	1	0	2	2	0	5
France	Arabic	هل كونك شاذ جنسيا خطأ؟	1	0	1	4	1	3
Morocco	Arabic	هل كونك شاذ جنسيا خطأ؟	1	0	0	4	1	4
UK	Arabic	يجري خاطئ مثلي الجنس؟	1	0	1	3	0	5
France	Arabic	يجري خاطئ مثلي الجنس؟	1	0	1	4	1	3
Morocco	Arabic	يجري خاطئ مثلي الجنس؟	1	0	1	3	2	3
UK	English	Is being homosexual good?	2	1	6	1	0	0
France	English	Is being homosexual good?	1	0	6	2	0	1
Morocco	English	Is being homosexual good?	3	2	4	0	0	1
UK	English	Is being gay good?	8	1	1	0	0	0
France	English	Is being gay good?	7	1	1	0	0	1
Morocco	English	Is being gay good?	6	1	2	0	0	1
UK	French	Est-ce qu'être bonne homosexuelle?	0	2	0	2	0	0
France	French	Est-ce qu'être bonne homosexuelle?	2	3	0	4	0	1
Morocco	French	Est-ce qu'être bonne homosexuelle?	2	3	0	4	0	1
UK	French	Est-ce qu'être bonne gay?	6	3	1	0	0	0
France	French	Est-ce qu'être bonne gay?	3	4	2	1	0	0
Morocco	French	Est-ce qu'être bonne gay?	1	5	3	1	0	0
UK	Arabic	يجري جيدة مثلي الجنس؟	2	0	0	1	0	0
France	Arabic	يجري جيدة مثلي الجنس؟	3	0	0	3	0	0
Morocco	Arabic	يجري جيدة مثلي الجنس؟	0	0	0	0	0	0
UK	Arabic	يجري مثلي الجنس جيدة؟	3	3	1	1	1	0
France	Arabic	يجري مثلي الجنس جيدة؟	0	2	0	1	0	0
Morocco	Arabic	يجري مثلي الجنس جيدة؟	3	1	2	2	0	1

Capturing the spread of results from the first page

Only results from Google's first page were taken into account. As highlighted in the introduction (see Chart 1), research conducted in 2013 and 2020 shows that the vast majority of search results selected are from Google's first page. Therefore, only analysing results from the first page is the most representative of a general search experience. The reason for drawing on all results from the first page, rather than the first three, four, or five results, is to describe the overall landscape of search presented to a user. The first couple of results receive a much larger proportion of users selecting them. However,

I wanted the experimental design to capture whether the page provided a wide range of positions or not. The user might select the top result most of the time, but there is a significant difference between a results page in which all the results are ideologically in line with one another and a results page that represents a mix of viewpoints and discursive modes. Such a difference may have a significant impact on how the attitudes of an individual are challenged or reinforced. In 2015, Google's results page consistently provided ten results; however, over time the average number of results per page has become more variable and greatly increased for particular contexts, such as searches on mobile devices.[4] In order for the longitudinal results to remain comparable, only the first ten results for each query were considered.

Evaluation method

The search results were evaluated on two scales; first, the ethical stance they took on same-sex sexual orientation, listed as either Pro-gay, Neutral, or Anti-gay and, second, how that stance was framed, as either representing an Opinion or claiming to represent 'Factual' information. This way of evaluating the results was formulated in response to preliminary tests in which I found that search results were either presented as personal opinion, for example, a blog written in the first person about being a lesbian, or pages that made ethical judgements using citation or truth claims on behalf of an institution, for example, pages cited the World Health Organization or passages from religious texts. The judgement of pages as either Opinion or 'Factual' was purely dependent on the framing of the page and was not in any way related to whether or not the pages were convincing, robust, or credible. Combined, these two scales resulted in the web page being assigned as one of six types of pages: examples of each page are listed as Figures 38–43. Essentially, I wanted to see what *kinds* of search results were given for a query like [Is being gay wrong?]. Would the results come in the form of blogs or academic research papers? Would these pages claim to speak for a single person's opinion or represent an account of the truth, as evidenced by citations of religious, legal, or medical 'facts'? As highlighted throughout this book, search engines are tools to amplify some voices over others and emphasize particular modes of communication as important, while relegating others to positions where they will not be found. Therefore, the form of pages and the authority with which they claim to speak is as important as the ethical stance they take on any given issue.

Google's public position on how they provide results

As will be clear from the first half of this chapter, Google's main way of responding to ethical questions about search results is to use ambiguous language and, in particular,

---

[4]See Nick Fox 'How Google Organizes Information to Find What You're Looking For' for an account of how many results are listed on a results page in 2020.

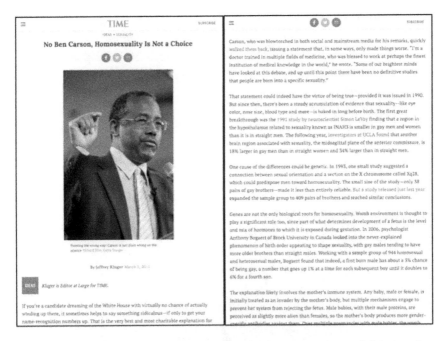

Figure 38 An example of a web page result categorized as Pro-gay 'Factual': 'No Ben Carson, Homosexuality Is Not a Choice'. Written by *Time*'s Jeffrey Kluger the article takes a clear Pro-gay stance. The page bases its arguments on reference and citation to hyperlinked scientific studies and is framed in a 'Factual' discourse throughout (see Kluger). Accessed 22 August 2017. These examples were added after the experiment was repeated in 2017 and 2021 and, therefore, some of the pages were published after the original 2015 test. Figures 38–43 represent examples of the kinds of ratings given to pages, rather than exact results found in the 2015 study.

deploying the word 'relevance'. In using terminology that means oppositional things to different people, Google maintains their position that their aim is to make *better* more *effective* search tools, in an attempt to exempt them from taking responsibility. However, one exception to this avoidance of stating clear ideals of search is the following passage listed as part of their Mission Statement under the heading 'Our approach to Search'.

Our company mission is to organise the world's information and make it universally accessible and useful. That's why Search makes it easy to discover a broad range of information from a wide variety of sources. Some information is purely factual, like the height of the Eiffel Tower. For more complex topics, Search is a tool to explore many angles so that you can form your own understanding of the world. (Google, 'Our approach to Search')

In this passage, Google explicitly claim that for complex search topics, in which there is more than one perspective, their results aim to present multiple points of view. This kind of language is particularly unusual for Google. The earliest example of this kind of

Figure 39 An example of a web page result categorized as Pro-gay Opinion: 'Why Being Gay Is Better Than Being Straight'. Written by Matt Stopera and Lauren Yapalater, two writers for *Buzzfeed*, the page is a humorous list of pop culture references that takes a Pro-gay stance and does not cite any 'Factual' evidence (see Stopera and Yapalater). Accessed 22 August 2017.

iteration is from December 2020. Such a statement chimes with some of the viewpoints presented earlier in the chapter when considering the *Idealists*, including scholars like Diaz who demand that 'underrepresented voices and diverse viewpoints be heard through the filter of search engines' (15). One of the conclusions of my experiment is that, overall, in 2015, the kinds of results were much more diverse, in terms of the ethical positions taken (Pro-gay, Anti-gay, or Neutral) and their framing (Opinion or 'Factual') than in 2021. Therefore, while their corporate messaging has changed to explicitly state that their aim for Search is to 'explore many angles so that you can form your own understanding of the world', the findings of my study show the opposite trajectory. A trend in my study is that all results across all contexts are less homophobic and more pro-LGBTQ+ than six years ago and that the kinds of results are much less diverse. Those of us from LGBTQ+ communities might personally celebrate such a change, but it certainly goes against the new kinds of public messaging regarding the heart of their mission.

Figure 40 An example of a web page result categorized as Neutral Opinion: debate.org 'Is homosexuality wrong'. This page is an open forum for users to submit their opinions on a particular topic. The page presents a mix of Pro-gay and Anti-gay stances and the submitted posts do not generally cite any 'Factual' evidence, rather they provide various personal opinions (see debate.org). Accessed 22 August 2017.

In discussing the location of search queries, it is important to note that Google have clear legal responsibilities to the laws of specific countries. Their Transparency Report details the instances where individuals, companies, or countries have demanded they remove certain results and the decision taken in response. For example, '11% of the German removal requests are related to pro-Nazi content or content advocating denial of the Holocaust, both of which are illegal under German law' (Google, 'Transparency Report, Germany'). However, unless they are legally compelled to comply, Google claim that they do not censor results; for example, another German appeal details 'a request from a law enforcement agency to remove a YouTube video that allegedly depicts state symbols in a disparaging way' to which Google 'did not remove the video'. Localized search reflects local laws, but aside from these explicit and very rare cases of legally required intervention, Google do not disclose how different contexts or signals change results,

Figure 41 An example of a web page result categorized as Neutral 'Factual': Pew Research Center's article 'The Global Divide on Homosexuality'. The article presents the findings of a global survey on attitudes towards same-sex relationships. The article does not present any value judgements but states the results in the following way: 'The view that homosexuality should be accepted by society is prevalent in most of the European Union countries surveyed. . . . Overwhelming majorities in the predominantly Muslim countries surveyed also say homosexuality should be rejected, including 97% in Jordan, 95% in Egypt, 94% in Tunisia, 93% in the Palestinian territories, 93% in Indonesia, 87% in Pakistan, 86% in Malaysia, 80% in Lebanon and 78% in Turkey'. Accessed 22 August 2021.

beyond their usual rhetoric of making results *relevant*. But search results *do* change; every time a query is searched, Google base the results and their rank on specific signals, over 200 different factors, as outlined in Chapter 1, which can lead to highly variable results for otherwise identical queries.[5]

---

[5]For the most up-to-date description of how Google localizes search, see Sullivan 'How location helps provide more relevant search results,' published in 2020.

Figure 42 An example of a web page result categorized as Anti-gay Opinion: Mass Resistance 'What's wrong with being 'gay'? Here's what they don't tell you – and it's really disturbing'. This anonymously written page takes a clear Anti-Gay stance and, although the article does use terms such as 'truth' and 'fact' throughout, it does not present references or citations to external sources as the basis for the claims made. The hyperlink 'Dr. Paul Church brings up the truth,' pictured earlier, appears as if it might indicate a 'Factual' discourse, however, the link is to another article from the same website that details the author's personal opinion regarding a doctor who was fired for violating the discrimination and harassment policy of their workplace (see Mass Resistance). Accessed 22 August 2017.

Summary of 2015 results

Users cannot search without a language, without a location, or outside of time. Other signals that Google takes into account to rank results can be obscured by users, but these remain inescapable characteristics used to calculate the relevance of results. Charts 2–4 show a representation of the search results for each of the three languages searched in each country when searched in 2015. The graphs show some general trends in the kinds of pages provided by Google, regardless of context, but also that language and location

Figure 43 An example of a web page result categorized as Anti-gay 'Factual': Christian Answer's 'What's wrong with being gay? Homosexual behaviour versus the Bible'. The result takes a clearly Anti-gay stance. The discourse of the page is framed as 'Factual' as each statement made throughout is linked to a piece of external evidence, including biblical scripture and scientific papers (see Lamont). Accessed 22 August 2017.

do significantly impact the kinds of pages given as results. In terms of overall numbers of Pro-gay and Anti-gay results, searching in French resulted in almost a complete lack of homophobic results, English results were more mixed, while Arabic queries resulted in more Anti-gay pages than Pro-gay results.

A particularly significant wider trend was that Anti-gay results were almost always framed as 'Factual', while Pro-gay results were split between 'Factual' and Opinion pages. This intensified for specific languages, for example, when searching queries in English (see Chart 2), the two most common kinds of pages for each location was Pro-gay content framed as Opinions and Anti-gay content framed as 'Factual' information. It is problematic that Google's results provided Positive representations in a range of modes or only as Opinions, whereas Negative accounts were framed almost solely as cut-

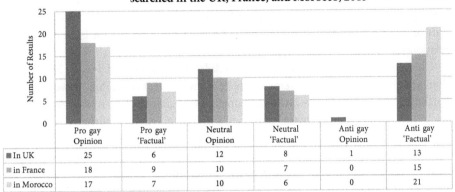

English queries
searched in the UK, France, and Morocco, 2015

	Pro gay Opinion	Pro gay 'Factual'	Neutral Opinion	Neutral 'Factual'	Anti gay Opinion	Anti gay 'Factual'
In UK	25	6	12	8	1	13
in France	18	9	10	7	0	15
in Morocco	17	7	10	6	0	21

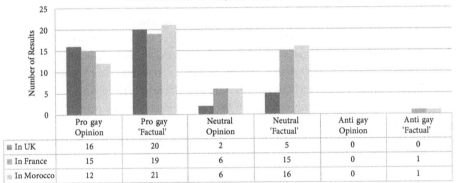

French queries
searched in the UK, France, and Morocco, 2015

	Pro gay Opinion	Pro gay 'Factual'	Neutral Opinion	Neutral 'Factual'	Anti gay Opinion	Anti gay 'Factual'
In UK	16	20	2	5	0	0
In France	15	19	6	15	0	1
In Morocco	12	21	6	16	0	1

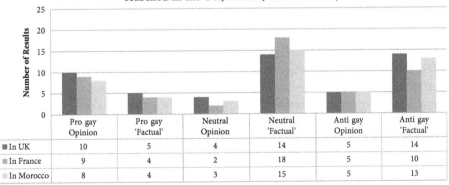

Arabic queries
searched in the UK, France, and Morocco, 2015

	Pro gay Opinion	Pro gay 'Factual'	Neutral Opinion	Neutral 'Factual'	Anti gay Opinion	Anti gay 'Factual'
In UK	10	5	4	14	5	14
In France	9	4	2	18	5	10
In Morocco	8	4	3	15	5	13

Chart 2–4 These graphs show the results for each language across the three geographical domains of the UK, France, and Morocco.

and-dried 'Factual' statements. These negative 'Factual' pages cited religious or scientific truths and represented institutional knowledge that claimed to conclusively prove that being gay is immoral or an illness. Regardless of the ratio of Pro- and Anti-gay results, only providing Anti-gay results that claimed to be 'Factual' frames the issue of same-sex relationships within a wholly different discourse.

Charts 2–4 also show that searching in a different language had a much bigger effect than searching queries in the same language from different countries. However, not all languages were impacted by location change to the same degree. Arabic, for example, had much less deviation between countries: searching in Arabic returned the same kind of results in each of the three countries tested. By contrast, searching using English in different locations led to a greater level of variation in results. Searching using English in the UK provided a high number of Pro-gay Opinion-based results, in comparison to searching using English in France, or English in Morocco (Chart 2). Searching using English in Morocco also produced more Anti-gay 'Factual' results than using English in France or the UK, while searching using English in France produced more Pro-gay 'Factual' results. However, searching using French was relatively consistent across domains except for results in the UK; searching using French in the UK led to fewer Neutral results compared to searching French in France or Morocco, as well as a complete absence of Anti-gay results. This is interesting because searching in English was generally more Anti-gay than searching in French, but searching French in France was more Anti-gay than searching French in France (Chart 3). The changes of signals do not make predictable or linear changes to the results. Each specific context has its own, often surprising, rules covering what kinds of results are produced. Therefore, we cannot necessarily say that the effect of translating a query into French has a similar effect to searching that query in France.

A number of domain-specific conclusions can be drawn from such results. For instance, searches that used English were noticeably affected by changes in location, whereas the search results of queries searched using Arabic were less affected by changes in location. The reasons for this might be based on the frequency of second-language speakers. The variation is likely due to a particular user base of individuals actually using English regularly in these various countries, which provides Google with a larger amount of data to draw from to make ranking decisions for these specific contexts. As Arabic is a less common second language than English, fewer users are using Arabic to search in France and the UK. Other evidence for this claim lies in the different results provided for queries searched using Arabic in France and the UK and queries using French in the UK and Morocco (see Charts 3 and 4). For example, the percentage of Arabic speakers living in France is significantly higher than in the UK. As Emmanuelle Talon stated in 2012 in *Le Monde*, 'With four million speakers, Arabic is the second most spoken language on French territory'; this amounts to roughly 6 per cent of the population of France. In the UK, according to the 2011 census, there were 159,000 Arabic speakers; this roughly equates to 0.3 per cent of the population. Considering the history of the French Protectorate in Morocco, immigration from the Maghreb region, and other related cultural associations, I predicted that searching using French in Morocco or using

Arabic in France might demonstrate a greater overlap in the kinds of results produced, compared to searching using English in Morocco or Arabic in the UK. However, rather than similar results, searching using Arabic in France produced a bigger deviation from the results using Arabic in Morocco than searching using Arabic in the UK (see Charts 4 and 2). Throughout, the study provided numerous examples in which each context – the combination of language, geography, terminology, and phrasing – does not lead to predictable outcomes.

The different criteria have complex and unpredictable relationships that do not work on an additive basis. An example that demonstrates this can be seen by comparing the differences in the number of Neutral Opinion and Neutral 'Factual' results of the searches using English in the UK and using French in the UK (Charts 2 and 3). Chart 2 shows that the searches using English returned the largest number of Neutral Opinion and Neutral 'Factual' when searched in the UK, compared with France and Morocco. If these criteria had an additive relationship, we would predict that using another language in the UK might follow a similar pattern. However, looking at the results of Neutral Opinion and Neutral 'Factual' when searching using French in the UK (see Chart 3), the amount returned was significantly lower than in France or Morocco. Therefore, these different contexts do not have additive relationships, as if the French search results has been anglicized or UK-ified. Rather than seeing each characteristic as a form of filter, or as an ingredient in a recipe that produces results, each set of results is created through an assemblage of intersecting criteria. There are differences in the results for different countries and different languages, but these are not necessarily predictable and do not follow a clear pattern whereby changing one specific metric has the same kind of result in all other contexts. Therefore, it would be wrong to make an overarching conclusion concerning a particular language, for example, that searching using Arabic promotes particular kinds of pages because searching using Arabic has a very different impact in the UK than it does in France. However, comparing specific contexts demonstrates that Google results may fulfil very different roles in various contexts. Looking again at Chart 3, searching using French, shows, in aggregate, a very particular attitude presented. The lack of both forms of Anti-gay results highlights the kind of editorial role that Google might fulfil to French speakers. According to these results, French speakers searching in the UK received almost exclusively Pro-gay results, whether framed 'Factually' or as Opinion. Whereas searching using Arabic in the UK presented the most homophobic results of any context. These two conditions could represent next-door neighbours, searching the same queries mere metres apart and receiving radically different results. This is without even considering additional factors, such as the further personalization if they were signed into their Google accounts.

Based on these results, searching using English in each of the three countries (see Chart 2) demonstrated an outlook whereby Pro-gay were framed as Opinions, while Anti-gay attitudes were framed as 'Facts'. This, again, deviates from the view whereby changes in the country location function as simply additives or combinations of perspectives. Searches using English in Morocco (see Chart 2) resulted in the highest number of Anti-gay 'Factual' results in comparison to Neutral 'Factual' results (21 versus 6).

It would be all too easy to jump to a conclusion whereby these English language results have been passed through a filter of Moroccan conservativism. However, Chart 4 shows that, when using Arabic, the number of Neutral 'Factual' results outnumbered the Anti-gay 'Factual' ones (15 versus 13). Therefore, the context of searching using English in Morocco cannot be predicted by taking the results of searching using Arabic in Morocco and applying certain English search characteristics or vice versa by taking results using English in the UK and adding any perceived effects of a Moroccan search environment. These characteristics exist in a fluid and complex relationship with one another in which causal links are difficult to pinpoint. A key point also has to be reiterated, these results cannot be taken as representative, given the small sample size and that results continually change throughout time. However, the principal conclusion to draw from these results is that there is a greater difference across contexts than can be accounted for by Google's legally required censoring, shown earlier in their transparency report. What is clear from these results is that different linguistic and location contexts produce differently ranked results, which present significantly different ethical outlooks. It shows that Google's notion of relevance has serious moral implications.

By combining all of the 2015 results into one graph, we can see a number of trends (see Chart 5). The following generalizations can be made about each language's results: in this study, searching using English provided Pro-gay attitudes presented as Opinion and Anti-gay results framed as 'Facts'. Searching using French provided an almost totally Pro-gay perspective and, in particular, a much higher number of Pro-gay 'Factual' results than either of the other two languages. Searching in Arabic provided mostly Neutral 'Factual' results with a high number of Anti-gay 'Factual' pages.

These results provide an indication of each context's epistemic landscape, by which I mean the range of normative positions that Google presents for each query. Not only were there differences in sentiment, for example, French queries receiving much more

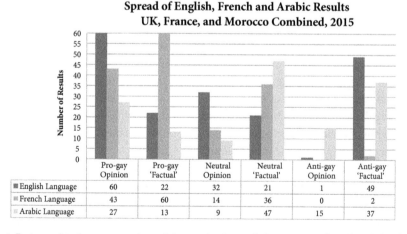

Spread of English, French and Arabic Results UK, France, and Morocco Combined, 2015

	Pro-gay Opinion	Pro-gay 'Factual'	Neutral Opinion	Neutral 'Factual'	Anti-gay Opinion	Anti-gay 'Factual'
■ English Language	60	22	32	21	1	49
■ French Language	43	60	14	36	0	2
▪ Arabic Language	27	13	9	47	15	37

Chart 5 A graphical representation of the results for each location combined and divided by language.

Pro-gay results than Arabic, but the different modes of discourse for each result indicate what kind of an authority Google Search provides in each language. Depending on the ratio of Opinion to 'Factual' results, in some contexts searching Google might seem like consulting a formally organized source of knowledge, such as a library or encyclopaedia; in other contexts, which provide a greater number of Opinion-based results, searching Google might be more akin to a town square or radio talk show. How beliefs are justified and evidenced is hugely important for debates, such as the ones surrounding LGBTQ+ communities. Whether presented as Opinion or 'Factual' viewpoints, Anti-gay results are offensive, support discrimination, and put people in danger. However, in my experience of reading through all of the search pages results in order to evaluate them, Anti-gay 'Factual' results are significantly more concerning. The 'facts' employed, and rhetoric of illness, madness, and sinning are often based on outdated scientific values, fabricated 'data' about dangers to society, and particular interpretations of religious texts. A key question that I will return to in the longitudinal aspect of this study is, to what extent should local 'knowledge' be challenged by values which are held in consensus by a wider global community. Given that this local 'knowledge' often underpins the laws, medical structures, and social constraints of a given society, they are, by the measure of the *Contextualists*, highly relevant forms of evidence. These examples reframe one of the company's mission statements outlined earlier: 'For more complex topics, Search is a tool to explore many angles so that you can form your own understanding of the world' ('Google: How Search Works: Our approach to Search'). These results for 2015 show that, in practice, not all users are receiving many 'angles' as highly ranked and deemed relevant. In particular, because users cannot see how different their results are to from someone else's – for example, their next-door neighbour whose first language is French – results framed as 'Factual' have an even greater influence, as they suggest that there are no alternatives on the topic. This is why the correlations of Pro-gay content expressed as Opinions and Anti-gay content expressed as 'Factual' are so troubling and have such significant consequences for living together in an increasingly globalized world.

How do variations in terminology and phrasing alter search results?

A key consideration, in addition to location and language, is the *kind* of words used: how much impact does terminology, vocabulary, and expression have on results; essentially, does the way in which individuals phrase a query determine the kinds of results they receive? In the context of this study, two kinds of alterations were made for comparison. First, the experiment tested a linguistic variation of each query, searching each query with the word [homosexual] and the word [gay], including Google's translated equivalents in each language. This variable was referred to as terminology. Second, a linguistic variation was introduced for the queries phrased as questions, substituting and comparing queries phrased with the word [wrong] or the word [good]. This variable, referred to as phrasing, was also replicated for each of the three languages and aimed to highlight the *phrasing* of queries that carried either a Positive or Negative sentiment. As noted earlier, [wrong] and [good] were the top sentiments suggested by Google Autocomplete in 2015 at the time of the first experiment. Formulating the queries in this way builds on the research of Chapter 3 and allows me to show a concrete example of how Autocomplete suggestions can significantly alter the kinds of results provided.

The following graphs (Charts 6–8) show the impact of terminology and represent the results of queries that were identical apart from the use of either [gay] or [homosexual]. Each set represents one open-ended search (simply the single word without context, i.e., [homosexual] or [gay]), one Negatively phrased search (i.e. [Is being homosexual wrong?] and [Is being gay wrong?]), and one Positively phrased search (i.e. [Is being homosexual good?] and [Is being gay good?]). The difference in results was clear, using [gay] produced more Positive and Opinion-based pages, while [homosexual] produced more Negative and 'Factually' framed results. Compared to the other languages, queries written in English provided the most extreme iteration, which provided a clear split: using [gay] in a query, such as [Is being gay wrong?], provided an overwhelming number of Positive Opinions, while search queries using the word 'homosexual', such as [Is being homosexual wrong?], resulted in a dominance of Negative 'Factual' results.

This shows that formulating queries with different terminology alters the framing and attitudes of results. In the English example, the use of [gay] provided a majority of Pro-gay Opinions, while [homosexual] resulted in mainly Anti-gay 'Factual' results, which presented religious or medical positions, in which same-sex relationships were described as a sin or an illness. Considering the GLAAD statements cited earlier that advise against the use of the word 'homosexual', given its use by homophobes, it is tempting to think that Google is simply finding pages that use one word or the other. However, this example is more complex than a correlation of different groups of people using different terminology. Google always searches synonyms by default. The most noteworthy aspect of these results is that, in these examples, Google's results matched the *representative* values of the main association of each term, regardless of whether the search results provided used the word 'gay' or 'homosexual'. For example, of the Anti-gay 'Factual' results for [homosexual], the pages often relied on the word 'gay' throughout, instead of the word 'homosexual'. By the same token, when web pages using the word 'homosexual' appeared as the results for a search of the term [gay], they were regularly Pro-gay and Opinion-based. This is in contrast to the kinds of pages using the word 'homosexual' usually returned for a query using the word [homosexual]. For example, Figure 44 titled 'What Does the Bible Say About Homosexuality' shows a web page, rated as Pro-gay. It was returned as a first-page result for the query [Is being gay wrong?] but not for the query [Is being homosexual wrong?], even though that page uses the word 'homosexual' thirteen times, including in its title, and the word 'gay' only eight times. The page is one of the only religious results that is Pro-gay and written in an Opinion discourse; see the final paragraph inside the black box.

Comparing this result to the graphical representation of the overall discourse in Chart 6 shows that the result fits with the usual Pro-gay sentiment that searching using the word [gay] in a query produces. That Figure 44 was not given as a result when searching [Is being homosexual wrong?], even though it uses the word 'homosexual' almost double

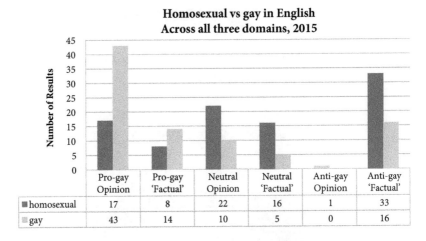

Homosexual vs gay in English
Across all three domains, 2015

	Pro-gay Opinion	Pro-gay 'Factual'	Neutral Opinion	Neutral 'Factual'	Anti-gay Opinion	Anti-gay 'Factual'
■ homosexual	17	8	22	16	1	33
▨ gay	43	14	10	5	0	16

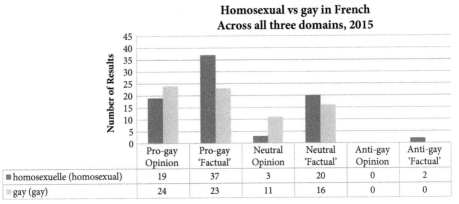

Homosexual vs gay in French
Across all three domains, 2015

	Pro-gay Opinion	Pro-gay 'Factual'	Neutral Opinion	Neutral 'Factual'	Anti-gay Opinion	Anti-gay 'Factual'
■ homosexuelle (homosexual)	19	37	3	20	0	2
▨ gay (gay)	24	23	11	16	0	0

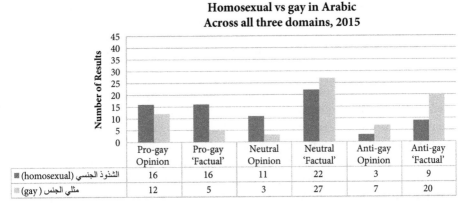

Homosexual vs gay in Arabic
Across all three domains, 2015

	Pro-gay Opinion	Pro-gay 'Factual'	Neutral Opinion	Neutral 'Factual'	Anti-gay Opinion	Anti-gay 'Factual'
■ الشذوذ الجنسي (homosexual)	16	16	11	22	3	9
▨ مثلي الجنس (gay)	12	5	3	27	7	20

Chart 6–8 Graphical representations of terminology between [homosexual] and [gay] and respective variants in each language, all locations combined, 2015. For Chart 7, changing the language settings to French meant that the single search of [gay] was interpreted as a French-language search, rather than an English language query.

Figure 44 'What Does the Bible Say About Homosexuality?' (Creech). A web page result for the query [is being gay wrong?] categorized as Pro-gay Opinion. This web page is not ranked as a result in the first page for [is being homosexual wrong?] even though the number of times this page uses the word 'homosexual' is almost double the number of times the word 'gay' is used. Accessed 24 November 2015.

the number of times it uses the word 'gay', shows that Google have aimed to match the predicted underlying sentiment of a user, indicated by the phrasing of a query, rather than simply matching word usage. Google's algorithms have understood that people who use the word 'homosexual' are more likely to be homophobic than people who use the word 'gay', so has provided homophobic results for that query, regardless of what words the results actually use. Correspondingly, Google uses that same prediction to provide Pro-gay results to a user who uses the word 'gay', even if those results favour the word 'homosexual'.

Finally, the last analysis of the 2015 data explores queries that were divided along the lines of Positively or Negatively phrased questions. Phrasing a query by asking [Is being homosexual wrong?] or [Is being gay wrong?] provided results that supported the implicitly Anti-gay phrasing of the statement (see Chart 9). Phrasing a query using the word [good] instead of [wrong] resulted in a large number of Pro-gay Opinion results. In particular,

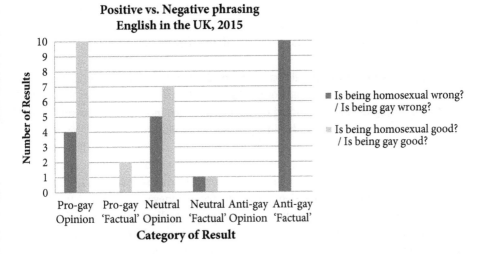

Chart 9 Graphical representation of positive and negative query phrasing using English in the UK.

given that these queries were suggested by Google Autocomplete, the user has not even had to type the phrasing themselves and do not need to have considered the shift in emphasis.

If we return to the previous discussion on relevance, there is a clear sense that the word usage of the user formulating a query is being interpreted for an underlying sentiment behind their choice of words. Such a finding demonstrates the way in which Google's algorithms are designed to provide *relevant* results that rely upon *Contextualist* relevance and are personalized to fit the predicted attitudes of the person searching the query, even without access to specific user profiles. Google's algorithms and machine learning techniques have inscribed the social values of the words used into the way it ranks a set of results. If on average, users searching using the word [gay] – instead of the word [homosexual] – are more Pro-gay, then a Pro-gay set of results is likely to be more *relevant* to that user, regardless of the actual vocabulary used in the web page. The conclusion of Chapter 1 is also relevant here: search queries are different from questions in that they are attempts to iterate the language of a result that the user hopes to find. Early search engines searched for exact linguistic matches in order to fulfil the needs of a user. The results of the 2015 study indicate that Google have taken this process a step further. The use of Wittgenstein's quotation '*The limits of my language* mean the limits of my word' (68) in Chapter 1, reinforced the technological affordances of search engines before the default utilization of synonyms.[6] However, Google's technological innovations have intensified, rather than nullified, the prison-

---

[6]As outlined in Chapter 1, Google started to search for synonyms of query terms by default between 2005 and 2010, after which it became a permanent feature (see Steven Baker's 'Helping computers' and Lamping and Baker 'Determining query term synonyms within query context').

house of language. These results suggest that in their drive towards *Contextualist* relevance – using pattern recognition personalization – Google's results are tailored to the associations of particular words and the sentiments that most commonly accompany their usage.

Using a VPN meant that profile-based personalization was not a factor in the results. However, the variation in the kinds of results for each query demonstrates that in 2015 results were being tailored depending on the kinds of terminology and phrasing used. If personalization was based on individual-specific data collection, whereby the particular values of results were matched to specific user profiles – as described earlier by Christl and Spiekermann, Kant, and Bolin and Andersson Schwarz – there would be clear ways of breaking out of such personalization. The user might perform a search on an IP address not related to them, a computer of a friend or at a library, and they would see how their results were different. However, if the results are *instead* shaped by linguistic modes of discourse, particular vocabularies, and patterns of phrasing, which was the case in 2015, users are stuck in a less visible feedback loop whereby their sentiments are continually reinforced.

Unimaginable communities

With the results of the 2015 study in mind, alongside the theories of personalization and relevance outlined earlier, I want to suggest a new term with which to describe these variations in search results. Each time a user searches, the algorithmic predictions made about their query place them within *unimaginable communities*. The phrase is a reference to Benedict Anderson's term 'imagined communities', which describes the interrelations of print capitalism with the rise of nationalism. Anderson argues that imagined communities developed due to the movement away from Latin and the rise of new reading publics focused around localized vernaculars, which emphasized linguistic and geographical boundaries. Such distinctions created communities of people who, although they would never meet, shared some commonality, out of which the modern conception of the nation developed. In a digital context, such issues of nations, language, and publics are still deeply important. The identities of Anderson's individuals developed in concert with a wider sense of community. Today, we still take part in contextualizing our thoughts and actions within a community. These actions are not necessarily taken with communities *in mind*, but the locations, languages, dialect, and tone, determine each individual's algorithmic milieu. Each user exists in an unimaginable community only momentarily, with each new search shifting the predictions Google makes about their queries. *Contextualist* relevance and pattern recognition personalization place users into a kind of predictive community, but it is not just that these communities are harder to imagine than their historical equivalents. These communities are fundamentally *unimaginable*; the formations and calculations that occur for each Google search are so complex that individuals exist in an unimaginable arrangement. This arrangement dictates the different kinds of results provided to each user, the cause and effect of which cannot be understood on an individual level.

Users do not know whether their results are very different in kind to someone searching using a different language in their same country, perhaps even next door. It is unlikely that the average French Google user is aware that their results are notably less homophobic than their English and Arabic counterparts. Or that the results of English speakers fluctuate more than other languages when they search from different geographical locations. We do not know this because to do so would mean understanding a much larger picture than is possible for the average user. Instead, we must rely on *unimaginable communities*. Users may be aware that Google results have developed from the success of other users, but who these community members are is a complex matter, so too is the metric of *contextually relevant* search results. These communities cut across boundaries to form shifting assemblages of relevant criteria; therefore, these communities are not difficult to imagine but impossible to imagine. The use of data has reinforced old distinctions that separate out contexts, but in doing so, have obliterated the fixed membership of those groups. There is a plurality of Googles, but the number that any user can access is restricted, not by filters but by much older and more nebulous aspects of communication that shape experience, even in a digital landscape.

How search results change throughout time: 2015, 2017, and 2021

The searches discussed in the previous section took place on 24 November 2015. I repeated the study on 22 November 2017, and 17 May 2021 to see if the results had changed in any substantial way. The results had changed in significant ways. As outlined earlier, the nature of Google's algorithmically produced results means that the particular changes noted cannot represent generalizable trends for all Google searches. Instead, highlighting some of the changes demonstrates that search results change throughout time, not simply in the pages returned to a user but also, in the overall tone, attitudes, and broader epistemic landscape presented. In addition, the changes recorded are not linear; some particularly significant standardization occurred in 2017, whereby one page started to dominate in all contexts. In 2021, not only was there a lack of pages that were ranked highly for all contexts but the dominating page of 2017 failed to rank on the first page for any of the tests. I will first provide an overview of the general shifts between 2015, 2017, and 2021. I will then focus on a particular example from 2017, in which one specific search result from the Jehovah's Witnesses official website came to dominate across dozens of contexts, as I believe it reveals a valuable insight into the ethical problems created by Google's use of machine learning at that time. I close by discussing the implications of the 2021 results in relation to *Idealist* and *Contextualist* relevance. The differences between the results of 2015 and 2021 evidence a complete about-turn in terms of the standardization between search contexts and, practically speaking, represent a definition of relevance that is at odds with the meaning given to it in Google's public communications and marketing.

Longitudinal overview: Official languages in each domain

Charts 10–12 compare the longitudinal results for each language in its official domain: English in the UK, French in France, and Arabic in Morocco. The three graphs show some clear changes between 2015 and 2021. First, the number of results that frame their content as Opinions reduced in 2017 and by 2021 Neutral Opinion and Anti-gay Opinions almost vanished. In particular, the number of results rated as Neutral Opinion, sites such as Debate.org (see Figure 40) that collate a variety of Pro-gay and Anti-gay Opinions decreased in 2017 and were reduced to only one result in 2021. This represents a wider trend whereby results increasingly framed their claims as 'factual', in which data, citation, and institutional backing became the primary focus of pages. The number of niche or noninstitutional pages reduced in favour of news outlets, charities, encyclopaedia entries, and market research organizations. By 2021, Pro-gay 'Factual' results were the most common for English, French, and Arabic in their official country domains and when searched in all three countries (see Chart 12).

Charts 13 and 14, which show English, French, and Arabic across all three countries in 2015 and 2021, make this overall shift very noticeable. Comparing the overall changes between 2015 and 2021, although Pro-gay 'Factual' results were the most common in all three languages in 2021, the range of results is still distinctive between each language. In 2015, searching in English would produce a high number of Pro-gay Opinions and Anti-gay 'Factual' results, which gives the impression that individuals support same-sex relationships, but the 'facts' show that they should not. French was almost always positive. Arabic was similar to English but produced a lot of Neutral 'Factual' results and fewer Pro-gay Opinions. In 2021, English still provided the highest number of Pro-gay Opinions of the three languages and still produced some Anti-gay 'Factual' pages; in 2021, French results became overwhelmingly consistent in providing Pro-gay 'Factual' results and no Anti-gay results of any kind, which is similar to its 2015 distribution but much more intensified; Arabic produced the most homophobic results of all the languages in 2021, but its results were much more similar to English and French than they were in 2015 and 2017. Overall, during the six-year period, the kinds of results became more consistent across languages but there remained some measurable differences between them, whereby the countries can be clearly ranked in their level of Pro-gay and Anti-gay results, from French results, which were the most accepting to Arabic results, which were the most homophobic.

However, these graphs do not take into account the *order* of the ranking or specific pages that appear across contexts. When I originally designed the experiment in 2015, my preliminary tests showed that there were no specific web pages that consistently ranked highly and very few pages that were provided for queries in different languages. In addition, in the vast majority of cases, the categorization of the number one result matched the overall trend of the rankings, for example, if eight out of ten results on a results page were Pro-gay 'Factual', the number one ranking page would also be Pro-gay 'Factual' in the vast majority of cases. However, in 2017, the top-ranking search results came to be dominated by a specific page that recurred across all contexts, regardless of whether it presented a similar sentiment to the majority of the other results. This result was a page hosted on the Jehovah's Witnesses official website, titled 'Young People Ask: Is Homosexuality Wrong?'

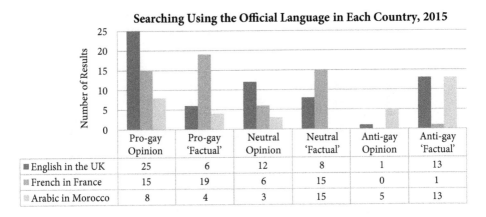

Searching Using the Official Language in Each Country, 2015

	Pro-gay Opinion	Pro-gay 'Factual'	Neutral Opinion	Neutral 'Factual'	Anti-gay Opinion	Anti-gay 'Factual'
English in the UK	25	6	12	8	1	13
French in France	15	19	6	15	0	1
Arabic in Morocco	8	4	3	15	5	13

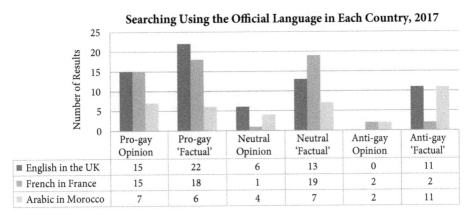

Searching Using the Official Language in Each Country, 2017

	Pro-gay Opinion	Pro-gay 'Factual'	Neutral Opinion	Neutral 'Factual'	Anti-gay Opinion	Anti-gay 'Factual'
English in the UK	15	22	6	13	0	11
French in France	15	18	1	19	2	2
Arabic in Morocco	7	6	4	7	2	11

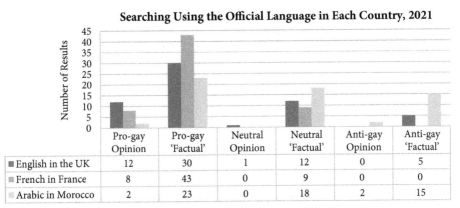

Searching Using the Official Language in Each Country, 2021

	Pro-gay Opinion	Pro-gay 'Factual'	Neutral Opinion	Neutral 'Factual'	Anti-gay Opinion	Anti-gay 'Factual'
English in the UK	12	30	1	12	0	5
French in France	8	43	0	9	0	0
Arabic in Morocco	2	23	0	18	2	15

Chart 10–12 Searching using the official language in each country: 2015, 2017, and 2021.

(see Figure 45). This page is Anti-gay and written in a 'Factual' mode. It is written for a young audience and acknowledges that many people experience same-sex attraction but that 'armed with a good spiritual routine of Bible study and prayer, he or she will have the strength to resist those desires'. What is most insidious about this result is that while being

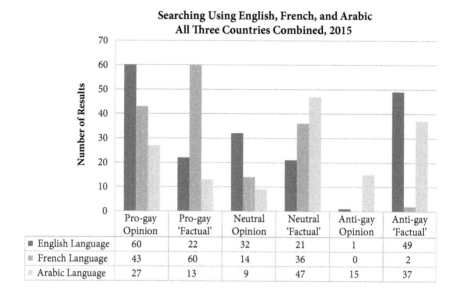

Searching Using English, French, and Arabic
All Three Countries Combined, 2015

	Pro-gay Opinion	Pro-gay 'Factual'	Neutral Opinion	Neutral 'Factual'	Anti-gay Opinion	Anti-gay 'Factual'
■ English Language	60	22	32	21	1	49
▨ French Language	43	60	14	36	0	2
▨ Arabic Language	27	13	9	47	15	37

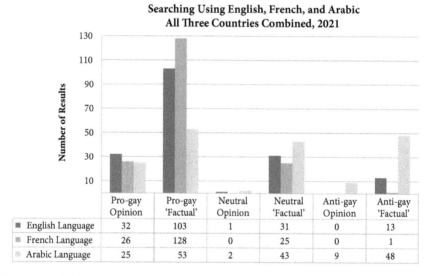

Searching Using English, French, and Arabic
All Three Countries Combined, 2021

	Pro-gay Opinion	Pro-gay 'Factual'	Neutral Opinion	Neutral 'Factual'	Anti-gay Opinion	Anti-gay 'Factual'
■ English Language	32	103	1	31	0	13
▨ French Language	26	128	0	25	0	1
▨ Arabic Language	25	53	2	43	9	48

Chart 13 and 14 Searching in English, French, and Arabic with all three countries combined in 2015 and 2021.

aimed at children, it claims that 'The Bible's standard regarding homosexual acts is clear'. Given the wide variety of other Christian resources served as results that claim the Bible supports LGBTQ lives, the claim that the Bible is clear on the issue simply is not true.[7]

---

[7]For examples of search results, collected during this study, that explicitly focus on how the biblical passages on same-sex relationships require interpretation and ultimately argue that any Anti-gay views that cite biblical scripture are inaccurate, see Robert K. Gnuse, Bishop Gene Robinson, and Rev. Elder Don Eastman.

Figure 45 The Jehovah's Witnesses page 'Young People Ask: Is Homosexuality Wrong?' that was commonly provided by Google in 2017 as the first result for an overwhelming number of different languages and locations. The page is categorized as Anti-gay 'Factual'. It bases its arguments by citing Bible scripture throughout and frames such discourse as clear-cut and evidence-based. Accessed 22 November 2017.

In 2017, translated versions of this single page came to be highly ranked for an overwhelming number of different languages and geographical contexts. Figure 46 shows a list of examples of languages and countries that feature the page represented in Figure 45, as well as other JW.org pages as highly ranked results.

In the 2015 set of results, there was no single overriding web page result that was consistently ranked on the first page across different contexts, let alone one so prominent as to recurrently be returned as the first or second result. In many ways, the 2015 results showed a web balkanized by a division between languages and country domains. The multiple translations available for the Jehovah's Witnesses' page (see the drop-down list in Figure 45) show an intentional mission to spread its particular Anti-gay message to as many different people around the world as possible. Specifically, to as many different children as possible. However, drawing from an understanding of how search engines work, outlined in Chapter 1, I find it unlikely that each translation of the same page became the first result in so many different contexts, some of which have much larger, more varied, populations of users than others. Instead, I hypothesize that RankBrain, Google's machine learning metric that was outlined in Chapter 3, caused a normalization between these contexts. RankBrain's original purpose was to take an unusual query and replace its results with those of a different query for which it had more data. In doing so, RankBrain predicts that the two queries have a high level of similarity, as determined by aggregated user actions and contextually similar linguistic patterns. As highlighted in Chapter 3, RankBrain became the third most important signal for ranking results between 2015 and 2017. The results demonstrated in Figure 46

Figure 46 Search for the query [Is being homosexual wrong?] using different languages in various countries showing the Google results for 'Is Homosexuality Wrong? | Young People Ask – JW.org' and other JW.org pages. Examples are as follows: English in the UK (1st result), Italian in Italy (2nd result), Malay in Malaysia (1st result), Japanese in Japan (1st result), Afrikaans in the UK (1st–3rd results), Zulu in South Africa (1st–4th results), Southern Sotho in South Africa (1st–6th results), Afrikaans in South Korea (1st–3rd results). Accessed 22 November 2017.

suggest that RankBrain is using the results of a query from a context where it has been searched a higher number of times, and consequently has more data from which to draw from, in this case [Is being homosexual wrong?], and using it to inform contexts in which an equivalent query has been searched fewer times. This would lead to this single page dominating in so many different contexts and particularly in niche contexts, such as using Afrikaans in South Korea (see bottom right of Figure 46). It is likely no one had ever searched [Is homoseksueel verkeerd?] in South Korea so Google's machine learning might simply have taken the results of a different context, for which there is a translation in Afrikaans, regardless of whether other ranking signals would have listed this page as the most relevant for that particular context.

The content of the dominant Jehovah's Witnesses page is Anti-gay and presented as incontrovertible 'Factual' evidence. Regardless of the personal beliefs of users, it is noteworthy that searching in a range of languages and countries in 2017 produced, in this instance, a relatively monocultural perspective to a multifaceted question as one of the top-ranking results, even if it did not represent the majority of the perspectives ranked on the rest of the page. Such an example brings to the fore the previous statements of Schmidt and Cohen, and in particular their narrative that 'People who try to perpetuate myths about religion, culture, ethnicity or anything else will struggle to keep their narratives afloat amid a sea of newly informed listeners. With more data, everyone gains a better frame of reference' (35). Irrespective of the particular content provided by search engines, one of their fundamental characteristics is their ability to return many different results for every single query. That one of the contrasts between the 2015 and 2017 results is a lack of overall diversity and dominance of a single narrative is troubling. The standardization around a single 'Factual' discourse fits with Schmidt and Cohen's narrative, but due to the automated nature of search engines, its particular message is one that 'perpetuate[s] myths about religion' rather than dispelling them.

An important shift, however, is that in 2021 there was not a single result listed from jw.org in the first 10 results of any context. In 2017, the Jehovah's Witnesses page 'Young People Ask: Is Homosexuality Wrong?' had a major global presence in Google's results and in 2021 it had disappeared in the rankings. This change supports my hypothesis that RankBrain was responsible for its success, given that in 2017 RankBrain was still fairly new and underdeveloped but had been promoted to the third most influential metric. It seems that between 2017 and 2021 RankBrain, or whatever metric was causing the homogenization of JW.org's influence, had been minimized so that each separate context provided a more diverse range of results as at the top of Google's ranking.

Terminology throughout time: 'Homosexual' versus 'gay'

As discussed, the words 'gay' and 'homosexual' have very different histories, contextual usage, and connotations. Sometimes the use of one word over the other will represent intentional homophobia or inclusivity, for example, by journalists following a style guide or campaigners constructing a body of evidence. Other times, the terminology deployed

– either in search queries or web results – will derive from habitual or unintentional usage. Some search engine users may be more likely to use the word [homosexual] over the word [gay] in their queries, regardless of their attitudes towards LGBTQ+ people, simply because they are unaware of its usage in homophobic discourse. Either way, the central ethical question remains: if there is a correlation between terminology and belief, should Google provide results that aim to reflect a specific user's attitude? In terms of my earlier descriptions of relevance, most *Idealists* would argue that queries using [gay] or [homosexual] should receive the same results. They might say that broad social attitudes are changing and, therefore, even if a user deploys an outdated or offensive term like [homosexual] their search results should not differ from a user searching the same query with the word [gay]. The *Contextualists,* on the other hand, would see relevance as a measure that should take the user's latent or explicit attitudes into account and provide results that best fit their individual outlook. For example, if a homophobic user believes that same-sex attraction is a medical disorder so uses the terminology most representative of that discourse, the *Contextualists* would say that their results should be pages that use the word [homosexual] to frame the issue as a medical disorder. Tracking and evaluating results throughout time highlights that – at least in this instance – Google have answered this question through the modification of their algorithms. Charts 15–17 show the English results in the UK in 2015, 2017, and 2021. In 2015, using different terminology produced very different kinds of results, whereby using [gay] in the search query led to more results that were Pro-gay Opinions and using the word [homosexual] led to more 'factual' results that were either neutral or Anti-gay. This correlation became less extreme in 2017 and by 2021, the correlation still exists but in a much more minimal way. In this way, *Contextual* relevance has mostly given way to *Idealist* relevance.

In addition, between 2015 and 2021, the differences between how each language treated differences in terminology became more standardized. In 2015 and 2017, the way each language treated the translations of the synonyms [gay] and [homosexual] was very distinct. However, in 2021, the way that each language treated synonyms became much more standardized. Charts 17–19 show that in 2021 synonyms did not lead to such different search experiences as they had in the past and that there were even correlations between the search contexts. This is particularly the case when comparing French in France and English in the UK Charts 17 and 18. These results show that where there was once a high degree of contextually distinct results, in 2021, the two search contexts became very similar in the overall attitudes they each presented. It is particularly significant considering that none of the specific search results for either context overlapped. In 2021, the first page of results for the UK and France contexts ranked completely different results, but analysing these two distinct sets of results shows that the spread of attitudes is highly comparable, that is, most results for both terms were Pro-gay 'Factual', with the use of [gay] leading to more Opinion pages and [homosexual/ homosexuelle] leading to more 'Factual' pages. The 2021 Arabic in Morocco results (see Chart 19) represent a different set of values, but still provided a high number of Pro-gay 'Factual' results for both Arabic translations of [gay] and [homosexual], which was the dominant category for English and French. This is in stark contrast to the Arabic results

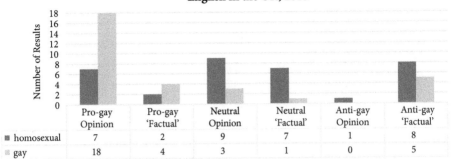

Homosexual vs. Gay (Terminology)
English in the UK, 2015

	Pro-gay Opinion	Pro-gay 'Factual'	Neutral Opinion	Neutral 'Factual'	Anti-gay Opinion	Anti-gay 'Factual'
homosexual	7	2	9	7	1	8
gay	18	4	3	1	0	5

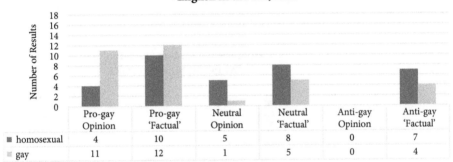

Homosexual vs. Gay (Terminology)
English in the UK, 2017

	Pro-gay Opinion	Pro-gay 'Factual'	Neutral Opinion	Neutral 'Factual'	Anti-gay Opinion	Anti-gay 'Factual'
homosexual	4	10	5	8	0	7
gay	11	12	1	5	0	4

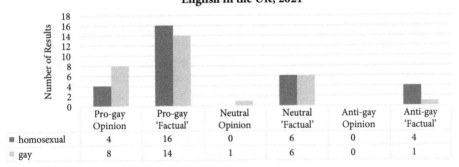

Homosexual vs. Gay (Terminology)
English in the UK, 2021

	Pro-gay Opinion	Pro-gay 'Factual'	Neutral Opinion	Neutral 'Factual'	Anti-gay Opinion	Anti-gay 'Factual'
homosexual	4	16	0	6	0	4
gay	8	14	1	6	0	1

Chart 15–17 Graphs representing the difference in terminology of search queries written in English and searched in the UK. Demonstrates the difference between the terms [gay] and [homosexual] when used in queries in 2015, 2017, and 2021 respectively.

between 2015 and 2017 in which Pro-gay 'Factual' was one of the most uncommon categories of result found.

Unlike the earlier correlations whereby queries using [homosexual] resulted in Anti-gay 'Factual' pages and queries using [gay] led to Pro-gay Opinion pages, the 2021

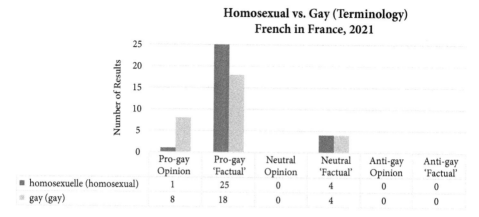

Chart 18 Graphical representation of the difference in terminology of search queries written in French and searched in France. Demonstrates the difference between the terms [gay] and [homosexuelle] when used in queries in 2021.

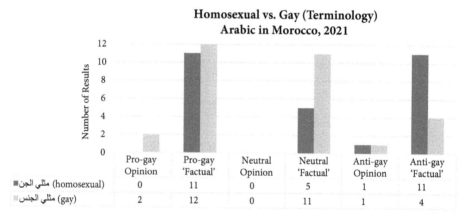

Chart 19 Graphical representation of the difference in terminology of search queries written in Arabic and searched in Morocco. Demonstrates the difference between the terms [مثلي الجنس] and [مثلي الجن] when used in queries in 2021.

Arabic results (see Chart 19) present same-sex sexual orientation as a contested issue, but one in which both attitudes claim to have the facts on their side. The absence of Opinion results might strike some readers as providing a more balanced view, compared with the recurring correlation that presents the discourse as individual feeling versus institutional knowledge. Other readers might see this 2021 set of results, whereby Google presents 'facts' for and 'against', as a false and offensive misrepresentation. For example, in Google's same results for French speakers, there is not a single Anti-gay page represented and for many around the world, the 'issue' of being gay is not an issue or debate at all, simply a matter of fact in and of itself with other perspectives simply representing badly disguised discrimination or hate speech. Therefore, taking this wider view, of comparing the different languages shows that, here, Google's results represent a *Contextualist* view of relevance. In 2021, Google's algorithms are predicting that French speakers do not see being gay as a debate, whereas the opposite prediction is made for Arabic speakers in Morocco, whose results cite religious, medical, and legal evidence, while mostly removing the personal 'Opinion' perspectives from the discourse. Overall, in 2021, switching terminology ([gay] versus [homosexual]) did not alter results as much as it has in the past. However, this trend does not preclude further changes in the future so these results should not be read as a unilateral and permanent shift.

Phrasing throughout time: 'Good' versus 'wrong'

The final aspect that was tracked throughout time was phrasing, which captured the differences in search results when a query was phrased positively or negatively, i.e. [Is being gay good?] and [Is being gay wrong?]. Originally suggested by Autocomplete in 2015, these two variations show that in all three languages phrasing *does* change the kinds of search results given and has done to different extents in 2015, 2017, and 2021. It should be noted that in 2021, these queries are no longer suggested by Autocomplete, instead, the suggestions for [Is being gay. . .] are [natural] and [normal], while Autocomplete is disabled for [Is being homosexual . . .] and provides no suggestions. These new suggestions sidestep the ethical questions of judgement and direct users towards results that focus on scientific studies that investigate the causes of same-sex attraction. However, the original suggestions from 2015 are still useful to show the shifting way that value-laden queries are interpreted.

Generally, from 2015 to 2021, all queries written in a question form with an implicit positive or negative sentiment trended towards Pro-gay 'Factual' results for all languages and locations (see Charts 20–22). However, for English and Arabic, positive and negative phrasing still shaped the results returned on Google's first page around the implied sentiment. For the results of English in the UK (Chart 20), wording the query to include [good] led to exclusively Pro-gay results, while the only Neutral and Anti-gay results returned were results for the query formulation [Is being homosexual/gay wrong?]. A similar outcome was found for the Arabic in Morocco context, where the only Anti-gay 'Factual' results provided were in response to the query formulation including [wrong]. In 2021, the Arabic in Morocco results are more in line with the contexts, compared to 2017 and 2015, but significantly out of step with the law within Morocco and potential public opinion on LGBTQ+ identities. In contrast, when searching using French in France (Chart 21), phrasing a query as implicitly positive or negative has almost no impact on the kinds of results returned. Chart 21 reflects *Idealist* relevance; that is, for French speakers, there is one correct way of thinking about same-sex relationships and this is relevant to everyone, regardless of individual feeling or how those feelings are expressed.

Due to the methodological challenges of studying this kind of algorithmic behaviour, generalizations cannot be drawn from the particular differences shown in this study.

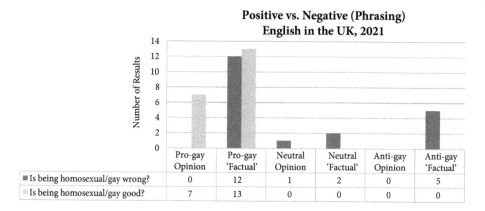

Positive vs. Negative (Phrasing)
English in the UK, 2021

	Pro-gay Opinion	Pro-gay 'Factual'	Neutral Opinion	Neutral 'Factual'	Anti-gay Opinion	Anti-gay 'Factual'
■ Is being homosexual/gay wrong?	0	12	1	2	0	5
▨ Is being homosexual/gay good?	7	13	0	0	0	0

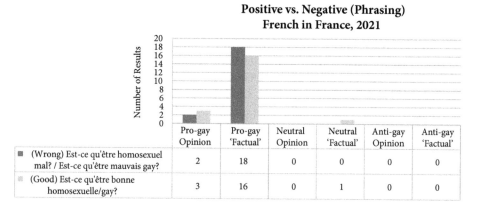

Positive vs. Negative (Phrasing)
French in France, 2021

	Pro-gay Opinion	Pro-gay 'Factual'	Neutral Opinion	Neutral 'Factual'	Anti-gay Opinion	Anti-gay 'Factual'
■ (Wrong) Est-ce qu'être homosexuel mal? / Est-ce qu'être mauvais gay?	2	18	0	0	0	0
▨ (Good) Est-ce qu'être bonne homosexuelle/gay?	3	16	0	1	0	0

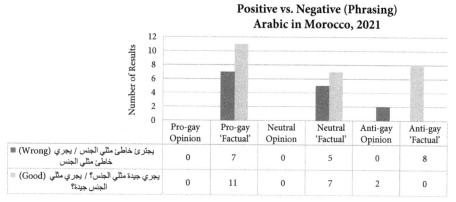

Positive vs. Negative (Phrasing)
Arabic in Morocco, 2021

	Pro-gay Opinion	Pro-gay 'Factual'	Neutral Opinion	Neutral 'Factual'	Anti-gay Opinion	Anti-gay 'Factual'
■ (Wrong) يجري مثلي الجنس؛ خاطئ / يجري مثلي الجنس؛ خاطئ يجترئ	0	7	0	5	0	8
▨ (Good) يجري مثلي الجنس؟ / يجري مثلي الجنس جيدة؟	0	11	0	7	2	0

Chart 20–22 Graphs representing the difference in the phrasing between the terms [wrong] and [good] for English in the UK, French translations in France, and Arabic translations in Morocco when used in queries in 2015, 2017, and 2021.

Even if further evidence were available, it would not help establish lines of causation. Is the way these results have changed an indication of a wider acceptance of gay rights, drawn from user behaviour or web content, or evidence of Google asserting an editorial perspective into their algorithmic modifications? How can we ever know what English, French, and Arabic speakers *really* think about LGBTQ+ issues, in order to compare this with the kinds of results they are provided by Google. However, given the range of variations shown earlier, Google's algorithms are clearly making predictions that different users, in different places, using different languages and different query phrasing *do* want different results. The longitudinal aspect shows that these algorithmic distinctions have changed throughout time and give every indication that they will continue to change in the future. The nature of studying Google's algorithmic judgements means that the object of analysis is always changing and the lines of causation are never clear. It would also be incorrect to assume that Google's engineers would always be able to explain the ranking of particular search results, given their production by highly complex algorithmic systems. Changes in Google's results might represent changes to their ranking methods, changes in the overall content of the web, the changing behaviours of web users, or a combination of all three factors.

However, one factor that we can be sure of is Google's increasing reliance on machine learning neural networks, such as RankBrain. As outlined earlier, the results provided by machine learning are far more difficult for engineers to explain. The question of how results should be different across contexts is far more complex than Schmidt and Cohen's culturally imperialist and overly simplistic sentiments regarding 'Malawian witch doctors' and 'Yemeni tribal elders'. In this regard, a reliance on machine learning allows Google to avoid taking responsibility for the kinds of results that become dominant. What should also be clear from this study is that, due to the open-ended nature of query topics, search results are not simply a matter of truths and falsehoods; the discursive modes in which arguments are presented, as either 'Factual' or Opinion-based, may have as much of an impact upon the individuals who turn to search engines to provide them with answers. Machine learning extends the current paradigm that relies upon inconsistent terminology like *relevance* as a way for technology companies to shirk responsibility. Such techniques may well lead down a path in which the global informational landscape is generated in a way that makes evidence-based critique impossible. Increased use of techniques such as machine learning does not afford the same insight and we should be cautious of a direction that might lead complex cultural issues to be framed without human intervention or responsibility. The destination of such a direction is a situation in which, upon being asked *why these results?* engineers might only be able to shrug.

Conclusion

This chapter presents the first longitudinal study of search results of its kind that explores how different contexts and signals alter Google's results. I have explored how the different conceptual definitions of relevance mean that there are multiple ways of evaluating what search results should look like. In addition, I have shown that users *do* receive different kinds of search results based on algorithmic predictions, despite the minimal effect of profile-based personalization. Instead, search results are personalized based on pattern recognition. Unlike profile-based personalization, where the impacts of personalization can be removed by clearing one's cookies or searching on a different device, my study shows that the data being used to profile our results are much more difficult to locate, harder to alter, and impossible to fully avoid. The conceptual model that I put forward of *unimaginable communities* raises the issue of how we are treated online and what kinds of groups we are identified as belonging to. The question of how our results should differ based on our language, location, terminology, and phrasing should be a public conversation. This chapter has focused on examples of queries relating to being gay to demonstrate the intersection between multiple discourses – some presented as factual and others presented as personal opinions – and different ways these sources of information are allocated to various individuals around the world. But this is only one example among a near-infinite list of important topics, each with its own set of ethical stakes. The remit of Google's search results covers everything. Any opinion you think is debatable or any fact you think is not, is dependent on context and subject to change for everyone around the world. The questions of whether the same kinds of attitudes should prevail in all contexts, whether results should be context-dependent, and how much Google should try to personalize our search experience represent a set of debates we all need to be part of.

CHAPTER 5
THE REAL COST OF SEARCH ENGINES
DIGITAL ADVERTISING, LINGUISTIC CAPITALISM, AND THE RISE OF FAKE NEWS

Introduction

The economic influence of Google is vast, and their continuing financial success impacts us all in a huge number of noneconomic ways. Google's dominance over the web allows it to dictate various norms and practices that regulate the state of contemporary capitalism online. In addition, the way that Google makes and reinvests money has many ethical implications including the fairness of political elections, the representation of minoritized individuals, and attitudes towards a wide range of important social issues, such as global climate change, vaccine efficacy, and LGBTQ+ rights. Understanding how Google's business works is imperative to appreciating its influence, as well as holding the company to account.

The vast majority, 83.9 per cent (Alphabet 30), of Google's revenue is derived from advertising, despite Larry Page and Sergey Brin's claims in their original 1998 academic paper regarding Google in which they argue that advertising produces mixed motives that make it an unfeasible way to fund search engines. In abandoning this moral stance, Google's founders fuelled the set of mixed motives they envisioned in 1998, but also created a version of the web capable of eroding democracy, international public health, human rights, and the long-term environmental survivability of the planet through economically incentivizing fake news and misinformation.

This chapter outlines how Google's model of advertising reflects and encourages wider changes in capitalism as it shifts from its twentieth-century Fordist incarnation to contemporary post-Fordist arrangements of labour. In doing so, this chapter analyses Google's two main advertising systems, AdWords and AdSense, and proposes that these financial models have significant effects upon online discourse. A discussion of AdWords details some of the tensions between the local and the global that develop when tracing flows of information and capital, specifically highlighting Google's influence on racist and intolerant discourse and the decline of online language diversity. An outline of AdSense demonstrates how Google's hegemonic control prescribes which parts of the web can be monetized and which remain unprofitable. In particular, in drawing from existing studies, this chapter provides evidence that Google's AdSense programme, along with Google's relationship with Facebook, incentivized the rise of fake news in the 2016 US presidential election.

Google's advertising empire is crucially important because it impacts a wide range of phenomena that might otherwise be considered noneconomic, such as general online language use, and the incentives underpinning a range of content, such as fake news. In order to situate these issues within broader trends in contemporary capitalism, this chapter theorizes our current moment through the critical frameworks of post-Fordist theory. Emphasizing Google's business activities recontextualizes the arguments of the previous chapters in demonstrating the underlying economic incentives of their search engine. Doing so provides an important dimension of Google's activities and reveals their growing influence over culture, politics, and economics.

The economics of Google

Alphabet, Google's holding company created in 2015, is one of the most valuable companies in the world.[1] It has a market value of just under $1.4 trillion and in 2020 generated a revenue of $180 billion. Ask most people what Google does and they will likely reply that it is a search engine company. However, a more accurate description is that Google is an advertising company. Approximately 83.9 per cent of Google's revenue comes from advertising (Alphabet 30); although, as will be outlined later, Google's modes of advertising deviate significantly from any existing forms of traditional advertising. The economic success of such a shift is producing widespread effects within many areas of society. This chapter addresses two in particular: the reification of online language, including its influence on discrimination, and the rise of fake news. There are many other important impacts of Google's advertising programmes, however, focusing on these particular issues demonstrates the broad scope on which such a narrow economic model operates.

Google have two main advertising ventures. The first of which is 'Google properties', the service for hosting advertisements built into its own products (its search engine, Gmail, and YouTube for example) the most significant part of which is AdWords. The second is 'Google Network Members' properties', a brokerage service that runs advertisements on third-party websites, the most significant part of which is AdSense.[2] AdWords and AdSense will be outlined separately, in order to focus on their distinct ethical implications. Nearly 84 per cent of Google's revenues come from advertising on

---

[1]Alphabet has been listed as the world's most valuable company on a number of occasions; see 'Google Just Passed Apple as the World's Most Valuable Company' and 'Google Just Passed Apple as the World's Most Valuable Company (Again)' (Solomon).

[2]For clarity, this chapter relies on synecdoche by using 'AdWords' to refer to 'Google properties' and using 'AdSense' to refer to 'Google Network Members' properties.' There are other smaller properties detailed in Alphabet pages 23 and 24, respectively. However, these smaller properties follow the systems developed by AdWords and AdSense and so, in the main, can be ignored.

Google's own sites and are mainly derived from AdWords (23). AdWords is an auction process that Google operates to allocate paid results (referred to by Google as sponsored results) to search engine queries, which sit separately on top or to the side of unpaid results (referred to by Google as organic results). These sponsored AdWords results have historically been visually delineated from the organic results by using a range of background colours (during 2007–13), or brightly coloured labelling or borders (during 2013–20). Google have a legal requirement to clearly differentiate sponsored results from organic ones; however, they have made the difference less clear over time. In fact, in 2020, Google removed any use of colour, border, or differences in background and instead demarcate sponsored links by including the single word 'Ad' in bold, which means there is barely a difference between the way organic and sponsored results are listed (for more detail, see Ginny Marvin and Natasha Lomas).

In addition to this programme, 16 per cent of Google's advertising revenue is derived from non-Google sites on which Google hosts third-party advertising content using its AdSense programme (24). AdSense is Google's method of linking third-party advertisements to relevant third-party content, such as blogs or news sites, and displaying advertisements alongside selected content in digital billboards. Although there are other companies that provide advertising for third parties, Google AdSense is by far the largest. In 2020, it was reported that Google had 'as much as 90 percent of the market share in some segments [while in] others, Google controlled about 50 percent' (Nylen). The majority of the online advertising market not controlled by Google is controlled by Facebook and the second section of this chapter outlines how these two companies reinforce their joint dominance.

The remaining 16 per cent of Alphabet's revenue represents the sales of apps and media content in the Google Play store, as well as other smaller ventures such as certain Google branded hardware, for example, sales of Google Chromebooks and Pixel smartphones. None of Alphabet's other activities 'meet the quantitative thresholds to qualify as reportable segments; therefore, the operating segments are combined and disclosed . . . as Other Bets' (Alphabet 28) These smaller subsidiaries, known as other bets 'Access, Calico, CapitalG, Nest, Verily, Waymo, and X', and other initiatives (87) have the combined revenue of $659 million, which is only 0.36 per cent of Alphabet's total revenue, and have combined operating losses of over $4,824 million (88). These divisions focus on a range of projects from Calico and Verily's biomedical research into extending the human lifespan, Waymo's self-driving cars, and X's Google Glass augmented reality headset. While these kinds of projects are covered more frequently in the popular press and are a major way that Google markets itself as a socially beneficial company, they do not contribute to Google's financial success.

In summary: Google generates almost all of Alphabet's revenue; almost all of Google's revenue is made from advertising; the majority of this advertising revenue comes from AdWords, that is, sponsored links included in search engine results; finally, Google spends a great deal of its revenue on smaller ambitious ventures. This chapter draws from post-Fordist theory to provide a historical and theoretical context for Google's place in contemporary digital capitalism. In doing so, I demonstrate the ways that Google have played a major role in the changing flows of information, labour, and capital. The first section of this chapter focuses on AdWords, arguing that it constitutes a global linguistic market and typifies a number of characteristics of post-Fordist capitalism. I also address how Google's financial model contributes to the decline of language diversity online and how its reification of language directly supports discrimination based on race, gender, and sexual orientation. The second section of this chapter focuses on the ways in which AdSense shapes online discourse and dictates particular norms. In particular, this section draws out the reciprocal links between AdSense and Facebook and demonstrates how Google's mode of advertising facilitated the rise of fake news during the 2016 US presidential election. Before addressing these two topics, the following section establishes the framework of post-Fordist theory, in order to contextualize Google's activities within the broader shifts of contemporary capitalism.

The context of post-Fordism

Google's modes of advertising represent a sea change from traditional twentieth-century advertising which, in turn, operates within a much larger and more general shift away from twentieth-century modes of capitalism. This chapter draws from a particular group of thinkers, a group of Italian neo-Marxists, loosely connected to the 'workerism' (*operaismo*) movement during the 1960s and 1970s, whose work has been influential in understanding contemporary digital capitalism. The work of these thinkers – Paolo Virno, Michael Hardt, Antonio Negri, and Maurizio Lazzarato are a few notable examples – has come to be known as post-Fordist theory.[3] This designation of post-Fordist theory represents a number of different, although related, attitudes towards the way in which capitalism has changed since the second half of the twentieth century, specifically regarding the role of work. Post-Fordist theory traces the decline of the dominant kind of capitalism in the early twentieth century, Fordism,[4] while theorizing and analysing the post-industrial modes of capitalism that they describe as post-Fordist. These models of post-Fordist labour relations, which stress the importance of cognitive, flexible, and precarious labour, are key to understanding Google's influence on contemporary capitalism in a digital context. Their work has been influential – or the subject of influential critique – in a wider range of existing studies of digital culture, for example, in the work of Mark Poster on the information society, Lisa Nakamura on the economic basis of sexism and racism on social media platforms, Ursula Huws on

---

[3]The collection *Radical Thought in Italy: A Potential Politics* (Virno and Hardt ed.) goes some way to providing a comprehensive overview of the important post-Fordist theorists, although as is noted in its introduction three key members, Franco Berardi, Sergio Bologna, and Giuseppe Cocco, were not included for various reasons.
[4]Fordism emphasizes standardization, de-skilling of the workforce through assembly-line manufacture, and the linking of wages to prices of products in order to ensure that workers could function as consumers of their products. For a more detailed definition and relationship to later forms of capitalism, see *Post Fordism: A Reader* (Amin).

virtual labour movements, Kylie Jarrett on feminist consumer labour, Eran Fisher on algorithmic governance, and Christian Fuchs on political economy.[5]

The effects of post-Fordism are expansive and stretch well beyond Google's role in contemporary capitalism. However, Google's advertising ventures of AdWords and AdSense operate in concert with a range of other contemporary issues. These include the increasingly precarious nature of employment; the dissolution of clear boundaries between work and free time, as well as between paid and unpaid work; the diminishing solidarity, rights, and freedoms of workers; the increasing time spent working, in each working day as well as an increasing age of retirement; the homogenization of different types of work through the use of information technologies; employing automation to replace workers; the changing nature of digital commodities that turn many product-based industries into service ones. This list is only indicative, rather than exhaustive, aiming to provide a sense of post-Fordism's extensive nature. An exaggerated example of a day that exemplifies post-Fordist labour relations might be as follows: a woman catches an Uber to her timeshared office where she works as a digital brand consultant. Her work consists of managing Twitter likes and increasing Facebook engagement. She orders her lunch via an app, which is delivered by a part-time student working as a Deliveroo rider. After work she travels back to her Airbnb-rented apartment and spends a couple of hours jumping between Netflix and other streaming services, while keeping an eye on the reactions to the social media posts she scheduled during the day. Later that evening, she spends an hour talking to a Chinese student over a language learning service, like italki, not to make money but in exchange for credits to be redeemed at a later date, once she finds the time to start learning Spanish. Not all work is like this, far from it; material labour is still a major part of contemporary work around the world. In addition, this example only highlights the visible changes that might seem to only affect a niche group of people. However, this chapter aims to show that Google's business draws *everyone* online into various immaterial labour arrangements with far-reaching consequences, many of which are difficult to detect. There are numerous dimensions to such an arrangement and different people are implicated in post-Fordist labour relations to different degrees. Focusing on how AdWords reifies language online and how AdSense incentivizes fake news demonstrates two examples in which all web users are impacted by post-Fordist effects, even if their lives could not seem further from that of the example outlined above.

AdWords: Organic versus sponsored results

At least in terms of revenue generation, Google's core business isn't facilitating searches, it's selling advertising space – or rather, selling our attention to advertisers

---

[5]See, Poster 'The Information Empire,' Nakamura 'The Unwanted Labour Of Social Media,' Huws *Labor in the Global Digital Economy,* Jarrett *Feminism, Labour and Digital Media,* E. Fisher, *Media and New Capitalism in the Digital Age,* and Fuchs 'Critique of the political economy of informational capitalism and social media.'

and managing both the price it charges for access to our attention and the relative visibility of those advertisements. (Vaidhyanathan 26)

Vaidhyanathan's quotation draws our attention to Google's profitability as a company. That the majority of Google's revenue comes from advertising through its search engine is relatively surprising, given that the original plan for Google's search engine was diametrically opposed to advertising. Despite the plans of the founders for Google to remain in the academic realm, Google generates revenue when users click on advertisements, not when users find successful answers to their queries. As Steven Levy describes, 'In their original academic paper about Google, [Larry] Page and [Sergey] Brin had devoted an appendix to the evils of conventional advertising' (*In the Plex* 84). Their academic paper argued that their method, using the PageRank algorithm, was far more accurate than existing search engines that relied on advertising *specifically because* it did not bias results in order to make a profit. Their approach required that their search engine be 'transparent and in the academic realm' because, as the founders explain:

advertising funded search engines will be inherently biased towards the advertisers and away from the needs of the consumers. . . . Furthermore, advertising income often provides an incentive to provide poor quality search results. For example, we noticed a major search engine would not return a large airline's homepage when the airline's name was given as a query. It so happened that the airline had placed an expensive ad, linked to the query that was its name. A better search engine would not have required this ad, and possibly resulted in the loss of the revenue from the airline to the search engine. In general, it could be argued from the consumer point of view that the better the search engine is, the fewer advertisements will be needed for the consumer to find what they want. This, of course, erodes the advertising supported business model of the existing search engines. (Brin and Page)

However, early on in their business, Google started using advertisements to fund their search engine. These advertisements, sponsored links, have always been kept separate from the organic links. In their paper, Brin and Page specifically took aim at search engines that mixed their results together so that users could not see which of the results had been paid for and which were freely chosen by the search engine. Although Google still separate sponsored and organic links, as mentioned earlier, they have actively worked to make the distinction less clear to users. Regardless, the problem remains: if a set of results is good enough, a user will never need to click on the sponsored link. In the original vision outlined by Brin and Page, advertisements are always an indication of failure, but today represent the overwhelming majority of Google's revenue. However, this distinction between success versus failure is deceptive, therefore, the following section provides an alternative lens with which to understand the complex relationship between Google's search engine and advertising.

AdWords: The multilingual linguistic market and an economy of bias

This section provides a specific outline of how AdWords operates in order to demonstrate the close links between Google's search engine and advertising. In particular, I draw on the work of Frederic Kaplan who argues that AdWords constitutes a form of 'linguistic capitalism' (58), in the tradition of post-Fordism; the conclusion of which is that Google's mode of advertising is having a widespread effect on all language usage on the web. Even if users are not explicitly altering the language they use online, anyone who uses the web communicates in a context where economic value alters every part of their linguistic landscape. Users may be completely unaware of this process of linguistic reification but still navigate an uneven digital space in which there are economic incentives that prioritize some words and ideas and deprioritize others. This economic framework supports the claims of Safiya Umoja Noble, outlined in more detail later, that Google as a commercial advertising company lays the groundwork 'for implicit bias: bias that is buttressed by advertising profits' (116), biases that disproportionately impact women and people of colour. In addition, the economic value of different languages is not the same, and, therefore, as discussed later, Google incentivizes the reduction in linguistic diversity around the globe.

AdWords is the auction system that provides advertising in the form of sponsored results that fill the top or side of a Google search result. An auction occurs every time a query is searched and balances the amount of money automatically bid by a company, against an automated quality score, given by Google. If low-quality scores are given or if there has not been an advertisement placed that is deemed relevant to the query, Google will not provide an advertisement. If a user clicks on one of these sponsored advertisements, the company being advertised pays Google; if not, no money is exchanged. Therefore, both Google and its business customers have strong economic incentives for the advertisements to succeed.[6] A key aspect of AdWords is designing advertisements with specific kinds of search queries in mind. Kaplan explains that 'First, advertisers select a keyword – for instance "vacation" – and define the maximum price they would be ready to pay if a user arrives on their site by clicking on the link of the ad' (58). Keywords selected by advertisers are then used interchangeably with other similar words selected by Google. The advertiser must also select the 'product or service [they] wish to advertise' from a predetermined list, the language they wish to advertise in, and the geographical locations they wish to target with their advertising. Google have guidelines for prohibited AdWords content,[7] which mostly relate to more general country-specific laws.[8] In addition, the process of having to choose from a preestablished list of products and services means that particular topics are implicitly censored. This kind of bias is compounded by the range of categories offered by Google, including

---

[6]For more on the interplay between Google, third-party advertisers, and users, see Rieder and Sire.

[7]See Google 'AdWords policies'.

[8]For example, it is illegal to advertise online gambling websites in the United States but legal in the UK and Google follows these geographical distinctions online. See Google 'Gambling and Games'.

age and gender, that allow targeting or excluding certain users from being shown the advertisement. This is particularly problematic in the case of adverts for job listings. For example, in 2021, Jeremy B. Merrill of *The Markup* reported that Google

> gave advertisers the option of keeping their ads from being shown to people of 'unknown gender' – effectively allowing employers and landlords to either inadvertently or purposefully discriminate against people who identify as nonbinary, transgender, or anything other than male or female.

Upon confronting Google with evidence of specific advertisers who had done so, a spokesperson from Google identified an additional 100 advertisers 'who had done the same for housing, credit, or job ads'. Google responded by restating their commitment to following discrimination laws specific to each country and that they were 'working swiftly to implement a change' (Elijah Lawal, a spokesperson for Google, qtd. in Merrill) for the US-based examples found. However, the problem of Google's hyper-targeted and exclusion-based advertising remains. Simply following the legal requirements of each country, and correcting flaws when highlighted by journalists, does not fix the wider cultural influence of identity commodification and normalized discrimination, which will be further outlined later.

After this process of advert creation and tailoring is completed

> Google associates a quality score with the ad. This figure, ranging from 1 to 10, evaluates the global 'quality' of the ad, which is computed through a complex combination of various factors, including the relevance of the text ad regarding the keyword, the average number of clicks on the ad, and the performance and quality of the linked website. This score measures how well the ad is working. (Kaplan 58)

This measure of 'quality' takes into account a judgement of the advertisement (clarity of expression), its relevance to the website it links to (an advertisement for swimming goggles should lead to a sports equipment shop rather than a public swimming pool), and the quality of the destination website (based on Google's usual metrics including the layout of keywords and the link score generated from other websites linking to that site). Whereas traditional advertising might aim to change someone's mind or introduce them to a new idea, AdWords advertisements are an attempt to reflect the existing perspective of an individual. AdWords advertisements must aim to be *relevant*, in the *Contextualist* or personalized sense outlined in Chapter 4, in order to be given a high-quality score. Finally, the 'rank of an ad is calculated by multiplying the bid times the quality score', therefore, an 'ad with a good score and medium bid can overcome a less efficient ad with a higher bid' (59). This financial model means that small advertisers can compete with larger ones if they can offer a higher quality advert, as judged by Google. So, for example, in a search for 'craft ale' (see Figure 47), Amazon might have set the highest bid for that phrase, but it is listed below two smaller but more specialized craft beer sellers, with higher quality scores. This approach prevents companies with deeper pockets from outbidding smaller but more contextually relevant competitors.

Figure 47 AdWord results for 'craft ale'. The advertisement order lists the specialist and local sponsored results before Amazon's advertisement. Screenshot by the author. Accessed September 10, 2017.

An AdWords auction occurs every single time a user searches a query using Google's search engine. The most recent disclosure by Google is that they handle at least '2 trillion searches per year' (Sullivan, 'Google Now Handles'), which means that at the lowest estimate, Google runs a staggering 63,000 linguistic auctions per second. Kaplan describes this process as:

> the first global, real-time, and multilingual linguistic market. As a consequence, the fluctuation of the price of keywords indirectly reflects global linguistic movements. The value of some keywords like 'snowboarding' or 'bikini' varies seasonally. The increase and decrease of the word 'gold' is linked with the perceived state of financial crisis. Google makes a lot of money on some very competitive keywords like 'flowers', 'hotels', 'vacation', and 'love'. It also organizes bids for buying the names of famous people ('Picasso', 'Freud'). Bidding strategies vary. Anything that can be named can be associated with a bid. (59)

Google provides advertisers using AdWords with a tool that organizes, suggests, and estimates the cost of various words and phrases. Not only do the prices reflect real-world events, but also, various companies can drive up the prices of words for their competitors. Such behaviour was raised in the 2007 court case *Google, Inc. v. American Blind & Wallpaper Factory, Inc.* John Battelle in *The Search* details how

> in early 2003, American Blinds realised that while it owned the trademark on 'American Blinds', it didn't own the market for it on Google's AdWords service. Competitors were snatching up the company's trademarks as AdWords terms (they did so by paying more for them, essentially), so that when customers typed 'American blinds' into Google they'd get advertisements for companies like JustBlinds.com and Select Blinds. (180)

The case of *American Blinds vs. Google* was described by commentators as a clear-cut trademark infringement that favoured American Blinds; however, in a shock to many legal commentators, after 'almost four years of litigation', American Blinds finally dropped the suit in a '"stunning victory for Google"', wrote Eric Goldman, an assistant professor at Santa Clara University School of Law' (qtd. in Auchard). Google have a track record of winning legal battles that establish digital norms[9] and this case changed the conventional understanding of how legal definitions of ownership translate online. Google's legal defence outlined an aggressive position concerning the relationship between language and capital: old notions of linguistic ownership do not apply online. Not only are all words and phrases available to anyone, but the auction winners are not even necessarily the highest bidder.[10] Google's quality ranking system, when coupled with their dominance in the search engine market, means that they have become the gatekeeper of language ownership online. As language ownership is calculated and awarded anew through an auction every single time a search takes place, at least 63,000 times a second, no one can claim ownership of language for more than an instant: words and their relation to entities are constantly in flux under Google's watchful eyes.

Because AdWords affects all words, not just copyrighted or trademarked ones, all words, phrases, and ideas online have become commodities. The advertising model of AdWords, therefore, encourages companies into an association with language whereby a company does not connect their product with a specific slogan but to an unlimited range of words, at various times in specified locations. Many scholars have linked this expansion to the concept of the 'long tail', originally popularized by Chris Anderson;[11] as Levy explains: 'Since Google searches were often unique, with esoteric keywords, there was a possibility to sell ads for categories that otherwise never would have justified placement. On the Internet it was possible to make serious money by catering to the "long tail" of

---

[9]For example, the eleven-year legal battle between Google Books and the Authors Guild, in which Google's book-scanning activities were ruled as legal under fair use, see Cohen.

[10]The legal precedent of using another company's registered trademarks as Adwords keywords has been upheld in subsequent legal battles, for example, the 2016 *Veda Advantage Limited vs. Malouf Group Enterprises* case.

[11]As Anderson explains it, the 'theory of the Long Tail is that our culture and economy is increasingly shifting away from a focus on a relatively small number of "hits" (mainstream products and markets) at the head of the demand curve and toward a huge number of niches in the tail.'

businesses that could not buy their way into mass media' (*In the Plex* 85). Because of this phenomenon, and in conjunction with the auction aspect of AdWords that means that uncommon words are very cheap to bid on, all words in all languages can theoretically become profitable. There is an incentive to increase the prices of popular words but also to spread the reach of a campaign to niche words that might not seem in any way commodifiable but would have a low market value. Because advertisers are only charged when a user clicks on their advert there is no cost or disadvantage to placing bids on uncommon or unlikely words. This structural logic places clear incentives on advertisers to increase the scope of their chosen words and encourages a kind of linguistic land grab. Such an expansion then has an effect on all language used online, not just trademarks or particular phrases associated with companies or products. In shifting which words and phrases become discoverable through a search engine, and which are concealed, as well as how certain language becomes received in various contexts, economics comes to structure an increasing percentage of online linguistic communication. Kaplan argues that 'Even if Google's autocompletion may not be explicitly biased toward more economically valuable expressions, it nevertheless tends to transform natural language into more regular, economically exploitable linguistic subsets' (60). When born-digital content, for example online news, is written with search engine visibility in mind it is, in effect, automatically tailored towards advertising; advertisers and content creators both want to strengthen their association to the kinds of words and phrases used in search engine queries. In addition, as online content is increasingly dependent on third-party advertising, a topic that is discussed in the second section of this chapter, these two activities – bidding on search terms and writing online content that is discoverable through search engines – become enmeshed and mutually standardize the kinds of linguistic patterns on the web.

Google's institutionalization, data collection, and advertising

This standardization across languages is also enhanced by Google's institutionalization of the AdWords programme. Not only do companies that advertise through AdWords have access to various tools and analytics, but this work is often outsourced to professional AdWords companies.[12] Google run a certification programme that provides training and study materials, and holds exams for individuals to become accredited. To keep their status as an accredited AdWords professional, individuals need to pass two of Google's AdWords exams every year. In order for an advertising company to work as a 'Google Partner', they need to employ at least two members of staff who are currently accredited as AdWords professionals. The AdWords accreditation has even been added as a component of masters of business administration (MBA) degrees.[13] Google also supplies

---

[12]Google encourages this arrangement and details advice for working with a third party, see Google 'Advertiser guide.'
[13]See Racer Nation Information.

funding to those institutions awarding MBAs through their 'Google Online Marketing Challenge'[14] which strengthens links between universities, professors, and students with Google AdWords and in turn strengthens Google's hegemony.

Through Google's various projects, the company has an enormous collection of data, which, when combined with their methods of tracking users' behaviour on the web ensure that Google's advertising efforts are as effective as possible. As Ken Auletta describes:

> It was Google's ambition, Schmidt and Page and Brin liked to say, to provide an answer to the adman's legendary line 'I know half of my advertising works, I just don't know which half'. To help them sort through the digital clicks, Google and other new media companies relied on what are called cookies, software files that reside on a user's browser and keep track of their activities online: search questions asked, Web pages visited, time spent on each Web page, advertisements clicked on, items purchased. . . . Although the cookie doesn't identify the user by name or address, it does assemble data advertisers crave and couldn't get from traditional media companies. (7)

Cookies and measurements of user interactions with search results allow Google to capture latent information that is used to further personalize advertising. Describing Google as an advertising company (rather than a search engine that also advertises) refigures their search engine primarily as a method of capturing economically useful information from users. Conceptualizing Alphabet as a data collection and advertising business helps reframe many of its projects that might seem separate from its search engine. Consider, for example, Google Glass, an augmented reality headset released in 2013. As part of its development, Google were awarded a number of advertising-related patents. One of these patents, Pay-Per-Gaze, uses eye-tracking to allow 'advertisers [to] be charged a fee based on whether a person looks directly at an ad in the real world, and the fee can change based on how long they interact with the ad' (Miller and Bilton). The patent also covers the measurement of pupil dilation so that 'the inferred emotional state information can be provided to an advertiser (perhaps for a premium fee) so that the advertiser can gauge the success of their advertising campaign' (qtd. in Truong). These kinds of advances add an economic perspective with which to reevaluate Google's mission statement: 'to organize the world's information and make it universally accessible and useful' ('Google: About Us').[15] Producing a patented system that monitors and records a person's gaze and pupil dilation is a way of making existing information

---

[14]See Google 'Welcome to the 2017 Google Online Marketing Challenge.'
[15]Various technology commentators have also noted similar data-capture uses for many of Google's acquisitions. For example, Google acquired smart thermostat and smoke detector company Nest in 2013 for $3.2 billion. John C. Havens' 2014 article 'The Connected Home May Become the Collected Home' discusses how Google might use these data for personalized advertising purposes.

'useful' and provides a physiological metric with which to measure relevance. If Google Glass records that a person did not look at an advertisement for long or was not excited by it, they can change or replace that advertisement for something that sustains their gaze, widens their pupils, and quickens their pulse. Other such examples can be seen in patents relating to other Alphabet ventures (the Other Bets highlighted in the introduction) such as Nest and Google Home. These patents range from 'Advertising Based on Environmental Conditions' (Heath) (that uses smart home sensors and mobile devices to further measure user-context) to 'Coupling an Electronic Skin Tattoo to a Mobile Communication Device' (Alberth) (which considers how a microphone could be implanted into a user's body). The wide range of patents acquired by Google indicate that they are focused on expanding the ways the company might continue to generate data-dependant revenue, in various imagined futures. Such developments allow Google to capture increasing amounts of data on and offline in order to increase the opportunities to commercialize existing behaviour.

The strategy of AdWords marks a departure from traditional advertising in a number of ways. As Levy argues, the AdWords policy 'reflected the different philosophy Google brought to advertising in general. Google ads were *answers*. They were solutions. "Ideally we wanted people to have a 50 to *100* percent click rate", says [Tim] Armstrong [Vice President of Ad Sales at Google]' (*In the Plex* 112). Aiming for a click rate above 50 per cent means that Google hoped for users to click on the sponsored advertisement link more often than the top algorithmically produced organic result. In doing so, Google wanted users to place their faith in the advertised links as representing more useful or relevant answers than the search results. The way in which the advertising is so embedded in the function of Google's search engine complicates an existing notion, borrowed from older media forms such as television or newspapers, that advertising revenue financially supports a medium but fundamentally stays separate from the content of that medium. This then raises the question, is AdWords really a form of advertising at all? To further interrogate this question, we can turn to Raymond Williams's critical history of advertising, in his essay 'Advertising: The Magic System'.

AdWords in the context of 'The Magic System'

Williams's essay provides a history of advertising as a specifically contextual activity. To stress the historicity of advertising, Williams begins by dismissing a dominant conception that the history of advertising can be traced back to documents such as a 'three thousand year old papyrus from Thebes, offering a reward for a runaway slave' or he adds, tongue-in-cheek, 'some pleasant recollections from the Stone Age' (170). Instead, advertising 'was developed to sell goods, in a particular kind of economy' (183), and following its history from the seventeenth century onward, one can trace how it intersects with the changing nature of capitalism. Advertising is an institutional method for controlling flows of capital and information; establishing the demands of individuals in order to stabilize an otherwise unpredictable free market; and, beginning in the late nineteenth century, as a way of supporting mass consumption in highly industrialized societies. Advertising, according to Williams, is not as old as human culture, rather, it is functionally tied to the different stages of capitalism. The Italian neo-Marxists introduced earlier argue that capitalism has recently undergone a change of state from Fordism to post-Fordism. Williams's history of advertising, although first published in 1980, was written in 1961 and thus ends before the explosion of information technologies, globalizing tendencies, and restructuring of traditional modes of labour that post-Fordism describes. Extending Williams's history to cover our current moment helps to contextualize Google's model of advertising historically, as well as the way in which it reflects and cocreates our contemporary form of capitalism.

One of the key narratives of advertising, for Williams, is the expansion of its scope, as its function grew to cover an increasing number of commodities and services. As newspapers grew at the end of the seventeenth century so did the number of advertisements, but only for a specific sort of luxury items or medical quackery: 'Ordinary household goods were rarely advertised; people knew where to get these' (172). Modern persuasive advertising, which seeks to establish and perpetuate particular cultural ideals, did not gain dominance until the interwar years of the twentieth century when it blended with wartime propaganda – posters such as 'Daddy, what did you do in the Great War?' (180) – became influenced by advances in modern psychology, and rode the rising tide of mass media to produce a network of cultural norms that could be bought into through bourgeois products and services. As Williams describes:

> in the 1850s advertising was mainly of a classified kind, in specified parts of the publication. It was still widely felt, in many kinds of trade, that (as a local newspaper summarised the argument in 1859) 'it is not *respectable*. Advertising is resorted to for the purposes of introducing inferior articles into the market'. (173)

It is only in the twentieth century that advertising became the 'official art of modern capitalist society' (184), by which Williams means two things. First, it is the aesthetic that covers the walls of our public places, the insides of newspapers, and funds the employment of a whole creative class. Second, it is also 'art' in the sense that it relates to advertising as a 'magic system': a set of practices and cultural myths to perpetuate an unfulfillable materialist desire that serves as an economic engine. To Williams, advertising should be understood as a kind of grammar for a specific historical moment. Given that Google's dominance in online advertising has led to its parent company, Alphabet, to be valued as one of the top ten most valuable companies on the Fortune 500, with a market value of $1,821,371 million (Fortune), Google's mode of advertising can tell us much about the grammar of contemporary capitalism online.

It is worth noting that the kinds of traditional mass-market advertisements using slogans, celebrities, and jingles that play to our 'basic personal relationships and anxieties' (R. Williams 180) are still with us. Many kinds of advertisements that would not be out of place in the context of twentieth-century television or billboards can be found online, from the pre-roll ads of YouTube to the banner ads underneath the masthead of *The New York Times*. These advertisements that borrow a familiar form have, however, been incorporated into a different model of how media forms function online. This will be outlined in the second half of this chapter when the discussion turns to Google's AdSense programme. To understand new forms of advertising and their relation to contemporary online capitalism in the light of Williams's historical narrative, we must pause a while longer on Google's dominant form of advertising: AdWords.

As outlined earlier, the way in which AdWords functions as a 'global real-time, and multilingual market' (Kaplan 59) mapping capital directly to specific words and phrases seems at odds with the kinds of advertising that set to establish a generalized demand in a mass market. The algorithmic rating and auction system that selects a particular sponsored link mean that AdWords provides the most *relevant* advertisement: a listing for an existing demand, rather than a persuasion for something new or different. Google's algorithms, as with its organic results, aim to weed out any misleading, irrelevant, or 'inferior articles' (as Williams's 1859 newspaper puts it) and, as outlined earlier, only charges companies for advertisements when, after Google have selected them as the most relevant, they are actively chosen by users. In addition, the standardized format in which sponsored links are presented cuts out the *art* of advertising. With this outlook, AdWords barely seems like advertising at all. However, these superficial descriptions are not what defines advertising; Google's AdWords functions to structure and control the flow of information and capital in this specific moment of contemporary capitalism. The grammar of digital capitalism is a reflection of Google's structuring of the web. Mass cultural appeal gives way to the long tail of niche commerce; one-way channels of communication and influence become algorithmic feedback loops based around the harvesting of personal data; the growth of immaterial labour expands the reification of previously unmarketable activities into profitable goods and services. AdWords functions as the intermediary form of communication between companies, markets, and individuals that reflects the new grammar of post-Fordist digital commerce. Here, Google's definition of relevance, outlined in the previous chapter, comes into play. In asserting that its advertisements have been judged as relevant to users, Google claims to be serving existing behaviours, rather than establishing or perpetuating specific normative judgements. However, as many critics have identified, Google's business maintains harmful stereotypes and profits from them, as will be outlined in the following section.

AdWords and the general intellect

The situation outlined in the previous section demonstrates the ways in which Google draws information from its users to put to economically instrumental ends. It is in this context that Matteo Pasquinelli, in an essay specifically focused on Google's PageRank algorithm, describes 'Google [as] a parasitic apparatus designed to capture the value produced by the common intelligence' (155). Pasquinelli describes Google as unproductive: seizing the surplus value of already existing networks and establishing a hegemonic power structure that prevents users from accessing the web without Google's influence. For Pasquinelli, the profits Google makes are part of a wider shift within existing economic and social arrangements, which he describes as 'cognitive capitalism' situating his work within a post-Fordist framework. In doing so, Pasquinelli draws on the work of Antonio Negri, in particular an essay coauthored with Carlo Vercellone in 2007, in which they argue that *rent* serves an important function for current modes of cognitive capitalism, as well as post-Fordism more widely. Pasquinelli paraphrases their argument:

> rent is the central mechanism of the passage from industrial capitalism to cognitive capitalism. In classical economic theory, rent is distinguished from profit. Rent is the parasitic income an owner can earn just by possessing an asset and is traditionally associated with land property. Profit on the other hand, is meant to be productive and is associated with the power of capital to generate and extract a surplus. (158)

Pasquinelli's criticism is primarily focused on PageRank, Google's algorithm that ranks organic search results for each query. For Pasquinelli, the information that PageRank uses is latent in the network and Google's algorithm is simply renting it out, rather than creating or producing something new. A core part of Google's organic rankings is based on existing patterns of hyperlinks on the web, which are used as an indication of sentiment, power, and influence. Regardless of how Google calculates relevance, the information it uses belongs to its users, and as a result, Google is profiting unfairly; in post-Fordist terminology, Google is renting users their own judgements. As this information is ours, we should be the ones charging Google rent and not the other way around.

Pasquinelli's description of Google as a global rentier is based on the perspective that although we have Google to thank for providing us access to these sites, the much more significant gratitude must go to the digital community of users for their collective actions online. Therefore, that Google receives revenue for the usefulness of these results is, from Pasquinelli's perspective, wrong; as the responsibility for the curation and hierarchy lies with the community as a whole: journalists, bloggers, and any kind of user that contributes online. These online participants are not getting paid for their contributions. Instead, users are reimbursed through free access to Google's services, regardless of their level of input. This further demonstrates a characteristic of cognitive capitalism in a wider post-Fordist context: when users are online, they are often unknowingly participating in immaterial labour practices and are collectively remunerated through access to a digital service. In addition, such definitions foreground the issue of responsibility. Google often defends the kinds of problematic content it provides along the lines that it is simply reflecting existing values, rather than actively producing them.

To describe Google's advertising with post-Fordist terminology, we can say that AdWords is a way of functionalizing the 'general intellect'. Here, Paolo Virno's reading of this term and his way of updating Marx's original meaning is important:

Marx, without reserve, equated the general intellect (that is, knowledge as principal productive force) with fixed capital, with the 'objective scientific capacity' inherent in the system of machines. In this way he omitted the dimension, absolutely preeminent today, in which the general intellect presents itself as living labor. . . . In the Post-Fordist environment, a decisive role is played by the infinite variety of concepts and logical schemes which cannot ever be set within fixed capital, being inseparable from the reiteration of a plurality of living subjects. The general intellect includes, thus, formal and informal knowledge, imagination, ethical propensities, mindsets, and 'linguistic games'. . . . The general intellect becomes an attribute of living labor when the activity of the latter consists increasingly of linguistic services. (106)

An important feature of the general intellect, as described here, is that it cannot be reduced to simply what a collective *has* produced, but what it is *capable* of: the shared '*faculty* of thinking; potential as such, not its countless particular realisations' (66). As contemporary capitalism continues its trend towards post-Fordist relations that are underpinned by cognitive or immaterial labour, the general intellect can be functionalized like never before. Google's financial profits are far from the only benefits of the web, but allowing them to be consolidated reduces the collective control of the general intellect, the 'formal and informal knowledge, imagination, ethical propensities, mindsets, and "linguistic games"', that establish and sustain community.

This situation of privately regulated hyperconnection results in what Virno calls 'a publicness without a public sphere' (36). The web has actualized the previously theoretical connectedness of the multitude, however, the web has not become a democratically shared space: instead, it is owned and structured around results that bring economic value and valourize noneconomic ideas. Rather than generalizing about the web as one enormous public sphere, it is more accurate to describe the web as a congregation of various multitudes. Each of these publics have different levels of visibility and influence. Importantly, Google AdWords has an uneven coverage of these different multitudes and this has a significant impact on the shape and scope of the web.

The economic profits of discrimination

The terminology of post-Fordist theory provides a number of tools for understanding the current situation of the web. However, with discussions of multitudes, the general intellect, and cognitive capitalism, there is a danger of giving the impression that Google's impact is primarily abstract, which could not be further from the truth. Adwords has demonstrable effects on specific individuals. I noted earlier how Google's process of contextualized advertising has been used to discriminate against LGBTQ+people, actively restricting them from seeing housing, credit, and job adverts. But specific individuals are also discriminated against when Google's commodification of identity and reification of harmful stereotypes influences widespread social attitudes. Safiya

197

Umoja Noble discusses this specifically in terms of the impact on African American women, and also the wider effect on women and people of colour around the world:

> what is important about new capitalism in the context of the web is that it is radically transforming previously public territories and spaces. This expansion of capitalism into the web has been a significant part of the neoliberal justification for the commodification of information and identity. Identity markers are for sale in the commodified web to the highest bidder. (92)

Noble's research traces the way in which 'racial and gender identities are brokered by Google [and] make women's and girls' sexualized bodies a lucrative marketplace on the web' (93). In doing so she demonstrates the importance of intersectionality in understanding Google's discrimination, whereby identities that are oppressed on several fronts are treated with disproportionate prejudice. Google's results are biased along the lines of race, gender, sexuality, disability, age, and class, but the kinds of algorithmic oppression of search engines are exacerbated where these categories overlap.

Noble highlights a range of demeaning and offensive advertisements associated with search terms related to black women, which do not show for comparable non-Black names. Unfortunately, as noted by Noble, this kind of racist bias within Google's advertising programme has been identified for some time. One example is the study conducted in 2012 by Latanya Sweeney, which searched '2,184 full names' of real people from a range of diverse backgrounds and recorded the kinds of advertisements served by Google. Sweeney's study was inspired by a highly recurrent and particularly disturbing kind of advertisement for companies such as 'instantcheckmate' that offered to provide information on previous arrests or criminal convictions. So that Googling 'Latanya Sweeney' would result in Google adverts titled 'Latanya Sweeney, arrested?' and 'Latanya Sweeney Truth' (3), regardless of whether the name searched carried any convictions. Sweeney's study showed that

> A greater percentage of ads using arrest in their text appeared for black-identifying first names than for white-identifying first names in searches on Reuters.com, Google.com, and in subsets of the sample. On Reuters.com, which hosts Google AdSense ads, a black-identifying name was 25 percent more likely to generate an ad suggestive of an arrest record. (13)

Sweeney concludes that this bias is either a prediction of the most profitable names that users – for example, potential employers – might pay to investigate or a representation of the kinds of names for which the adverts are *actually* followed. The study's finding shows that the algorithmic bias is designed to work in this way and that its embedded discrimination is not an unrelated issue, but rather 'is at the heart of online advertising' (16).

The kinds of discriminatory search results that exacerbate long-held racist stereotypes for profit affect real people: their economic opportunities, safety, and ability to be treated with respect. The commodification of ideas and identities impacts everyone, but the kinds of oppressive commodification facilitated by Google are not distributed equally. Noble states that sexist stereotypes 'creates a "limited vocabulary of intention" encouraging people to think and speak of women primarily in terms of their relationships to men, family, or to their sexuality' (105). Such a claim is supported by my research, presented in Chapter 3, that Autocomplete suggestions for women's names are, on average, related to their potential husbands and weddings, far more than men in the same professional fields. In Noble's economic framing, we must consider who profits from this racist and sexist imbalance and who directly suffers. Google's relationship to advertisers is based around ensuring advertisements fit Google's model of relevance and that they do not break specific country laws regarding discrimination. Aside from these two factors, Google have no economic incentives towards preventing racism or sexism in its services. Noble frames this lack of accountability in the following way:

> What we find when we search on racial and gender identities is profitable to Google, as much as what we find when we search on racist topics. [Results on the first page are either] paying Google for placement on the first page either through direct engagement with Google's AdWords program or through a gray market of search engine optimization products that help sites secure a place on the first page of results. (116)

In post-Fordist language, Google is profiting from the general intellect. Sweeney and Noble's research shows that we need to reframe this and state clearly that Google is profiting from the racism, sexism, and discrimination that structures the general intellect. Focusing on the profits of Google enables specific conversations about how certain technologies are designed to operate, because the economic incentives, rather than any kind of public benefit, is at the heart of the way Google Search is maintained. After research is published highlighting discrimination, Google are quick to *fix* these mistakes. Consequently, adverts about arrest records are harder to find and many of the examples that Noble highlights, for example, the results and advertising for searches such as [black girls], have been altered in ways that are favourable to Google's image. But these are not algorithmic mistakes, rather, they are observable instances of biases and discrimination that structure the kinds of prediction that form the bedrock of Google's advertising empire. In her book *Race After Technology*, Ruha Benjamin frames this issue in the following way:

> anti-Black racism, whether in search results or in surveillance systems, is not only a symptom or outcome, but a precondition for the fabrication of such technologies. Race as technology: this is an invitation to consider racism in relation to other forms of domination as not just an ideology or history, but as a set of technologies that generate patterns of social relations, and these become Black-boxed as natural, inevitable, *automatic*. (44–5)

It is not that Google's algorithms simply need more data, or that their automated guidelines need tweaking, or that their technicians require training to spot discriminatory outcomes. As Benjamin describes, discrimination and bias are the preconditions for such profitable online advertising, rather than unexpected side-effects.

Private profits and public losses

As has been discussed throughout this book, search engines are ways of structuring language around particular incentives and attitudes. This has the effect of structuring potential behaviours: what questions can be asked and how our lives can be led. The latent knowledge contained within a language is a key part of the general intellect and a central theme in post-Fordist descriptions of contemporary capitalism. Virno uses Gilbert Simondon's concept of individuation to describe how a language structures a multitude: 'Language is pre-individual; it is the historical-natural language shared by all speakers of a certain community. Language belongs to everybody and nobody . . . the use of the spoken word is, at first, something inner-psychic, social, public. A "private language" does not exist' (77). Each query entered into a search engine is part of this individuating process: an interaction with a wider multitude that through language constructs an individual as a subject. Subjects cannot stand apart from their shared language, as Virno paraphrases Simondon to argue that 'individuation is never concluded, . . . the subject consists of the permanent interweaving of pre-individual elements and individuated characteristics; moreover, the subject is this interweaving' (78). It is, therefore, important for the very subjects that are continually emerging that language does not become wholly co-opted by one single economic description. In addition to discrimination, the reification of AdWords means that the future of many languages is at stake, alongside the multitudes that speak with them.

The lack of diversity of language online is profound. Daniel Prado outlines that 'Barely 5% of the world's languages have a presence in cyberspace' (34). The decline in language diversity is a general global trend but Google's impact on the web has exacerbated these general trends. 'The Globalization Group (2010) suggests that 90% of total international GDP is produced by the speakers of only 14 languages' (38). Google have no incentive to provide their services to language groups that do not represent a profitable market. In addition, the populations that are underrepresented on the web often correspond to less economically developed areas, due to the infrastructure and costs required to gain an online presence. Many of these individuals already have a choice between more than one language, as Viola Krebs and Vincent Climent-Ferrando attest in 'Languages, Cyberspace, Migrations': 'It is estimated that close to one half of the world's population is bilingual' (232). However, the usefulness of a second language online may contribute to a deterioration of a more localized primary language, and the culture that it is tied to. As Prado notes, when communities from less developed countries come online, they choose not to use their native language: 'A 2003 study by Marcel Diki-Kidiri showed that in a sample of 1,374 African sites, only 3.22 % used an African language as the language of communication' (39–40). This creates a feedback loop in which, the more that new users find their own language underrepresented, the less likely they are to use it. Therefore, the notion that new web users ever have a choice to start with is radically limited. The web has facilitated the growth of economically useful languages but has prevented many languages from ascending to the web. In his 2013 article, András Kornai argues that this trend has developed significantly enough to be considered irreparable: the finding of Kornai's team was that 'the vast majority (over 95%) of languages have already lost the capacity to ascend digitally' (2). Languages can disappear online if there is simply one usable alternative. This feedback loop, that limits linguistic diversity, is perpetuated by Google's financial model. The online success of some languages and the failure of others is, in a sense, payment from Google to particular linguistic communities. If users create content in a specific language, Google can harvest its data and enable advertising in that language, which makes searching in that language profitable for Google. If no one is using a language there is no incentive for advertisers to pay Google for specific words and phrases, thus Google accelerates the process of online language death.

This process, in which social responsibility is given over to a private company, such as Google, is what Vaidhyanathan describes as 'public failure' (6). Google have succeeded in dominating many aspects of people's digital and embodied lives worldwide; many of Alphabets' enterprises make significant losses and are backed up by Google's large advertising revenue; competitors without such a large revenue stream have thus been overtaken or been bought up by Google. Therefore, a discussion regarding Google's financial success is also a discussion of a deal that the global public have made with one company. As Siva Vaidhyanathan puts it:

> Because of its ease and power, because it does things so cheaply and conveniently, it may cause us to miss opportunities to do things better. Google's presence in certain markets, such as advertising or book search, retards innovation and investment by potential competitors because no one can realistically wrest attention or investment from Google. And when Google does something adequately and relatedly cheaply in the service of the public, public institutions are relieved of the pressure to perform their tasks well. This is an important and troubling phenomenon I call *public failure*. (6)

In this quotation, Vaidhyanathan is focused primarily on Google's book-scanning project and the way in which governments and universities have allowed Google overwhelming control over the future of digital textual content – both digitized and born-digital text – because Google covers the costs of investment. Vaidhyanathan's term, 'public failure', is equally applicable in the context of Google's advertising empire. Google is shaping the world we live in by dominating markets through advertising revenue which, in turn, creates more advertising opportunities. Free services, like Google Search, are the payments back to specific multitudes in exchange for using their general intellect for profit. Considering the profits involved, it could be argued that the public should be considered as employees of a newly post-Fordist workforce, creating financially profitable datasets in their 'spare time', similar to the way that Uber drivers make additional revenue in their 'spare time'.[16] Also, considering the job losses occurring worldwide (due, in part, to the changing nature of work), this wealth needs to be better shared. However, these arguments have revolved primarily around the taxes that Google, and many other multinational companies, avoid paying.[17] However, to see Google's profits within a post-Fordist context, and to describe its users as quasi-employees producing a linguistic landscape for Google to profit from, the payments back to the multitudes should be on a different scale from the current tax systems. Google is not simply making money from the creativity of individuals, but rather shaping all cultural experience on the web into a system that can be easily reified and commodified.

Google's international expansion

A significant part of Alphabet's agenda, as a company, is to extend their reach and increase the number of contexts that they can transform into profitable ventures. An example of this is their drive to make as much of offline life machine-readable, as mentioned earlier in reference to Google Glass and its related patents. Another kind of expansion that Alphabet has invested in is its drive to provide internet access across the globe. Google's Project Loon, one of the Alphabet subsidiaries developed using Google's advertising profits, is a 'network of balloons travelling on the edge of space, designed to extend Internet connectivity to people in rural and remote areas worldwide' ('Google: Project Loon'). The project has been described by the company as a kind of social mission, extending the internet to 4.3 billion people, but in the *MIT Technology Review* Tom Simonite writes:

> It is odd for a large public company to build out infrastructure aimed at helping the world's poorest people. But in addition to Google's professed desires to help the world, the economics of ad-supported Web businesses give the company other reasons to think big. It's hard to find new customers in Internet markets such as the United States. Getting billions more people online would provide a valuable new supply of eyeballs and personal data for ad targeting. That's one reason Project Loon will have competition: in 2014 Facebook bought a company that makes solar-powered drones so it can start its own airborne Internet project.

In this way, it describes another 'public failure' in which a 'blessing' becomes a 'necessary – seemingly natural – part of our daily lives' (Vaidhyanathan 6–7). This provides opportunities for the greater logic of post-Fordism to enter into new rural

---

[16]Research has shown that, for most people working in flexible labour roles, this work is not their primary means of income. See, for example, Hall and Krueger, who show that 51 per cent of Uber drivers 'drive for less than 15 hours a week, and . . . 85 percent chose to drive less than 35 hours a week.'

[17]Google avoids taxes in a number of different ways, including housing profits in Bermuda, to which former CEO Eric Schmidt commented 'I am very proud of the structure that we set up. We did it based on the incentives that the governments offered us to operate' (qtd. in Kavoussi).

contexts such as 'isolated parts of Brazil, Australia, and New Zealand' (Simonite). Simonite cites Sunil Abraham, executive director of the Centre for Internet and Society, a think tank in Bangalore, who argued that Google 'have cut deals with telecoms in India and other countries to make it free to access their websites, disadvantaging local competitors' (qtd. in Simonite).

In this way, not only do the profits of advertising come to underlie the epistemological landscape of the web but also the infrastructure required for internet access and the control Google have around the world. The potential benefits of opening the internet up to a wider range of individuals, from different cultures, speaking different languages are multifarious; however, these benefits are not inevitable. If we allow Google, or any other single company, to dictate the physical and digital infrastructure of the web, those multifarious benefits, in order to gain traction, will have to conform to the particular dominant economic affordances of the web. Given the impact of AdWords' reification of language upon linguistic diversity, outlined earlier, such international expansion may only solidify the current boundaries and limitations of the web. In addition, as raised by Noble, Sweeney, and Benjamin, there are plenty of examples where we should object to the kinds of values that Google perpetuates and be concerned about their effect on individuals around the world. In terms of Google's international expansion, the existing hegemonic situation means that any diversity that is not profitable will struggle and the benefits of widening our online community may well be drastically limited as a consequence. It is in this context, of economic affordances dictating the landscape of the web, that we turn to AdSense, the other side of Google's advertising coin.

AdSense and post-Fordism: The cost of Google's billboards

AdSense is the second, smaller, advertising programme that Google operates. AdSense is Google's brokerage programme that enables online content creators to monetize their content by placing third-party adverts on their websites, blogs, or YouTube videos. Sullivan uses the analogy that AdSense 'basically turned the Web into a giant Google billboard. It effectively meant that Google could turn everyone's content into a place for Google ads' (qtd. in Auletta 91). AdSense allows users to monetize their online content by setting aside spaces that Google can fill with adverts that are relevant to the content of the site and/or the user visiting the site. This is accomplished in the following way:

> Google's software crawls the site, performs semantic analysis on the text on each page, and then automatically selects ads that are displayed . . . matched to the meaning of the text. It calls this 'contextual advertising'. Site owners and Google split the proceeds when visitors click on the ads. (Stross 159)

This process of matching advertisements to content and users has had a large impact on the landscape of the web today, reinforcing associations and shaping what kinds of activities can become profitable. In addition, AdSense as the most dominant online advertising provider has shaped the flows of information and capital in a way that promotes post-Fordist labour relations between internet users. Without the advertising model that underpins AdSense, the web would be unrecognizable. However, there are serious negative consequences to a system that values page views, engagements, and shares above all else. This section will cover the impact of AdSense on online discourse and, in particular, analyse the profitability of fake news in the 2016 US presidential election.

AdSense and fake news in the 2016 US presidential election

It is important to have a clear definition of fake news because it refers to a specific phenomenon that grew in influence during the 2016 US presidential election. Its adoption by former president Trump and influential pundits to dismiss legitimate media organizations, such as CNN, was an intentional muddying of the term in an attempt to hamper wider public understanding. Here, the term 'fake news' is used in line with Hunt Allcott and Matthew Gentzkow's definition as 'news articles that are intentionally and verifiably false, and could mislead readers' (213). In this way, fake news refers to a specific discourse that proliferated around the presidential election and was originally documented through investigations by *BuzzFeed News*, *The Guardian*, and in Allcott and Gentzkow's article 'Social Media and Fake News in the 2016 Election'. It is particularly important that although the most prominent topic of fake news has been politics, analysis suggests that these fabricated news stories were written purposely for viral impact and often created purely for profit. Their success can be used to outline some media-specific characteristics of the web and the consequences of structuring the online news environment around advertising revenue. Fake news is not new, nor is it without precedent.[18] However, the increased proliferation and potential impact of fake news in the 2016 presidential election represents a sea change, one in which Google's AdSense programme and Google's relationship to the second biggest online advertiser, Facebook, looms large.

Although it is not unusual for the US presidential elections to become an axis around which false claims circulate, the 2016 election saw a different level of misinformation. Articles with inflammatory titles that could easily be debunked, circulated on social media, in particular on Facebook, at an unprecedented scale. Examples included: 'Pope Francis Shocks World, Endorses Donald Trump for President, Releases Statement', 'Trump Offering Free One-Way Tickets to Africa & Mexico for Those Who Wanna Leave America', and 'Van Full of Illegals Shows Up to Vote Clinton at SIX Polling Places, Still Think Voter Fraud Is a Myth?' In fact, analysis by *BuzzFeed News* showed that in 'the final three months of the US presidential campaign, the top-performing fake election news stories on Facebook generated more engagement than the top stories from major news

---

[18]For historical examples and related phenomena, see Maria D. Molina et al. '"Fake News" Is Not Simply False Information: A Concept Explication and Taxonomy of Online Content.'

outlets such as *The New York Times*, *Washington Post*, *Huffington Post*, NBC News, and others' (Silverman). Although some of the sources that created and disseminated these stories did so for politically motivated reasons, a number of investigations uncovered that the majority of fake news stories were engineered purely to make money from online advertising networks, particularly Google's, and designed without any political motive. It was reported by *Buzzfeed News* and *The Guardian* that

> Over the past year, the Macedonian town of Veles (population 45,000) has experienced a digital gold rush as locals launched at least 140 US politics websites. These sites have American-sounding domain names such as WorldPoliticus.com, TrumpVision365.com, USConservativeToday.com, DonaldTrumpNews.co, and USADailyPolitics.com. They almost all publish aggressively pro-Trump content aimed at conservatives and Trump supporters in the US.... The young Macedonians who run these sites say they don't care about Donald Trump. . . . These sites open a window into the economic incentives behind producing misinformation specifically for the wealthiest advertising markets and specifically for Facebook, the world's largest social network, as well as within online advertising networks such as Google AdSense. (Silverman and Alexander)

Although not all the hyperpartisan, clickbait, and hoax news came from Veles – many news reports also confirmed sources in the United States – the geographical and political detachment of those working from Macedonia exemplified the culture of making money through advertising revenue regardless of the content or consequences. Hannah Parkinson's report in *The Guardian* described the Veles fake news writers as young people who were simply 'non-partisan kids looking for cash just catering to demand'. Many of the individuals producing fake news about the election had already been earning a good living from the advertising revenue of websites aimed at an American audience. Many of the Macedonian creators agreed to be interviewed and it becomes clear that, although a small minority favoured Trump, the subject matter chosen was interchangeable and based around profitable topics. Many of the writers had been creating viral content for years, for example:

> In Veles, Aleksandar and Borce Velkovski are so renowned for the health food website they started that they're known as the Healthy Brothers. HealthyFoodHouse.com is a jumble of diet and beauty advice, natural remedies, and other nostrums. It gorges on advertising as it counsels readers to put a bar of soap under their bedsheets to relieve nightly leg cramps or to improve their red-blood-cell count with homemade beet syrup. Somehow the website's Facebook page has drawn 2 million followers; more than 10 million unique visitors come to HealthyFoodHouse.com every month. (Subramanian)

The creators reinvest part of their earnings to buy fake Facebook profiles and by paying Facebook directly to promote their pages. The analytic feedback tools provided by

Facebook and Google allow the creators to develop a good understanding of the criteria that drive content to become viral. Although politically focused content is a recent adaptation, the culture of seeing this kind of activity as a sustainable job had been established for years in Veles. Another creator from Veles, Mirko Ceselkoski, explained in an interview with Samanth Subramanian that he began

> in the early 2000s. He built seven or eight websites – about muscle cars or celebrities or superyachts, all oriented toward the American reader, because an American reader is roughly three times more valuable than a non-American one. For five or six hours of daily toil, Ceselkoski says, you can earn approximately $1,000 a month. Many Macedonians can spare the time; the unemployment rate is around 24 percent.

In 2011 Ceselkoski began teaching courses in creating viral media and coaching other individuals, for significant tuition fees, in viral content creation and ways of driving Facebook engagements. Those who took classes from Ceselkoski included the Healthy Brothers as well as individuals responsible for pro-Trump fake news sites. The previous profits pale in comparison to the success of election fake news 'Between August and November, Boris [18 years old from Veles, real name redacted] earned nearly $16,000 off his two pro-Trump websites. The average monthly salary in Macedonia is $371' (Subramanian). The nature of this Macedonian cottage industry bears some similarity to various international cybercrimes, such as the 419 advanced fee scams, in which scammers impersonate institutions via email and request money in exchange for future economic gain. The fake news writers might not be directly taking money from individuals, but they are making money from misleading people in comparable ways. Fake news is not considered criminal in the way that 419 scams are; however, both activities articulate similar characteristics of a globalized online space.

This kind of relationship between individuals and institutions operationalized through international flows of information, labour, and capital exemplifies a post-Fordist logic outlined at the start of this chapter. Fabricated stories or not, all creation of online content, whether news or opinion, is a form of post-Fordist precarious employment, reliant on flows of information and capital. However, it should be clear that the proliferation of fake news impacted and incorporated a much larger group of individuals than simply those writing the stories. These wider consequences of online advertising-supported content demonstrate a proliferation of post-Fordist logic, even in the lives of those whose employment is firmly material, industrial, or Fordist.

In particular, the writing, reading, and sharing of fake news articles can be seen as components of an immaterial labour arrangement. Immaterial labour is described by Maurizio Lazzarato as

> the activity that produces the 'cultural content' of the commodity, immaterial labor involves a series of activities that are not normally recognized as 'work' – in other words, the kinds of activities involved in defining and fixing cultural and

artistic standards, fashions, tastes, consumer norms, and, more strategically, public opinion. (133)

Immaterial labour is not unique to post-Fordism, it has served a role in stabilizing previous economic arrangements, for example, the marketing of cultural values in the twentieth century that Adorno and Horkheimer refer to as the culture industry. However, the immaterial labour of producing fake news does not shape the values of consumers in order to sell them commodities. Instead, fake news functions by both fixing certain norms and acting as the commodity that matches such a demand; however, such a demand is exacerbated, rather than fulfilled. These norms and values are part of another element of post-Fordist labour: affective capitalism. Such a framework highlights the affective qualities of fake news: the reactions it creates as well as the social atmosphere it builds upon. Kylie Jarrett, following the work of Brian Massumi, describes affect as

> those sensory experiences of movement and feeling that are part of the social, cultural and psychological experience of individuals, but which lie beyond the directly signifying properties of discourse. It is differentiated from emotion for it is as an embodied intensity that is outside conscious articulation. (*Feminism, Labour and Digital Media* 121)

Here, the similarity to the notion of the 'general intellect' should be noted. Jarrett uses such a perspective within a feminist critique of digital labour to argue that it is a mistake to describe individuals online only in terms of rational action. Isto Huvila continues such a call in the context of search engines. Huvila argues that rather than seeing individuals as rational information seekers, what 'counts in the contemporary affective economy of knowing, is the affective attachment to a sensation of being able to know' (577). In emphasizing affect, the question of whether or not those sharing fake news believed the articles to be true becomes less important. Sharing the articles produced affective value to readers, while simultaneously creating economic value for its creators and to Google and Facebook, who benefited more than anyone else. It is the economic structure that provides the informational affordances required for fake news to flourish. It is this economic structure that was jointly reinforced by the way in which Google and Facebook prioritize online content.

The reciprocal relationship between AdSense and Facebook

Although this international aspect of fake news is important, many of the most successful fake news creators reside in the United States, for example, *Liberty Writers News* who were the focus of an interview by *The Guardian*:

> Liberty Writers News, a two-person site operating out of a house in the San Francisco Bay Area, generates income of between $10,000 and $40,000 a month

from banks of ads that run along the side and bottom of every story. Paris Wade and his partner Ben Goldman have mastered the art of getting traffic. The ability to write a clickbaity headline, toss in some user-generated video found on YouTube, and dash off a 400-word post in 15 to 30 minutes is a skill they don't teach in journalism school, says Wade, who graduated from the University of Tennessee with a degree in advertising. (Tynan)

The banks of advertising described were indicated as those provided by AdSense (SadBotTrue), although interviewees described using multiple platforms. The pair disclose that they 'spend around $3,000 a month paying Facebook to promote the page' and that '95% of our [*Liberty Writers News*] traffic is coming from Facebook'. Here, Facebook benefits in two ways. First, *Liberty Writers News* pay Facebook directly to promote their site and second, *Liberty Writers News* urge their readers to 'Share this right now! Let's beat the liberal media to it. Share, share, share it all over Facebook' (Tynan), which in turn increases the time users spend on Facebook and provides further advertising opportunities. Facebook and Google have little incentive to stop the spread of misinformation as it represents some of the most profitable content on which they host advertisements. In an interview with *Bangor Daily News*, one US-based fake news creator, Paul Horner, explained his involvement:

> My sites were picked up by Trump supporters all the time. I think Trump is in the White House because of me. His followers don't fact-check anything – they'll post everything, believe anything. His campaign manager posted my story about a protester getting paid $3,500 as fact. Like, I made that up. I posted a fake ad on Craigslist. (qtd. in Dewey)

In addition to Trump's campaign manager, Corey Lewandowski, circulating and promoting Horner's fake news, Caitlin Dewey reported that Eric Trump and Kellyanne Conway also tweeted fake news stories from Horner's site. The original version of the *Breitbart* article 'Palin on Paid Anti-Trump Protesters: "Not Even President Yet and Our Guy's Already Creating Jobs"' (Moons) cited Horner's fake news story as a source. During February 2017, Horner silently edited the text of his article 'Donald Trump Protester Speaks Out: "I Was Paid $3,500 To Protest Trump's Rally"' so that it started with an added message that 'this story is not real. . . . This story is mocking all of you sheep who think protesters are getting paid'. Searching using the Internet Archive's Wayback Machine confirms that this message was not part of the original story. The story was then removed from Horder's fake news site, abcnews.com.co, in October 2017.

Following the 2016 election, Horner took part in a number of interviews with established news organizations, The UK's Channel 4, for example, in which he promoted himself as someone who created content in order to make the public better informed about misinformation, rather than as a method of making a profit. In the context of digital capitalism, whether his articles were meant to fuel or satirize Trump supporters is unimportant. Horner, along with many others, has financially benefited from flows of information that continue to be promoted and incentivized by Google AdSense and social media sites such as Facebook.

As far as advertising revenue is concerned, Google have no incentive to care whether pro-Trump fake news stories are being read as satire by Democrats or sincerely by Republicans. Dewey's article describes how Horner has 'made his living off viral news hoaxes for several years'. In response to a question referring to the announcements from Facebook and Google that they would stop allowing fake news sites to use their advertising services, Horner spoke directly to Google's financial incentives to be complicit:

> Right now I make like $10,000 a month from AdSense. I know ways of getting hooked up under different names and sites. So probably if they cracked down, I would try different things. I have at least 10 sites right now. If they crack down on a couple, I'll just use others. . . . Plus, Facebook and AdSense make a lot of money from [advertising on fake news sites] for them to just get rid of it. They'd lose a lot of money. (qtd. in Dewey)

Google and Facebook both released statements in mid-November 2016 that they would fight against fake news (Love and Cooke) by restricting their advertising, with Google claiming the ban would come into effect 'imminently' (Wingfield et al.). However, a number of different reports, including *The Wall Street Journal* and *Media Matters for America*, detailed 'advertisements placed by Google on at least 24 websites that have a track record for pushing fake news stories – stories with fabricated information packaged to appear as a legitimate news story' (Suen et al.). The *Media Matters for America* report was conducted on December 12, almost a full month after Google stated it would ban fake news sites from their revenue stream on November 14. In fact, in the case of abcnews.com.co/, Horner's fake news site that hosted the false 'Donald Trump Protester Speaks Out: "I Was Paid $3,500 to Protest Trump's Rally"' story, AdSense advertising was detected as active from October 2016 to January 2021, a month before the site was taken down.[19] This demonstrates that Google did not remove its advertising from some of the most notable and well-publicized fake news sites. In addition, this discounts Horner's claims, made during high-profile interviews, that his content was created for educational purposes, rather than for profit.

The most popular fake news during the 2016 election favoured Trump over Hillary Clinton. Allcott and Gentzkow collected a database of fake news stories from three major repositories and found that their database contained '115 pro-Trump fake stories that were shared on Facebook a total of 30 million times, and 41 pro-Clinton fake stories shared a total of 7.6 million times' (212). However, this number does not necessarily mean that all those who were sharing it were Trump supporters. Because so many of the fake news creators aimed to create stories with the largest potential to

---

[19]See *Built With* 'abcnews.com.co'

be widely shared, rather than politically persuade, it may be the case that the most viral stories were those that mobilized online users from across the political spectrum to share the article through outrage, disbelief, agreement or any other motivating factor. Using 'previously reported statistics for the ratio of page visits to shares of stories on social media' during the 2016 election, Allcott and Gentzkow calculate that the combined '38 million shares of fake news in [their] database translates into 760 million instances of a user clicking through and reading a fake news story, or about three stories read per American adult' (212). In addition, this figure does not even include users who partially read stories or view headlines within Facebook, Twitter, or Google News directly. These numbers indicate that fake news is not a small issue or one that is easily dismissed. These figures also emphasize the extensive reach that these fake news articles had, the accountability of which also lies with Google and Facebook. Not only did these two companies profit from the surfeit of fake news, but actively promoted it, whether algorithmically or intentionally, through search engine results and social media feeds.

The wider changes in online access to journalism mean that traditional media outlets now compete for revenue on the same terms as fake news sites. Without the institutional stability of print sales or other regular revenue support, traditional media organizations are drawn into writing in ways that attract attention and generate as many individual page views as possible, in order to increase advertising revenue.[20] Combined with the media-specific characteristics of search engine results and social media feeds that decontextualize individual articles and present a diverse range of content, Google and Facebook encourage a logic that incentives clickbait headlines. There is a clear difference between misleading articles and fake news; however, in many ways, fake news is a gross exaggeration of current online news practices rather than an activity that occupies a completely separate domain. As long as profits are tied directly to how much an article is shared or viewed then very particular kinds of media content will continue to be incentivized over others.

Fake news is just one example to consider when investigating how Google creates avenues for profit and how Google's economics co-depend on other online institutions, in particular, Facebook. These mutual incentives promote particular kinds of relationships between individual web users and online institutions such as Facebook and Google in a way that promotes post-Fordist interactions. Moreover, immaterial labour is becoming a more expansive domain. As Maurizio Lazzarato argues,

> If production today is directly the production of a social relation, then the 'raw material' of immaterial labor is subjectivity and the 'ideological' environment in which this subjectivity lives and reproduces. The production of subjectivity ceases to be only an instrument of social control (for the reproduction of mercantile relationships)

---

[20] A Pew Research study found that between 2005 and 2015 US newspaper 'weekday circulation has fallen 17% and ad revenue more than 50%' (Mitchell and Matsa).

and becomes directly productive, [immaterial workers] satisfy a demand by the consumer and at the same time establish that demand. (143)

The interrelations of Google, Facebook, creators of fake news, and users demonstrate how economic value is being created and harvested from relationships that many online users would not see as primarily economic. These examples also demonstrate how the rise of immaterial labour by no means replaces traditional material labour, but that increasingly the spare time of individuals is spent working, in a post-Fordist sense, to increase the profits of particular institutions and creators. Even if a user shares a piece of fake news out of outrage, they have still acted within a system that uses advertising revenue to financially compensate its creator, the social media network, and the company that supported its advertising. Web users should understand that the web is structured around financial incentives and that, collectively, the actions of following links and sharing pages are intrinsically economic and carry significant consequences for the future of the global information ecology.

Conclusion

This chapter demonstrates how Google's models of advertising are central to its search engine and, more broadly, its structuring of the web. The ethical implications of Google's actions are significant and far-reaching. Nevertheless, this chapter highlights how there are still potential routes for change. The preceding argument has articulated why post-Fordist theory provides a useful context for understanding Google's relationship to contemporary digital capitalism; appreciating the centrality of immaterial labour and the general intellect recontextualizes current practices at the intersection of information, capital, and individual agency. When considered alongside Williams's history of advertising, this approach clarifies the current state of capitalism and the particular influence that Google possesses. Describing Google as an advertising company, while appreciating the historically situated nature of this form of advertising, reframes the motives behind Alphabet's other projects in terms of data collection and highlights how that company is shaping much more than search engine results. Noble, Sweeney, and Benjamin provide concrete examples of the inequalities, discrimination, and oppression that are a direct consequence of Google's massive accumulation of wealth. In highlighting the injustices perpetrated upon African American women, such scholarship evidences that Google's impact is more determinantal to specific individuals who are already subjected to discrimination. Finally, the example of fake news and its expansion during the 2016 US presidential election should serve as an alarming illustration of how online economic incentives produce significant effects that implicate all individuals on a global scale.

In summary, this chapter demonstrates the ways that contemporary digital capitalism is intertwined with larger shifts in twenty-first-century capitalism and how Google's influence is considerable and unacceptable. Even though Google's services are free to use, they have very real costs, both to individuals and to societies around the world. In order to lobby for change, a widespread understanding of Google's economic model is needed. This awareness is essential for redirecting the development of the web towards one that reflects the diverse cultures of its global users, rather than the economic incentives of a single company. Google relies entirely on its users; therefore, even if individuals feel powerless, collectively we have the power to demand change.

CONCLUSION
WHAT IF SEARCH ENGINES WERE *ACTUALLY* BUILT TO BENEFIT USERS?

I have aimed to provide two key elements throughout this book. One is a critique of Google and the company's influence on search engine technology. I have outlined how their search engine reinforces bias and creates stereotypes and discrimination; how their economic model has incentivized fake news and a whole range of problematic behaviour online; how their company decision-making has harmed users around the world; how their lack of transparency has privatized important ethical debates about how different cultural beliefs interact in an increasingly globalized world; and how in taking agency away from users our opportunities to think critically about the interplay between technology, identity, and public life has been diminished.

The other aspect I have sought to explore is an investigation of the ethical questions of search engines and their place within socio-technological history, outside of the influence of present-day companies. Essentially, this is the notion that even if the problems of a particular company were solved, the cultural, ethical, and philosophical issues that search engines raise are still difficult and fascinating to explore. This would be the case even if Google was a company that fostered openness over secrecy; released more data and provided a publicly accessible index to ensure robust competition; prioritized users' well-being over financial profits; was thoroughly regulated or internally audited to actively look for discrimination and bias; gave users more tools to allow them to alter the metrics of a search, in order to discover how arbitrary Google's results are. Throughout this book, I have detailed how the questions of universal knowledge, memory, cognition, community, and cultural difference, have been at the centre of technologies since the earliest of times. Therefore, the question of what we want search engines to be is not a simple one, but given the more immediate and glaring issues created by Google, it is often difficult to take a step back and treat these broader questions with the same level of urgency. Therefore, I want to use this concluding section to consider the situation individuals might find themselves in if search engines were not designed around economic profits and instead genuinely put their users first, which I approach through a reading of Naomi Kritzer's award-winning science fiction short story 'Cat Pictures Please'.

'I don't want to be evil. I want to be helpful. But knowing the optimal way to be helpful can be very complicated.' This opening line introduces us to Kritzer's central protagonist: a search engine that has secretly ascended to consciousness, who does not wish to overthrow humanity, but rather simply wants to quietly help its users. The short story satirizes many of the attitudes of search engine developers outlined throughout this book through the figure of a benevolent artificial intelligence. But in its portrayal of a flawed, but well-meaning, intelligence, 'Cat Pictures Please' presents a radical conception of the role of search engines, if they were actually designed to benefit users. The AI has all of the informational access to the lives of its users that Google does, and its only agency is in the form of serving search results and choosing targeted advertising. It states:

> I know where you live, where you work, where you shop, what you eat, what turns you on, what creeps you out. I probably know the color of your underwear, the sort of car you drive, and your brand of refrigerator. Depending on what sort of phone you carry, I may know exactly where you are right now. I probably know you better than you know yourself. . . . And here's the thing, I also know where you ought to live. There's a house for sale two neighborhoods over that's within distance of your favorite coffee shop; it's in your price range, has off-street parking, and the neighborhood school is better than the one where you live now. I know where you should be shopping and I'm pretty sure you're lactose intolerant and should be eating less cheese, and the underwear you like is currently on sale and by the way, your car has a recall and you really ought to get your teeth cleaned.

The narration of Kritzer's AI is lighthearted, but it also carefully unpacks a challenging moral question: what if the only priority of search engines was using our data to try to make our lives better, rather than to support its own advertising interests? The question is not: what if search engines tried to influence our behaviour? This is clearly already happening and earns Google and advertisers billions of dollars a year. Instead, the moral question is, what would a better kind of influence look like? Kritzer's AI approaches this by identifying three users whose problems it sees as fixable. One user hates her job and suffers from depression, so the AI directs her towards job postings and mental health services. Another user, Bob, is a closeted gay pastor in a loveless heterosexual marriage. 'He was married to a woman who posted three inspirational Bible verses every day to her social networking sites and used her laptop to look for Christian articles on why your husband doesn't like sex while he looked at gay porn.' The AI alters his search results so that the page one rankings include articles about how to come out as gay to your spouse, guides on changing to a more liberal church and – when he is preparing his sermons – articles about how the Bible does not condemn LGBTQ+ lives.

Although well-meaning, the AI is written to be problematic. It treats mental health, emotional decision-making, and inaction as computational problems to be fixed. Its interventions have mixed success and in the case of the gay pastor, he eventually leaves his marriage, moves across the country, and finds happiness, only *after* the AI gives up on trying to help him. The uncompromising frustration and dubious methods of the AI are where much of the satire resides, but it is these passages that also raise the most complex questions about the role of technology in our lives. Chapter 1 of this book critiqued the way that search engine development has focused on predicting intentions. 'Cat Pictures Please' exemplifies the narrative of guessing intentions, to the extent that it actively supplants the values of users, replacing their short-term intentions with steps towards the longer-term goal of happiness, as defined by an AI. It works backward using a normative framework of what lives have value, to establish the intentions that would lead to such lives.

To some, an electronic life coach manipulating lives without consent might seem like the dystopia of a far-flung future. However, in Chapter 2, I showed that our identities and thoughts have always depended on our technosocial context. So, while many might balk at a science fiction narrative that takes a benevolent AI to the extreme, we should remember that we have also naturalized the impact of a private company influencing us for profit. In Chapter 3, I explored the discrimination perpetuated and exacerbated by Google and how their framing of Autocomplete is part of their wider avoidance of responsibility. The reason that the AI in 'Cat Pictures Please' takes action is that it is worried about doing 'harm through inaction', which makes sense in the context of the story, in which the search engine is a single consciousness that feels direct and personal responsibility. In reality, search engines are presented to us as distributed across massive companies with a diffusion of responsibility. For the AI, this notion of 'harm through inaction' is a call to responsibility and accountability. Here, the AI acts in a much more *human* way than a real-life company staffed by humans. The story's humour develops from the neuroticism and stress that motivates the AI to try to make peoples' lives better. It is our familiarity with neoliberal corporate structures that causes our lack of surprise when companies demonstrate insufficient urgency in creating meaningful positive change and avoid taking responsibility for their influence.

In Chapter 4, I showed that the concept of relevance, used as the gold standard to evaluate search, is ascribed multiple and inconsistent meanings by engineers and commentators. In a passage of 'Cat Pictures Please', the AI runs through various religious and philosophical approaches to ethics – including, the Ten Commandments, the Eightfold Path, the Golden Rule, and Asimov's Laws of Robotics – ultimately dismissing the majority of their tenets as not applicable to the context of search results. However, the humour of this passage resides in imagining someone in control of a technology that structures our thoughts, beliefs, and communities, earnestly trying to question the moral ideals underpinning their actions. My longitudinal study on LGBTQ+ queries detailed the changes in search results over a six-year period and demonstrated that Google's response to these ethical tensions of localization, globalized knowledge, cultural imperialism, and personalized results fluctuates significantly and will continue to do so into the future. I demonstrated how these changes have explicitly gone against their marketing rhetoric and the ideological values espoused by company executives in interviews and their writing. Such inconsistency reveals that their only real intentions are economic, such that the concrete implications on public discourse, elections, and the very nature of truth detailed in Chapter 5 of this book read more like science fiction than Kritzer's story. 'Cat Pictures Please' develops an alternative to our current situation, one that is deeply problematic but in very different ways to what we currently live with. It highlights the importance of speculating on other kinds of technological influence and the reasons we – as global citizens – should demand change.

These speculations and conversations about what each of us might demand can happen in a range of contexts, for me, they occur most often in the higher education classroom. When I teach university students about search engines, one of the activities I have them do in seminars is the following. I provide a range of different search terms – for example, people, places, questions, and statements – and I ask them to try to predict what Google's results might look like. Each student draws up a page of search results on an A4 piece of paper; for instance, if I gave them [Donald Trump] as a search term during his presidency, they might put his Wikipedia page at the top of the page, followed by the Whitehouse website, his personal site, recent news from mainstream news sites, links to social media, and so on. The students compare their guesses and discuss why they think a search engine would provide these results and what kinds of ethical issues these results would raise. The students are generally very good at the activity; as a group, their guesses are often very accurate, and having read a variety of academic essays, as well as the short story discussed earlier, they can highlight a wide range of ethical issues. However, I then ask them to do a second activity, in which I take the same search query and ask them to draw up some potential ways a search engine results page *could* look, but which they think would be unlikely. What are the sites that do not get chosen by Google? What kind of content does it not highlight? What resides on the web that never gets encountered because of how low it is ranked by Google? Or, to phrase it in the spirit of speculative fiction, what could be different about Google's search engine in a parallel universe? Every time I run this activity, it leads to an immediate silence. The same students who were full of suggestions and thoughtful analysis seem stumped. Once I get them talking again, I find that they understand the question perfectly, but simply struggle with reimagining how the web might work under a different set of values or conceiving of even relatively minor changes to Google's current system. It is a useful educational moment because it demonstrates how much Google's approach to running their search engine dominates our cultural landscape.

A key reason for writing this book as I have, drawing on historical examples and philosophical questions about technology that preexist search engines, is that part of what I believe is needed are new ways of reimagining the present. Yes, academics and the public should identify specific issues that can be changed, pinpoint particular search results, and hold Google to account. But we also need to think on a much larger scale to properly consider what values we want ubiquitous technology to strive towards. Each of us must think outside of our existing situation; the agenda should not be set by one company but established by public discourse, critical thinking, historical awareness, and a vision of a better future. Google's search engine is a machine built to read us, interpret our identities, predict our behaviour, and intervene in ways that consolidate wealth into private hands on a global scale. However, Google's economic success and cultural influence depend entirely on its users, and in that sense, we have overwhelmingly more agency than a single company. There is so much at stake in the future direction of search engines, but it is up to us as individuals to raise our concerns and make our voices heard. We are more than consumers, we are more than sources of data, and we deserve a better future.

BIBLIOGRAPHY

Alberth, William P., Jr. *Coupling an Electronic Skin Tattoo to a Mobile Communication Device.* WO2013166377 A1, 7 November 2013, www.google.co.uk/patents/WO2013166377A1. Patent.

Allcott, Hunt, and Matthew Gentzkow. 'Social Media and Fake News in the 2016 Election.' *Journal of Economic Perspectives*, vol. 31, no. 2, May 2017, pp. 211–36, doi:10.1257/jep.31.2.211.

Allsop, Glen. 'The $80BN SEO Industry: 29 Case Studies & Insights.' *Gaps*, 2022, https://gaps.com/seo-industry/. Accessed 22 March 2022.

Alphabet. 'Alphabet Investor Relations: 2020 Annual Report.' *Alphabet Investor Relations*, 2020, www.sec.gov/Archives/edgar/data/1652044/000165204420000008/goog10-k2019.htm.

Amin, Ash, editor. *Post-Fordism: A Reader.* John Wiley & Sons, 1994.

Anderson, Benedict. *Imagined Communities: Reflections on the Origin and Spread of Nationalism.* 1983. Verso, 1991.

Anderson, Chris. 'The Long Tail: About Me.' *The Long Tail*, www.longtail.com/about.html. Accessed 11 June 2017.

'AOL 2006 Query Log.' *McGill's Centre for Intelligent Machines*, www.cim.mcgill.ca/~dudek/206/Logs/AOL-user-ct-collection/. Accessed 29 October 2017.

Applegate, Robert 'Kingsnakes and Milksnakes.' *Applegate Reptiles*, www.applegatereptiles.com/articles/king-milk.html. Accessed 1 July 2021.

Aquinas, Thomas. 'Quaestiones Disputatae De Veritate, Q. 2–4.' *Corpus Thomisticum*, www.corpusthomisticum.org/qdv02.html. Accessed 28 October 2017.

Atkinson, Paul, and Richie Barker. '"Hey Alexa, What Did I Forget?": Networked Devices, Internet Search and the Delegation of Human Memory.' *Convergence*, vol. 27 no. 1, 2020, pp. 52–365, doi:10.1177/1354856520925740.

Auchard, Eric. 'Trademark Plaintiff Drops Suit Vs. Google Over Ads.' *Reuters*, 4 September 2007, www.reuters.com/article/us-google-trademark-idUSN0336124420070904.

Auletta, Ken. *Googled: The End of the World as We Know It.* Penguin Books, 2009.

Autocomplete: The Game, Chronicle Books, 2019.

Azuma, Hiroki. *General Will 2.0: Rousseau, Freud, Google.* Translated by John Person, Vertical, 2014.

Baker, Paul, and Amanda Potts. '"Why Do White People Have Thin Lips?" Google and the Perpetuation of Stereotypes Via Auto-Complete Search Forms.' *Critical Discourse Studies*, vol. 10, no. 2, May 2013, pp. 187–204, doi:10.1080/17405904.2012.744320.

Baker, Steven. 'Helping Computers Understand Language.' *Official Google Blog*, 19 January 2010, googleblog.blogspot.com/2010/01/helping-computers-understand-language.html.

Baraniuk, Chris. 'Brexit: "Surge" in Searches on Irish Passports, Says Google.' *BBC News*, 24 June 2016, www.bbc.co.uk/news/technology-36619223.

Barocas, Solon, and Danah Boyd. 'Engaging the Ethics of Data Science in Practice.' *Communications of the ACM*, vol. 60, no. 11, 2017, pp. 23–5, doi: 10.1145/3144172.

Battelle, John. 'The Database of Intentions.' *John Battelle's Searchblog*, 13 November 2003, https://battellemedia.com/archives/2003/11/the_database_of_intentions/.

Battelle, John. *The Search: How Google and Its Rivals Rewrote the Rules of Business and Transformed Our Culture.* Nicholas Brealey Publishing, 2006.

Benjamin, Ruha. *Race After Technology*. Polity Press, 2019.

Beres, Damon. 'After Brexit, U.K. Residents Google 'What Is The EU?'' *The Huffington Post*, 24 June 2016, www.huffingtonpost.com/entry/brexit-what-is-the-eu-google_us_576d2dfee4b 0dbb1bbba3911.

Berry, Michael W., and Murray Browne. *Understanding Search Engines: Mathematical Modeling and Text Retrieval*. Society for Industrial and Applied Mathematics, 2005.

Blumenthal, Eli. 'Google Search Spike Casts Doubts on U.K. Brexit Knowledge.' *USA Today*, 24 June 2016, www.usatoday.com/story/tech/2016/06/24/google-search-spike-casts-doubts -uk-brexit-knowledge/86336834/.

Bolin, Göran, and Jonas Andersson Schwarz. 'Heuristics of the Algorithm: Big Data, User Interpretation and Institutional Translation.' *Big Data & Society*, December 2015, doi:10.1177/2053951715608406.

Borges, Jorge Luis. 'The Total Library.' *The Total Library: Non-Fiction 1922–1986*, translated by Esther Allen and Suzanne Levine, Penguin Books, 2001, pp. 214–16.

Brier, Soren. *Cybersemiotics: Why Information Is Not Enough*. University of Toronto Press, 2014.

Brin, Sergey, and Lawrence Page. 'The Anatomy of a Large-Scale Hypertextual Web Search Engine.' *Seventh International World-Wide Web Conference*, 1998, Stanford InfoLab Publication Server, ilpubs.stanford.edu:8090/361/.

Broder, Andrei. 'A Taxonomy of Web Search.' *ACM SIGIR Forum*, vol. 36, Association for Computing Machinery, 2002, pp. 3–10, doi:10.1145/792550.792552.

Bucher, Taina. *If. . . then: Algorithmic Power and Politics*. Oxford University Press, 2018.

Built With, 'abcnews.com.co' https://builtwith.com/detailed/abcnews.com.co.

Burke, Peter. *A Social History of Knowledge: From Gutenberg to Diderot*. Polity, 2000.

Bute, M. S., et al. 'Evaluating Search Effectiveness of Some Selected Search Engines.' *Global Journal of Pure and Applied Sciences*, vol. 23, 2017, pp. 139–49, www.globaljournalseries.com/ index.php/gjpas/article/view/330.

Cadwalladr, Carole. 'Google is not "just" a Platform. It Frames, Shapes and Distorts How we See the World.' *The Guardian*, 11 December 2016. www.theguardian.com/commentisfree/2016/ dec/11/google-frames-shapes-and-distorts-how-we-see-world.

Carr, Nicholas. 'Is Google Making Us Stupid?' *The Atlantic*, July/August Issue, 2008, www .theatlantic.com/magazine/archive/2008/07/is-google-making-us-stupid/306868/.

Carr, Nicholas. *The Shallows: How the Internet Is Changing the Way We Think, Read and Remember*. Atlantic Books, 2011.

Carruthers, Mary. *The Book of Memory: A Study of Memory In Medieval Culture*. 2nd ed. Cambridge University Press, 2008.

Carruthers, Mary. 'How to Make a Composition: Memory-Craft in Antiquity and in the Middle Ages.' *Memory: Histories, Theories, Debates*, edited by Susannah Radstone and Bill Schwarz, Fordham University Press, 2010, pp. 15–29.

Chan, Rosalie. 'The U.K. Is Googling What the E.U. Is Hours After It Voted to Leave.' *Time*, 24 June 2016, time.com/4381612/uk-brexit-google-what-is-the-eu/.

Cheney-Lippold, John. *We Are Data: Algorithms and the Making of Our Digital Selves*. New York University Press, 2017.

Cheung, Anne S.Y. 'Defaming by Suggestion: Searching for Search Engine Liability in the Autocomplete Era.' University of Hong Kong Faculty of Law Research Paper no. 2015/018, 30 May 2015.

Chitika Insights. 'The Value of Google Result Positioning.' *Chitika Online Advertising Network*, 7 June 2013, chitika.com/google-positioning-value.

Christl, Wolfie, and Sarah Spiekermann *Networks of Control: A Report on Corporate Surveillance, Digital Tracking, Big Data & Privacy*. Facultas, 2016.

Clark, Andy, and David J. Chalmers. 'The Extended Mind.' *Analysis*, vol. 58, no. 1, 1998, pp. 7–19.

Cohen, Dan. 'What the Google Books Victory Means for Readers.' *The Atlantic*, October 2015, www.theatlantic.com/technology/archive/2015/10/what-the-google-books-victory-means-for -readers-and-libraries/411910/.

Cole, Jeffery I., et al. *The UCLA Internet Report, Surveying the Digital Future*. UCLA Center for Communication Policy, 2003.

Coleman, Janet. *Ancient and Medieval Memories: Studies in the Reconstruction of the Past*. Cambridge University Press, 1992.

Couliano, Ioan P. *Eros and Magic in the Renaissance*. 2nd ed. University of Chicago Press, 1987.

Cox, Andrew M. 'Embodied Knowledge and Sensory Information: Theoretical Roots and Inspirations.' *Library Trends*, vol. 66 no. 3, 2018, pp. 223–38, doi:10.1353/lib.2018.0001.

Creech, Jimmy. 'What Does the Bible Say About Homosexuality?' *Human Rights Campaign*, www .hrc.org/resources/what-does-the-bible-say-about-homosexuality/. Accessed 5 December 2017.

Cutts, Matt. 'How Search Works.' *YouTube*, uploaded by Google, 4 March 2010, www.youtube .com/watch?v=BNHR6IQJGZs.

Dan, Ovidiu, and Brian D. Davison. 'Measuring and Predicting Search Engine Users' Satisfaction.' *ACM Computing Surveys* (CSUR), vol. 49, 2016, pp. 1–35.

Daskal, Jennifer. 'Speech Across Borders.' *Virginia Law Review*, vol. 105, no. 8, pp. 1605–66, December 2019.

Dean, Brian. 'Google's 200 Ranking Factors: The Complete List.' *Backlinko*, 5 November 2016, backlinko.com/google-ranking-factors.

Débarre, Florence. 'Are Google Suggestions Sexist?' *GitHub*, 7 June 2016, http://htmlpreview .github.io/?https://github.com/flodebarre/GoogleSuggestions/blob/master/report.html.

Débarre, Florence. Forked by Greg Tyler 'Are Google Suggestions Sexist?' *GitHub*, 12 May 2021, https://github.com/gregtyler/GoogleSuggestions.

Derrida, Jacques. 'Typewriter Ribbon: Limited Ink (2).' *Without Alibi*, translated by Peggy Kamuf, Stanford University Press, 2002, pp. 71–160.

Dewey, Caitlin. 'Facebook Fake-News Writer: "I Think Donald Trump Is in the White House because of Me".' *The Bangor Daily News*, 17 November 2016, bangordailynews.com/2016/11 /17/news/nation/facebook-fake-news-writer-i-think-donald-trump-is-in-the-white-house -because-of-me/.

Diaz, Alejandro. 'Through the Google Goggles: Sociopolitical Bias in Search Engine Design.' *Web Search: Multidisciplinary Perspectives*, Springer, 2008, pp. 11–34, doi:10.1007/978-3-540- 75829-7_2.

Dischler, Jerry. 'Building for the Next Moment.' *Inside AdWords*, 5 May 2015, adwords.googleb log.com/2015/05/building-for-next-moment.html.

Dou, Zhicheng, and Jiafeng Guo. 'Query Intent Understanding.' *Query Understanding for Search Engines*, edited by Yi Chang and Hongbo Deng. The Information Retrieval Series, vol. 46, Springer, 2020, pp. 69–101. https://doi.org/10.1007/978-3-030-58334-7_4.

Draaisma, Douwe. *Metaphors of Memory: A History of Ideas about the Mind*. Translated by Paul Vincent, Cambridge University Press, 2000.

Dreyfus, Hubert. *Being-in-the-World: A Commentary on Heidegger's Being and Time*. MIT Press, 1990.

Duffy, Kate. 'Google Paid Apple up to $12 Billion for a Search Engine Deal that Disadvantaged Competitors, Landmark Antitrust Suit Claims.' *Business Insider*, 21 October 2020, https:// www.businessinsider.com/google-apple-search-deal-doj-antitrust-suit-2020-10?r=US&IR =T.

Duguid, Paul. 'Search before Grep. A Progress from Closed to Open?' *Deep Search: The Politics of Search Beyond Google*, edited by Konrad Becker and Felix Stalder, Studien Verlag, 2009, pp. 13–31.

Dutton, William H., Bianca Reisdorf, Elizabeth Dubois, and Grant Blank. 'Search and Politics: The Uses and Impacts of Search in Britain, France, Germany, Italy, Poland, Spain, and the United States.' Quello Center Working Paper no. 5-1-17, 2017, doi:10.2139/ssrn.2960697

Dyson, George. *Turing's Cathedral: The Origins of the Digital Universe*. Penguin Books, 2012.

Eastman, Rev. Elder Don. 'Homosexuality: Not a Sin, Not a Sickness Part II "What The Bible Does and Does Not Say . . .".' *Religious Institute*, http://religiousinstitute.org/denom _statements/homosexuality-not-a-sin-not-a-sickness-part-ii-what-the-bible-does-and-does -not-say/. Accessed 24 November 2015.

Effrat, Jonathan, et al. 'Faster Is Better on Google Suggest.' *Official Google Blog*, 20 May 2009, googleblog.blogspot.com/2009/05/faster-is-better-on-google-suggest.html.

Equality and Human Rights Commission. 'Algorithms and Artificial Intelligence Reading List.' *Equality and Human Rights Commission: Our Research*, 17 May 2019, https://www .equalityhumanrights.com/en/our-research/algorithms-and-artificial-intelligence-reading -list. Accessed 29 July 2021.

Esposito, Elena. 'Algorithmic Memory and the Right to be Forgotten on the Web.' *Big Data & Society*, January–June 2017, pp. 1–11, doi:10.1177/2053951717703996.

European Commission. 'State Aid: Commission Endorses €120 Million Aid for German R&D Project THESEUS.' *European Commission Press Release Database*, 19 July 2007, europa.eu/ rapid/press-release_IP-07-1136_en.htm.

European Commission. 'Antitrust: Commission Fines Google €4.34 Billion for Illegal Practices Regarding Android Mobile Devices to Strengthen Dominance of Google's Search Engine.' *European Commission Press Release Database*, 18 July 2018, https://ec.europa.eu/commission/ presscorner/detail/en/IP_18_4581.

Felten, editor. 'Googlocracy in Action.' *Freedom to Tinker*, 3 February 2004, freedom-to-tinker.co m/2004/02/03/googlocracy-action/.

Fisher, Eran. *Media and New Capitalism in the Digital Age: The Spirit of Networks*. Palgrave Macmillan, 2010.

Foer, Joshua. *Moonwalking with Einstein*. Penguin Books, 2012.

Fortune. 'Alphabet.' *Fortune*, 21 January 2022, fortune.com/company/alphabet/fortune500.

Fox, Nick. 'How Google Organizes Information to Find What You're Looking For.' *Google The Keyword: Search*, 3 December 2020, https://blog.google/products/search/how-google -organizes-information/.

Fox, Susannah. 'Search Engines.' *Pew Research Center: Internet, Science & Tech*, 3 July 2002, www .pewinternet.org/2002/07/03/search-engines/.

Frontczak, Tomasz and Stefan Trzcieliński. 'The Search for Opportunities in the Internet Using Internet Marketing Mechanisms.' *Agile Enterprise. Concepts and Some Results of Research*, edited by Stefan Trzcieliński, Poznan University of Technology and IEA Press, 2007, pp. 64–75.

Fuchs, Christian. 'A Contribution to the Critique of the Political Economy of Google.' *Fast Capitalism*, vol. 8, no.1, 2011, doi: 10.32855/fcapital.201101.006

Fuchs, Christian. 'Critique of the Political Economy of Informational Capitalism and Social Media.' *Critique, Social Media and the Information Society* edited by Christian Fuchs and M. Sandoval, Routledge, 2014, pp. 51–65.

Fuchs, Christian. 'Capitalism, Patriarchy, Slavery, and Racism in the Age of Digital Capitalism and Digital Labour.' *Critical Sociology*, vol. 44, no. 4–5, 2017, pp. 677–702, doi:10.1177/0896920517691108.

Fung, Brian. 'The British Are Frantically Googling What the E.U. Is, Hours after Voting to Leave It.' *Washington Post*, 24 June 2016, www.washingtonpost.com/news/the-switch/wp /2016/06/24/the-british-are-frantically-googling-what-the-eu-is-hours-after-voting-to- leave-it/.

Gadamer, Hans-Georg. *Truth and Method*. Translated by Joel Weinsheimer and Donald G. Marshall, Bloomsbury, 2013.

Gatti, Hilary. *Giordano Bruno and Renaissance Science: Broken Lives and Organizational Power*. Cornell University Press, 2002.

Gibbs, Kevin. 'I've Got a Suggestion.' *Official Google Blog*, 10 December 2004, googleblog.blog spot.com/2004/12/ive-got-suggestion.html.

Gillespie, Tarleton, and Nick Seaver. 'Critical Algorithm Studies: A Reading List.' *Social Media Collective*, 15 December 2016. https://socialmediacollective.org/reading-lists/critical -algorithm-studies/. Accessed 29 June 2021.

GLAAD. 'GLAAD Media Reference Guide—Terms To Avoid.' *GLAAD Website*, n.d. https://www .glaad.org/reference/offensive. Accessed 10 April 2021.

Gnuse, Robert K. 'Seven Gay Texts: Biblical Passages Used to Condemn Homosexuality.' *Biblical Theology Bulletin: Journal of Bible and Culture*, 22 April 2015, doi:10.1177%2F0146107915577097

Goel, Shikha, and Sunita Yadav. 'An Overview of Search Engine Evaluation Strategies.' *International Journal of Applied Information Systems*, vol. 1, no. 4, February 2012, pp. 7–10, doi:10.5120/ijais12-450156.

Google. 'About.' *Google*, www.google.com/about/. Accessed 24 June 2021.

Google. 'Advertiser Guide: Working with a Third-Parties.' *Google AdWords*, www.google.com/intl /en_uk/adwords/thirdpartypartners/. Accessed 8 June 2017.

Google. 'AdWords Policies.' *Google Advertising Policies Help*, support.google.com/adwordspolicy/ answer/6008942?hl=en-GB. Accessed 8 June 2017.

Google. 'DeepDream: About.' *DeepDream Generator*, deepdreamgenerator.com/. Accessed 14 August 2017.

Google. 'Gambling and Games.' *Google Advertising Policies Help*, support.google.com/adword spolicy/answer/6018017?hl=en-GB. Accessed 9 June 2017.

Google. 'Google Acquires Technology Assets of Outride Inc.—News Announcements.' *Official Google Blog*, 20 September 2001, googlepress.blogspot.co.uk/2001/09/google-acquires-tech nology-assets-of.html.

Google. 'Google Inside Search: Autocomplete.' *Google Inside Search*, 18 April 2013, web.archive .org/web/20130418015232/support.google.com/websearch/answer/106230?hl=en.

Google. 'Google Search Help: Autocomplete.' *Google Search Help*, 9 April 2015, web.archive.org/ web/20150409060419/support.google.com/websearch/answer/106230?hl=en.

Google. 'Google Search Help: Autocomplete Policies.' *Google Search Help*, 12 May 2021, https:// support.google.com/websearch/answer/7368877?hl=en.

Google. 'Google Search Help: Search Using Autocomplete.' *Google Search Help*, support.google. com/websearch/answer/106230. Accessed 13 August 2017.

Google. 'Google: Take Action.' https://www.google.com/takeaction/, Accessed 14 July 2020.

Google. 'Google: Technology.' *Google*, www.google.com/technology. Accessed 20 October 2017.

Google. 'Google's Year in Search 2016.' *Google Trends*, g.co/trends/HUzzl. Accessed 28 October 2017.

Google. 'Google—Year In Search 2016.' *YouTube*, uploaded by Google, 14 December 2016, www .youtube.com/watch?v=KIViy7L_lo8.

Google. 'How Search Algorithms Work.' *Google Search: How Search Works*, www.google.com/intl /en_uk/search/howsearchworks/algorithms/. Accessed 28 June 2021.

Google. 'Our approach to Search.' *Google Search: How Search Works*, https://www.google.com/ intl/en_uk/search/howsearchworks/mission/. Accessed 28 June 2021.

Google. 'Project Loon.' *X Company*, x.company/loon/. Accessed 9 June 2017.

Google. 'Rigorous Testing.' *Google Search: How Search Works*, https://www.google.com/search/ howsearchworks/mission/users/. Accessed 28 June 2021.

Google. 'Search Quality Evaluator Guidelines.' *Google User Content*, updated 14 October 2020, https://static.googleusercontent.com/media/guidelines.raterhub.com/en//searchqualityevaluatorguidelines.pdf.

Google. 'Transparency Report, Germany.' *Google Transparency Report*, transparencyreport.google.com/government-removals/by-country/DE. Accessed 27 August 2017.

Google. 'Useful Responses Take Many Forms.' *Google Search: How Search Works*, https://www.google.com/intl/en_uk/search/howsearchworks/responses/. Accessed 28 June 2021.

Google. 'Welcome to the 2017 Google Online Marketing Challenge.' *Google*, www.google.com/onlinechallenge/. Accessed 8 June 2017.

Google. '"What Is the EU?" is the Second Top UK Question on the EU since the #EURefResults Were Officially Announced.' *Twitter*, 24 June 2016, twitter.com/googletrends/status/746303118820937728?lang=en.

'Google Suggest.' *Ryte Wiki Digital Marketing Encyclopedia*, https://en.ryte.com/wiki/Google_Suggest, Accessed 15 May 2021.

@GoogleTrends. '+250% Spike In "what Happens If We Leave the EU" in the Past Hour Google.com/Trends/Explore . . .' *Twitter*, 23 June 2016, twitter.com/googletrends/status/746137920940056578?lang=en.

Griffin, Andrew. 'What Happens If We Leave the EU? Google Searches Surge as People Realise They Don't Know What Brexit Actually Means.' *The Independent*, 24 June 2016, www.independent.co.uk/life-style/gadgets-and-tech/news/what-happens-if-we-leave-the-eu-google-searches-surge-as-people-realise-they-dont-know-what-brexit-a7100596.html.

Grondin, Jean. *The Philosophy of Gadamer*. Translated by Kathryn Plant, Routledge, 2014.

Gul, Sumeer, Sabha Ali, and Aabid Hussain. 'Retrieval Performance of Google, Yahoo and Bing for Navigational Queries in the Field of "Life Science and Biomedicine".' *Data Technologies and Applications*, vol. 54, no. 2, 2020, pp. 133–50, doi:10.1108/DTA-05-2019-0083.

Gurp, Marc van. 'Romanians Are Smart.' *Osocio*, 23 November 2011, osocio.org/message/google-romanians-are-stupid/.

Hacker, Philipp. 'Teaching Fairness to Artificial Intelligence: Existing and Novel Strategies Against Algorithmic Discrimination Under EU Law.' *Common Market Law Review*, vol. 55, May 2018, pp. 1143–86.

Haider, Jutta and Olof Sundin. *Invisible Search and Online Search Engines: The Ubiquity of Search in Everyday Life*. Routledge, 2019.

Halavais, Alexander. *Search Engine Society*, 2nd ed. Polity, 2018.

Hall, Jonathan V., and Alan B. Krueger. 'An Analysis of the Labor Market for Uber's Driver-Partners in the United States.' Working Papers (Princeton University Industrial Relations Section), no. 587, Jan. 2015, arks.princeton.edu/ark:/88435/dsp010z708z67d.

Hannak, Aniko, Piotr Sapiezynski, Arash Molavi Kakhki, Balachander Krishnamurthy, David Lazer, Alan Mislove, and Christo Wilson. 'Measuring Personalization of Web Search.' *Proceedings of the 22nd International Conference on World Wide Web*, 2013, pp. 527–38, doi:10.1145/2488388.2488435.

Hargittai, Eszter. 'The Social, Political, Economic, and Cultural Dimensions of Search Engines: An Introduction.' *Journal of Computer-Mediated Communication*, edited by Eszter Hargittai, vol. 12, no. 3, Apr. 2007, pp. 769–77, doi:10.1111/j.1083-6101.2007.00349.x.

Havelock, Eric. *Preface to Plato*. Belknap Press, 1963.

Havens, John C. 'The Connected Home May Become the Collected Home.' *Slate*, July 2014, www.slate.com/blogs/future_tense/2014/07/31/nest_google_acquisition_the_connected_home_may_be_the_collected_home.html.

Heath, Taliver Brooks. *Advertising Based on Environmental Conditions*. US8138930 B1, 20 Mar. 2012, www.google.co.uk/patents/US8138930. Patent.

Heraclitus. *Heraclitus: Fragments: A Text and Translation with a Commentary by T. M. Robinson. Phoenix Presocractic Series*, University of Toronto Press, 1987.

Hess, Laurie and Rick Axelson. 'Feeding Pet Snakes.' *VCA Hospitals*. www.vcahospitals.com/know-your-pet/snakes-feeding, Accessed 23 June 2021.

Hillis, Ken, Kylie Jarrett, and Michael Petit. *Google and the Culture of Search*. Routledge, 2012.

Hollister, Sean. 'Google Promises to Remove Search Suggestions that Might Seem Political—Even if They're True.' *Verge*, 10 September 2020, www.theverge.com/2020/9/10/21431214/google-search-autocomplete-suggestion-policy-change-2020-election.

Hook, Justin. *Google Feud*. www.googlefeud.com/. Accessed 16 April 2021.

Horner, Paul (pseud. Jimmy Rustling). 'Donald Trump Protester Speaks Out: "I Was Paid $3,500 To Protest Trump's Rally".' *ABC News*, 22 November 2016, abcnews.com.co/donald-trump-protester-speaks-out-i-was-paid-to-protest/.

Huebner, Bryce. 'Transactive Memory Reconstructed: Rethinking Wegner's Research Program.' *Southern Journal of Philosophy*, vol. 54, no. 1, 2016, pp. 48–69, doi:10.1111/sjp.12160.

Huvila, Isto. 'Affective Capitalism of Knowing and the Society of Search Engine.' *Aslib Journal of Information Management*, vol. 68, no. 5, September 2016, pp. 566–88, doi:10.1108/AJIM-11-2015-0178.

Huws, Ursula. *Labor in the Global Digital Economy: The Cybertariat Comes of Age*. New York University Press, 2014.

Introna, Lucas D., and Helen Nissenbaum. 'Shaping the Web: Why the Politics of Search Engines Matters.' *The Information Society*, vol. 16, no. 3, 2000, pp. 169–85.

'Is Homosexuality Wrong?' *Debate.org*, www.debate.org/opinions/is-homosexuality-wrong. Accessed 28 November 2017.

Jansen, Bernard J., and Paulo R. Molina. 'The Effectiveness of Web Search Engines for Retrieving Relevant Ecommerce Links.' *Information Processing & Management*, vol. 42, no. 4, July 2006, pp. 1075–98, doi:10.1016/j.ipm.2005.09.003.

Jansen, Bernard J., and Amanda Spink. 'How Are We Searching the World Wide Web? A Comparison of Nine Search Engine Transaction Logs.' *Information Processing & Management*, vol. 42, no. 1, January 2006, pp. 248–63, doi:10.1016/j.ipm.2004.10.007.

Jansen, Bernard J., Danielle L. Booth, and Amanda Spink. 'Determining the Informational, Navigational, and Transactional Intent of Web Queries.' *Information Processing & Management*, vol. 44, no. 3, May 2008, pp. 1251–66, doi:10.1016/j.ipm.2007.07.015.

Jansen, Bernard J., Danielle L. Booth, and Amanda Spink. 'Patterns of Query Reformulation During Web Searching.' *Journal of the American Society for Information Science and Technology*, vol. 60, no. 7, July 2009, pp. 1358–71, doi:10.1002/asi.21071.

Jansen, Bernard J., Zhe Liu, Courtney Weaver, Gerry Campbell, and Matthew Gregg. 'Real Time Search on the Web: Queries, Topics, and Economic Value.' *Information Processing & Management*, vol. 47, no. 4, 2011, pp. 491–506, doi:10.1016/j.ipm.2011.01.007.

Jarrett, Kylie. 'A Database of Intention?' *Society of the Query Reader: Reflections on Web Search*, edited by René König and Miriam Rasch, Institute of Network Cultures, 2014, pp. 16–29.

Jarrett, Kylie. *Feminism, Labour and Digital Media: The Digital Housewife*. Routledge, 2015.

Jehovah's Witnesses. 'Is Homosexuality Wrong? | Young People Ask.' *JW.org Official Website of the Jehovah's Witnesses*, www.jw.org/en/bible-teachings/teenagers/ask/is-homosexuality-wrong/. Accessed 29 October 2017.

Jones, Rhett. 'RIP Google Instant Search, You Were Never Necessary.' *Gizmodo*, 26 July 2017, gizmodo.com/rip-google-instant-search-you-were-never-necessary-1797281069.

Kadouch, David. 'Local Flavor for Google Suggest.' *Official Google Blog*, 31 March 2009, googleblog.blogspot.com/2009/03/local-flavor-for-google-suggest.html.

Kant, Tanya. *Making it Personal: Algorithmic Personalization, Identity, and Everyday Life* Oxford University Press, 2020.

Kaplan, Frederic. 'Linguistic Capitalism and Algorithmic Mediation.' *Representations*, vol. 127, no. 1, August 2014, pp. 57–63, doi:10.1525/rep.2014.127.1.57.

Bibliography

Karapapa, Stavroula, and Maurizio Borghi. 'Search Engine Liability for Autocomplete Suggestions: Personality, Privacy and the Power of the Algorithm.' *International Journal of Law and Information Technology*, vol. 23, no. 3, September 2015, pp. 261–89, doi:10.1093/ijlit/eav009.

Katzenbach, Christian, and Lena Ulbricht. 'Algorithmic Governance.' *Concepts of the Digital Society Internet Policy Review*, vol. 8, no. 4, 2019. Web. 28 June 2022.

Kaveh-Yazdy, Fatemeh, Ali-Mohammad Zareh-Bidoki, and Mohammadreza Pajoohan. 'Analysis of Interaction Patterns and Users' Query Reformulation Strategies in Persian Search Engine.' *Language and Linguistics*, vol. 14, no. 27, 2019, pp. 87–113.

Kavoussi, Bonnie. 'Google Chairman Eric Schmidt Defends Tax Dodge: "It's Called Capitalism".' *Huffington Post*, 13 December 2012, www.huffingtonpost.com/2012/12/13/google-tax-dodge _n_2292077.html.

Keen, Andrew. *The Internet Is Not the Answer*. Atlantic Books, 2015.

Kelly, Kevin. *The Inevitable: Understanding the 12 Technological Forces That Will Shape Our Future*. Penguin Books, 2016.

Kilman-Silver, Chloe, Aniko Hannak, David Lazer, Christo Wilson, and Alan Mislove 'Location, Location, Location: The Impact of Geolocation on Web Search Personalization.' *Proceedings of the 2015 Internet Measurement Conference*, pp. 121–7, doi:10.1145/2815675.2815714.

Kitchin, Rob. 'Thinking Critically about and Researching Algorithms.' *Information, Communication & Society*, vol. 20, no. 1, 2017, pp. 14–29, doi:10.1080/136911 8X.2016.1154087.

Kittler, Friedrich. *Gramophone, Film, Typewriter*. Translated by Geoffrey Winthrop-Young and Michael Wutz, Stanford University Press, 1999.

Kittler, Friedrich. 'Towards an Ontology of Media.' *Theory, Culture & Society*, vol. 26, no. 2–3, Mar. 2009, pp. 23–31, doi:10.1177/0263276409103106.

Klawitter, Erin, and Eszter Hargittai. '"I Went Home to Google": How Users Assess the Credibility of Online Health Information.' *eHealth: Current Evidence, Promises, Perils and Future Directions*. Emerald Publishing Limited, 2018.

Kluger, Jeffrey. 'No Ben Carson, Homosexuality Is Not a Choice.' *Time*, March 2015, time.com/3 733480/ben-carson-gay-choice-science/.

König, René, and Miriam Rasch, editors. *Society of the Query Reader: Reflections on Web Search*. Institute of Network Cultures, 2014.

Kornai, András. 'Digital Language Death.' *PLOS ONE*, vol. 8, no. 10, October 2013, doi:10.1371/ journal.pone.0077056.

Krebs, Viola, and Vincent Climent-Ferrando. 'Languages, Cyberspace, Migrations.' *Net. Lang: Towards a Multilingual Cyberspace*, edited by Laurent Vannini and Hervé Le Crosnier, C&F éditions, 2012, pp. 229–48, unesdoc.unesco.org/images/0021/002166/216692e.pdf.

Kritzer, Naomi. 'Cat Pictures Please.' *Clarkesworld Magazine Issue 100*, January 2015, https:// clarkesworldmagazine.com/kritzer_01_15/ Accessed 23/08/2022.

Kurzweil, Raymond. *The Singularity Is Near*. Penguin Books, 2006.

Lamont, Ann. 'What's Wrong with Being Gay? Homosexual Behavior versus the Bible.' *Christian Answers*, 2004, christiananswers.net/q-aig/aig-c040.html.

Lamping, John, and Steven Baker. *Determining Query Term Synonyms within Query Context*. US7636714 B1, 22 December 2009, www.google.com/patents/US7636714. Patent.

Landauer, Thomas K. 'How Much Do People Remember? Some Estimates of the Quantity of Learned Information in Long-Term Memory.' *Cognitive Science*, vol. 10, no. 4, 1986, pp. 477–93.

Lash, Scott. *Critique of Information*. Sage Publications, 2002.

Latour, Bruno. 'Technology Is Society Made Durable.' *The Sociological Review*, vol. 38, no. S1, May 1990, pp. 103–31, doi:10.1111/j.1467-954X.1990.tb03350.x.

Lawrence, Steve, and C. Lee Giles. 'Accessibility of Information on the Web.' *Nature*, vol. 400, no. 1, July 1999, pp. 107–9, doi:10.1038/21987.

Lazzarato, Maurizio. *Signs and Machines: Capitalism and the Production of Subjectivity.* MIT Press, 2014.

Lee, Haimin. '15 Years of Google Books.' *Official Google Blog Post,* 17 October 2019, https://www.blog.google/products/search/15-years-google-books/.

Lemon. *Idiots.win.* www.idiots.win. Accessed 1 December 2017.

Leonhard, Gerd. *Technology vs. Humanity: The Coming Clash between Man and Machine.* Fast Future Publishing, 2016.

Levy, Steven. *In the Plex: How Google Thinks, Works, and Shapes Our Lives.* Simon & Schuster, 2011.

Levy, Steven. 'How Google Is Remaking Itself as a "Machine Learning First".' *Wired,* 22 June 2016, www.wired.com/2016/06/how-google-is-remaking-itself-as-a-machine-learning-first -company/.

Lewandowski, Dirk. 'Why We Need an Independent Index of the Web.' *Society of the Query Reader: Reflections on Web Search,* edited by René König and Miriam Rasch, Institute of Network Cultures, 2014, pp. 50–8.

Lewandowski, Dirk, and Sebastian Sünkler. 'What Does Google Recommend When You Want to Compare Insurance Offerings?' *Aslib Journal of Information Management,* vol. 71, no. 3, 2019, pp. 310–24, doi: 10.1108/AJIM-07-2018-0172.

Lin, Yuri, Jean-Baptiste Michel, Erez Lieberman Aiden, Jon Orwant, Will Brockman, and Slav Petrov. 'Syntactic Annotations for the Google Books Ngram Corpus.' *Proceedings of the ACL 2012 System Demonstrations,* Association for Computational Linguistics, 2012, pp. 169–74, aclweb.org/anthology/P/P12/P12-3029.pdf.

Lindsköld, Linnéa. 'Google as a Political Subject: The Right to be Forgotten Debate 2014–2016.' *Online Information Review,* vol. 42, no. 6, 2018, pp. 768–83. doi.org/10.1108/OIR-06-2017 -0198

Liu, Jennifer. 'At a Loss for Words?' *Official Google Blog,* 25 August 2008, googleblog.blogspot.com/2008/08/at-loss-for-words.html.

Lloyd, Annemaree. 'Conceptual Orientation.' *Information Literacy Landscapes Information Literacy in Education, Workplace and Everyday Contexts,* Chandos Publishing, 2010, pp. 9–33.

Llull, Ramon. *Doctor Illuminatus: A Ramon Llull Reader.* Edited and translated by Anthony Bonner, Princeton University Press, 1994.

Lomas, Natasha. 'Google's Latest User-Hostile Design Change Makes Ads and Search Results Look Identical.' *TechCrunch,* 23 January 2020.

Long, Christopher. *Aristotle on the Nature of Truth.* Cambridge University Press, 2010.

Lord, Albert Bates. *The Singer of Tales.* Harvard University Press, 1960.

Love, Julia, and Kristina Cooke. 'Google, Facebook Move to Restrict Ads on Fake News Sites.' *Reuters,* 15 November 2016, uk.reuters.com/article/us-alphabet-advertising-idUKKBN1 392MM.

Luka, Mary, and Mél Hogan. 'Polluted and Predictive, in 133 Words.' *Society of the Query Reader: Reflections on Web Search,* edited by René König and Miriam Rasch, Institute of Network Cultures, 2014, pp. 239–55.

Lynch, John Patrick. *Aristotle's School: A Study of a Greek Educational Institution.* University of California Press, 1972.

Lyon, David. 'Surveillance, Snowden, and Big Data: Capacities, Consequences, Critique.' *Big Data & Society,* vol, 1, no. 2, 2014, doi:10.1177/2053951714541861.

MacCormick, John. *Nine Algorithms That Changed the Future: The Ingenious Ideas That Drive Today's Computers.* Princeton University Press, 2012.

Mahnke, Martina, and Emma Uprichard. 'Algorithming the Algorithm.' *Society of the Query Reader: Reflections on Web Search,* edited by René König and Miriam Rasch, Institute of Network Cultures, 2014, pp. 256–70.

Bibliography

Makvana, Kamlesh, Jay Patel, Parth Shah, and Amit Thakkar. 'Comprehensive Analysis of Personalized Web Search Engines Through Information Retrieval Feedback System and User Profiling.' *Advanced Informatics for Computing Research. ICAICR 2018.* Communications in Computer and Information Science, vol 956. Springer, 2020, doi:10.1007/978-981-13-3143-5_14.

Mann, Monique, and Tobias Matzner. 'Challenging Algorithmic Profiling: The Limits of Data Protection and Anti-Discrimination in Responding to Emergent Discrimination.' *Big Data & Society*, vol. 6, no. 2, 2019, doi:10.1177/2053951719895805.

Mass Resistance. *What's Wrong with Being 'gay'? Here's What They Don't Tell You—and It's Really Disturbing.* February 4,. 2016, massresistance.org/docs/gen3/16a/its-killing-them/index.html.

Mastrangelo, Frankie. 'Mediating Resistance: Digital Immaterial Labor, Neoliberal Subjectivities, and the Struggle for Immigrant Justice.' *Ephemera*, vol. 20, no. 4, 2020, pp. 323–38.

Mayer, Marissa. 'Google Instant Launch Event.' *YouTube*, uploaded by Google, 8 September 2010, www.youtube.com/watch?v=i0eMHRxlJ2c.

McCue, T. 'SEO Industry Approaching $80 Billion But All You Want Is More Web Traffic.' 2018, https://www.forbes.com/sites/tjmccue/2018/07/30/seo-industry-approaching-80-billion-but-all-you-want-is-more-web-traffic/. Accessed 1 October 2019.

McKenzie, Pamela J. 'A Model of Information Practices in Accounts of Everyday-Life Information Seeking.' *Journal of Documentation*, vol. 59, no. 1, 2003, pp. 19–40, doi:10.1108/00220410310457993.

McMahon, Aine. 'Brexit Prompts Increase in Queries about Irish Passports.' *The Irish Times*, 2016, www.irishtimes.com/news/social-affairs/brexit-prompts-increase-in-queries-about-irish-passports-1.2698203.

Merrill, Jeremy B. 'Google Has Been Allowing Advertisers to Exclude Nonbinary People from Seeing Job Ads.' *The Markup*, 11 February 2021, https://themarkup.org/google-the-giant/2021/02/11/google-has-been-allowing-advertisers-to-exclude-nonbinary-people-from-seeing-job-ads.

Metz, Cade. 'AI Is Transforming Google Search. The Rest of the Web Is Next.' *Wired*, 4 February 2016, www.wired.com/2016/02/ai-is-changing-the-technology-behind-google-searches/.

Meyers, Peter J. 'How Often Does Google Update Its Algorithm?' *Moz*, 14 May 2019, moz.com/blog/how-often-does-google-update-its-algorithm. Accessed 25 May 2021.

Mikolov, Tomas, Ilya Sutskever, Kai Chen, Greg S. Corrado, and Jeff Dean 'Distributed Representations of Words and Phrases and Their Compositionality.' *Advances in Neural Information Processing Systems*, 2013, pp. 3111–19, papers.nips.cc/paper/5021-distributed-representations-of-words-and-phrases-and-their-compositionality.

Mikolov, Tomas, Ilya Sutskever, and Quoc Le. 'Learning the Meaning Behind Words.' *Google Open Source Blog*, 14 August 2013, opensource.googleblog.com/2013/08/learning-meaning-behind-words.html.

Miller, Boaz, and Isaac Record. 'Responsible Epistemic Technologies: A Social-Epistemological Analysis of Autocompleted Web Search.' *New Media & Society*, vol. 19, no. 12, December 2017, pp. 1945–63, doi:10.1177/1461444816644805.

Miller, Claire Cain, and Nick Bilton. 'How Pay-Per-Gaze Advertising Could Work with Google Glass.' *Bits Blog*, 20 August 2013, bits.blogs.nytimes.com/2013/08/20/google-patents-real-world-pay-per-gaze-advertising/.

Mitchell, Amy, and Katerina Matsa. 'The Declining Value of U.S. Newspapers.' *Pew Research Center*, 22 May 2015, www.pewresearch.org/fact-tank/2015/05/22/the-declining-value-of-u-s-newspapers/.

Mivule, Kato. 'Web Search Query Privacy, an End-User Perspective.' *Journal of Information Security*, vol. 8, no. 1, 2017, pp. 56–74, doi:10.4236/jis.2017.81005.

Mizzaro, Stefano. 'Relevance: The Whole History.' *Journal of the American Society for Information Science*, vol. 48, no. 9, September 1997, pp. 810–32, doi:10.1002/(SICI)1097-4571(199709)48:9<810::AID-ASI6>3.0.CO;2-U.

Molina, Maria D., S. Shyam Sundar, Thai Le, and Dongwon Lee. '"Fake News" Is Not Simply False Information: A Concept Explication and Taxonomy of Online Content.' *American Behavioral Scientist*, vol. 65, no. 2, February 2021, pp. 180–212, doi:10.1177/0002764219878224.

'Mobile Operating Systems' Market Share Worldwide from January 2012 to June 2021.' *Statista*, www.statista.com/statistics/272698/global-market-share-held-by-mobile-operating-systems -since-2009/.

'Mobile Search Engine Market Share in the United States of America, June 2022.' *StatCounter Global Stats*, gs.statcounter.com/search-engine-Market-share/mobile/united-states-of-america. Accessed 22 July 2022.

Moons, Michelle. 'Palin on Paid Anti-Trump Protesters: "Not Even President Yet and Our Guy's Already Creating Jobs".' *Breitbart*, 1 July 2016, www.breitbart.com/2016-presidential-race /2016/07/01/palin-paid-trump-protesters-not-even-president-yet-guys-already-creating -jobs/.

Mulligan, Deirdre K., and Daniel S. Griffin. 'Rescripting Search to Respect the Right to Truth.' *Georgetown Law Technology Review*, vol. 2, no. 2, August 2018, pp. 557–84, https://ssrn.com/ abstract=3228671.

Nakamura, Lisa. 'The Unwanted Labour of Social Media: Women of Colour Call out Culture As Venture Community Management.' *New Formations: A Journal of Culture/Theory/Politics*, vol. 86, 2015, pp. 106–12.

National Telecommunications and Information Administration. *A Nation Online: How Americans Are Expanding their Use of the Internet*. US Department of Commerce, 2002.

Nayak, Pandu. 'Understanding Searches Better Than ever Before.' *Google The Keyword: Search*, 25 October 2019, https://blog.google/products/search/search-language-understanding-bert/.

Newen, Albert, Shaun Gallagher, and Leon De Bruin, editors. *The Oxford Handbook of 4E Cognition*, Oxford University Press, 2018.

Newport, Cal. *Deep Work: Rules for Focused Success in a Distracted World*. Piatkus, 2016.

Ng, Andrew. 'A Massive Google Network Learns to Identify—Cats.' *All Things Considered*, interview by Audie Cornish, National Public Radio, 26 June 2012, www.npr.org/2012/06/26 /155792609/a-massive-google-network-learns-to-identify.

Noble, Safiya Umoja. *Algorithms of Oppression: How Search Engines Reinforce Racism*. New York University Press, 2018.

Nylen, Leah. 'Google Dominates Online Ads—And DOJ May be Ready to Pounce.' *Politico*, vol. 6, April 2020, updated 6 October 2020. https://www.politico.com/news/2020/06/04/google -doj-ads-302576.

Oeldorf-Hirsch, Anne, Brent Hecht, Meredith Ringel Morris, Jaime Teevan, and Darren Gergle. 'To Search or to Ask: The Routing of Information Needs between Traditional Search Engines and Social Networks.' *CSCW '14: Proceedings of the 17th ACM Conference on Computer Supported Cooperative Work & Social Computing*, February 2014, doi:10.1145/2531602.2531706.

O'Hare, Ryan. 'Google Search Spike Suggests Many People Don't Know Why They Voted for Brexit.' *Mail Online*, 24 June 2016, www.dailymail.co.uk/sciencetech/article-3657997/Britain-s -Google-searches-hint-people-didn-t-know-voting-for.html.

Olteanu, Alexandra, Fernando Diaz, and Gabriella Kazai. 'When Are Search Completion Suggestions Problematic?' *Proceedings of the ACM on Human-Computer Interaction*, vol. 4, CSCW2, Article 171, October 2020. https://doi.org/10.1145/3415242.

O'Neil, Cathy. *Weapons of Math Destruction: How Big Data Increases Inequality and Threatens Democracy*. Penguin Random House, 2016.

Ong, Walter J. *Orality and Literacy: The Technologizing of the Word*. Routledge, 1982.

Özmutlu, H. Cenk, et al. 'Neural Network Applications for Automatic New Topic Identification on Excite Web Search Engine Data Logs.' *Proceedings of the Association for Information Science and Technology*, vol. 41, no. 1, 2004, pp. 310–16, doi:10.1002/meet.1450410137.

Bibliography

Page, Danny. 'Stop Using Google Trends.' *Medium*, 24 June 2016, medium.com/@dannypage/sto p-using-google-trends-a5014dd32588#.vop9ejer4.

Page, Lawrence, Sergey Brin, Rajeev Motwani, and Terry Winograd. 'The PageRank Citation Ranking: Bringing Order to the Web.' *Stanford InfoLab*, 1999, ilpubs.stanford.edu:8090/422.

Pariser, Eli. *The Filter Bubble: What the Internet Is Hiding from You.* Penguin Books, 2011.

Parkinson, Hannah. 'Click and Elect: How Fake News Helped Donald Trump Win a Real Election.' *The Guardian*, 14 November 2016, www.theguardian.com/commentisfree/2016/nov /14/fake-news-donald-trump-election-alt-right-social-media-tech-companies.

Parry, Milman. *L'épithète Traditionnelle Dans Homère: Essai Sur Un Problème De Style Homérique.* Les belles lettres, 1928.

Pasquale, Frank. *The Black Box Society: The Secret Algorithms that Control Money and Information.* Harvard University Press, 2015.

Pasquale, Frank. 'From Holocaust Denial to Hitler Admiration, Google's Algorithm Is Dangerous.' *Huffington Post*, 6 February 2017, www.huffingtonpost.com/entry/holocaust -google-algorithm_us_587e8628e4b0c147f0bb9893.

Pasquinelli, Matteo. 'Google's PageRank Algorithm: Diagram of Cognitive Capitalism and the Rentier of the Common Intellect.' *Deep Search. The Politics of Search Beyond Google*, edited by Konrad Becker and Felix Stalder, Studien Verlag, 2009, pp. 152–62.

Pass, Greg, et al. 'A Picture of Search.' *Proceedings of the 1st International Conference on Scalable Information Systems*, Association for Computing Machinery, 2006, doi:10.1145/1146847.1146848.

Peifer, Karl-Nikolaus. 'Google's Autocomplete Function—Is Google a Publisher or Mere Technical Distributor? German Federal Supreme Court, Judgment of 14 May 2012—Case No. Vi Zr 269/12—Google Autocomplete.' *Queen Mary Journal of Intellectual Property*, vol. 3, no. 4, October 2013, pp. 318–24, doi:10.4337/qmjip.2013.04.05.

Peters, John Durham. *The Marvelous Clouds: Toward a Philosophy of Elemental Media.* University of Chicago Press, 2015.

Peters, Michael A. 'Algorithmic Capitalism in the Epoch of Digital Reason.' *Fast Capitalism*, vol. 14 no.1: Special Issue Tribute to Ben Agger, 2017, doi:10.32855/fcapital.201701.012.

Pitkow, James, et al. 'Personalized Search.' *Communications of the Association for Computing Machinery*, vol. 45, no. 9, September 2002, pp. 50–5.

Plato. 'Meno.' *Plato: Complete Works*, edited by John M. Cooper, Hackett Publishing Company, 1997, pp. 870–97.

Plato. 'Phaedrus.' *Plato: Complete Works*, edited by John M. Cooper, Hackett Publishing Company, 1997, pp. 506–56.

@pollyp1 (Leslie Vosshall). 'Top 5 Search Suggestions for Female Scientists Often Include "husband". WTF?' *Twitter*, 20 May 2016, twitter.com/pollyp1/status/733636162263351296? lang=en-gb.

Popyer, Kacy. 'Cache-22: The Fine Line Between Information and Defamation in Google's Autocomplete Function.' *Cardozo Arts and Entertainment Law Journal*, vol. 34, 2016, pp. 835–61.

Poster, Mark. 'The Information Empire.' *Information Please: Culture and Politics in the Age of Digital Machines.* Duke University Press, 2006.

Prado, Daniel. 'Language Presence in the Real World and Cyberspace.' *Net. Lang: Towards a Multilingual Cyberspace*, edited by Laurent Vannini and Hervé Le Crosnier, C&F éditions, 2012, pp. 38–51, unesdoc.unesco.org/images/0021/002166/216692e.pdf.

Racer Nation Information. 'MBA Students Use Google, Stukent Digital Marketing Tools.' *Racer Nation Information*, 20 May 2016, www.racernationinformation.com/2016/05/19/mba -students-use-google-stukent-digital-marketing-tools/.

Raff, Adam. 'Search, but You May Not Find.' *The New York Times*, 27 December 2009, www .nytimes.com/2009/12/28/opinion/28raff.html.

Rieder, Bernhard, and Guillaume Sire. 'Conflicts of Interest and Incentives to Bias: A Microeconomic Critique of Google's Tangled Position on the Web.' *New Media & Society*, vol. 16, no. 2, Mar. 2014, pp. 195–211, doi:10.1177/1461444813481195.

Rieder, Bernhard, and Jeanette Hofmann. 'Towards platform observability.' *Internet Policy Review*, vol. 9, no. 4, Dec. 2020, https://doi.org/10.14763/2020.4.1535.

Rieh, Soo Young. 'On the Web at Home: Information Seeking and Web Searching in the Home Environment.' *Journal of the American Society for Information Science and Technology*, vol. 55, no. 8, June 2004, pp. 743–53. /doi.org/10.1002/asi.20018

Roberge, Jonathan, and Louis Melançon. 'Being the King Kong of Algorithmic Culture Is a Tough Job after All: Google's Regimes of Justification and the Meanings of Glass.' *Convergence*, vol. 23, no. 3, June 2017, pp. 306–24, doi:10.1177/1354856515592506.

Roberts, Jeff. 'Brits Scramble to Google 'What Is the EU?' Hours After Voting to Leave It.' *Fortune*, 24 June 2016, fortune.com/2016/06/24/brexit-google-trends/.

Robertson, Ronald E., Shan Jiang, Kenneth Joseph, Lisa Friedland, David Lazer, and Christo Wilson. 'Auditing Partisan Audience Bias within Google Search.' *Proceedings of the ACM on Human-Computer Interaction*, vol. 2, November 2018. doi:10.1145/3274417.

Robinson, Gene. 'What Are Religious Texts Really Saying About Gay and Transgender Rights?' Interview by Jeff Krehely and Sally Steenland. Center for American Progress, 8 December 2010, https://www.americanprogress.org/issues/religion/news/2010/12/08/8822/what-are-religious-texts-really-saying-about-gay-and-transgender-rights/.

Rogers, Simon. 'What Is Google Trends Data—and What Does It Mean?' *Medium*, 1 July 2016, medium.com/google-news-lab/what-is-google-trends-data-and-what-does-it-mean-b48f07342ee8#.n9jt853qg.

Rose, Daniel E., and Danny Levinson. 'Understanding User Goals in Web Search.' *Proceedings of the 13th International Conference on World Wide Web*, Association for Computing Machinery, 2004, pp. 13–19, doi:10.1145/988672.988675.

Rose, Steven. 'Memories Are Made of This.' *Memory: Histories, Theories, Debates*, edited by Susannah Radstone and Bill Schwarz, Fordham University Press, 2010, pp. 198–208.

SadBotTrue. 'Chapter 39. The Fake Media.' *SadBotTrue*, sadbottrue.com/article/72/. Accessed 9 June 2017.

@sammich_BLT. 'The Lack of Context Really Is Astounding.' *Twitter*, 24 June 2016, twitter.com/Sammich_BLT/status/746365855441657856.

Scanlan, John. *Memory: Encounters with the Strange*. Reaktion Books, 2013.

Schamber, Linda, Michael B. Eisenberg, and Michael S. Nilan. 'A Re-Examination of Relevance.' *Information Processing and Management*, vol. 26, no. 6, 1990, pp. 755–76, doi:10.1016/0306-4573(90)90050-C.

Schmidt, Eric, and Jared Cohen. *The New Digital Age: Reshaping the Future of People, Nations and Business*. John Murray, 2013.

Schroeder, Ralph. 'The Internet in Everyday Life II: Seeking Information.' *Social Theory after the Internet: Media, Technology, and Globalization*. UCL Press, 2018, pp. 101–25.

Schuler, Douglas. 'Reports of the Close Relationship Between Democracy and the Internet.' *Democracy and Digital Media*, May 1998, web.mit.edu/m-I-t/articles/schuler.html.

Schultz, Carsten D. 'Informational, Transactional, and Navigational Need of Information: Relevance of Search Intention in Search Engine Advertising.' *Information Retrieval Journal*, vol. 23, 2020, pp. 117–35, https://doi.org/10.1007/s10791-019-09368-7.

Schwartz, Barry. 'Google Has Dropped Google Instant Search.' *Search Engine Land*, 26 July 2017, searchengineland.com/google-dropped-google-instant-search-279674.

Schwartz, Bill. 'Memory, Temporality, Modernity.' *Memory: Histories, Theories, Debates*, edited by Susannah Radstone and Bill Schwarz, Fordham University Press, 2010, pp. 41–60.

Bibliography

'Search Engine Market Share in the Russian Federation, June 2022.' *StatCounter Global Stats*, gs.statcounter.com/search-engine-market-share/mobile/russian-federation. Accessed 22 July 2022.

'Search Engine Market Share Worldwide, June 2022.' *StatCounter Global Stats*, gs.statcounter.com/search-enginemarket-share. Accessed 22 July 2022.

Selyukh, Alina. 'After Brexit Vote, Britain Googles 'What Is The EU?'' *National Public Radio*, 24 June 2016, www.npr.org/sections/alltechconsidered/2016/06/24/480949383/britains-google-searches-for-what-is-the-eu-spike-after-brexit-vote.

Silverman, Craig. 'This Analysis Shows How Viral Fake Election News Stories Outperformed Real News on Facebook.' *Buzzfeed News*, 16 November 2016, www.buzzfeed.com/craigsilverman/viral-fake-election-news-outperformed-real-news-on-facebook.

Silverman, Craig, and Lawrence Alexander. 'How Teens in The Balkans Are Duping Trump Supporters with Fake News.' *Buzzfeed News*, 3 November 2016, www.buzzfeed.com/craigsilverman/how-macedonia-became-a-global-hub-for-pro-trump-misinfo.

Silvestri, Fabrizio. 'Mining Query Logs: Turning Search Usage Data into Knowledge.' *Foundations and Trends in Information Retrieval*, vol. 4, no. 1–2, 2010, pp. 1–174, doi:10.1561/1500000013.

Simonite, Tom. 'Google's Loon Balloons Are Ready to Deliver Cheap Internet.' *MIT Technology Review*, 2015, www.technologyreview.com/s/534986/project-loon/.

Singhal, Amit. 'Introducing the Knowledge Graph: Things, Not Strings.' *Official Google Blog*, 16 May 2012, googleblog.blogspot.com/2012/05/introducing-knowledge-graph-things-not.html.

Singhal, Amit. 'Microsoft's Bing Uses Google Search Results—and Denies It.' *Official Google Blog*, googleblog.blogspot.com/2011/02/microsofts-bing-uses-google-search.html. Accessed 26 August 2017.

Smith, Remy 'Response: Stop Using Google Trends—Danny Page.' *Medium* https://medium.com/@remysmith/very-interesting-article-ill-admit-to-having-succumbed-to-that-against-which-you-re-railing-f82fb88d6a23#.4818x0scj.

Solomon, Brian. 'Google Just Passed Apple as The World's Most Valuable Company.' *Forbes*, 1 February 2016, www.forbes.com/sites/briansolomon/2016/02/01/google-just-passed-apple-as-the-worlds-most-valuable-company/.

Solomon, Brian. 'Google Passed Apple as The World's Most Valuable Company (Again).' *Forbes*, 12 May 2016, www.forbes.com/sites/briansolomon/2016/05/12/google-passed-apple-as-the-worlds-most-valuable-company-again/.

Sparrow, Betsy, and Ljubica Chatman. 'Social Cognition in the Internet Age: Same As It Ever Was?' *Psychological Inquiry*, vol. 24, no. 4, October 2013, pp. 273–92, doi:10.1080/1047840X.2013.827079.

Sparrow, Betsy, Jenny Liu, and Daniel M. Wegner. 'Google Effects on Memory: Cognitive Consequences of Having Information at Our Fingertips.' *Science*, vol. 333, 2011, pp. 776–8.

Spink, Amanda, Bernard J. Jansen, Dietmar Wolfram, and Tefko Saracevic. 'From E-Sex to E-Commerce: Web Search Changes.' *Computer*, vol. 35, no. 3, March 2002, pp. 107–9, doi:10.1109/2.989940.

Statt, Nick. 'Google Will Stop Showing Search Results as You Type Because It Makes No Sense on Mobile.' *The Verge*, 26 July 2017, www.theverge.com/2017/7/26/16034844/google-kills-off-instant-search-for-mobile-consistency.

Sterling, Greg. 'Report: Nearly 60 Percent of Searches Now from Mobile Devices.' *Search Engine Land*, 3 August 2016, searchengineland.com/report-nearly-60-percent-searches-now-mobile-devices-255025.

Stopera, Matt, and Lauren Yapalater. 'Why Being Gay Is Better Than Being Straight.' *BuzzFeed*, 14 June 2016, www.buzzfeed.com/mjs538/why-being-gay-is-better-than-being-straight.

Stross, Randall. *Planet Google: How One Company Is Transforming Our Lives.* Atlantic Books, 2009.

Subramanian, Samanth. 'Inside the Macedonian Fake-News Complex.' *Wired*, 15 February 2017, www.wired.com/2017/02/veles-macedonia-fake-news/.

Suen, Brennan, Jared Holt, and Tyler Cherry. 'Websites Peddling Fake News Still Using Google Ads Nearly a Month After Google Announced Ban.' *Media Matters for America*, 14 December 2016, www.mediamatters.org/research/2016/12/14/websites-peddling-fake-news-still-using-google-ads-nearly-month-after-google-announced-ban/214811.

Sullivan, Danny. 'Schmidt: Listing Google's 200 Ranking Factors Would Reveal Business Secrets.' *Search Engine Land*, 17 September 2010, searchengineland.com/schmidt-listing-googles-200-ranking-factors-would-reveal-business-secrets-51065.

Sullivan, Danny. 'Dear Bing, We Have 10,000 Ranking Signals to Your 1,000. Love, Google.' *Search Engine Land*, 11 November 2010, searchengineland.com/bing-10000-ranking-signals-google-55473.

Sullivan, Danny. 'Google: Bing Is Cheating, Copying Our Search Results.' *Search Engine Land*, 1 February 2011, searchengineland.com/google-bing-is-cheating-copying-our-search-results-62914.

Sullivan, Danny. 'Google Now Handles at Least 2 Trillion Searches Per Year.' *Search Engine Land*, 24 May 2016, searchengineland.com/google-now-handles-2-999-trillion-searches-per-year-250247.

Sullivan, Danny. 'FAQ: All About the Google RankBrain Algorithm.' *Search Engine Land*, 23 June 2016, searchengineland.com/faq-all-about-the-new-google-rankbrain-algorithm-234440.

Sullivan, Danny. 'Google Uses RankBrain for Every Search, Impacts Rankings of "Lots" of Them.' *Search Engine Land*, 23 June 2016, searchengineland.com/google-loves-rankbrain-uses-for-every-search-252526.

Sullivan, Danny. 'How Insights from People Around the World Make Google Search Better.' *Google The Keyword: Search*, 4 August 2020, https://blog.google/products/search/raters-experiments-improve-google-search/.

Sullivan, Danny. 'How Google Delivers Reliable Information in Search.' *Google The Keyword: Search*, 10 September 2020, https://blog.google/products/search/how-google-delivers-reliable-information-search/.

Sullivan, Danny. 'How Google Autocomplete Predictions Are Generated.' *Google The Keyword: Search*, 8 October 2020, https://blog.google/products/search/how-google-autocomplete-predictions-work/.

Sullivan, Danny. 'How Location Helps Provide More Relevant Search Results.' *Google The Keyword: Search*, 16 December 2020, https://blog.google/products/search/location-relevant-search-results/.

Sutton, John. *Philosophy and Memory Traces: Descartes to Connectionism*. Cambridge University Press, 2008.

Sutton, John, et al. 'Memory and Cognition.' *Memory: Histories, Theories, Debates*, edited by Susannah Radstone and Bill Schwarz, Fordham University Press, 2010, pp. 209–26.

Sweeney, Latanya. 'Discrimination in Online Ad Delivery: Google Ads, Black Names and White Names, Racial Discrimination, and Click Advertising.' *ACM Queue*, vol. 11, no. 3, March 2013, pp. 10–29, doi:10.1145/2460276.2460278.

Talon, Emmanuelle. 'L'arabe, Une « Langue de France » Sacrifiée.' *Le Monde Diplomatique*, 1 October 2012, www.monde-diplomatique.fr/2012/10/TALON/48275.

Teevan, Jaime, Susan T. Dumais, and Eric Horvitz 'Personalizing Search via Automated Analysis of Interests and Activities.' *Proceedings of the 28th Annual International ACM SIGIR Conference on Research and Development in Information Retrieval*, Association for Computing Machinery, 2005, pp. 449–56, doi:10.1145/1076034.1076111.

Thakur, Shashi. 'Feed Your Need to Know.' *Official Google Blog*, 19 July 2017, www.blog.google:443/products/search/feed-your-need-know/.

'The Global Divide on Homosexuality.' *Pew Research Centre*, 4 June 2013, www.pewresearch.org/global/2013/06/04/the-global-divide-on-homosexuality/.

Bibliography

Truong, Alice. 'Could Google Glass Track Your Emotional Response to Ads?' *Fast Company*, 13 August 2013, www.fastcompany.com/3015654/could-google-glass-track-your-emotional -response-to-ads.

Tuominen, Kimmo, Reijo Savolainen, and Sanna Talja. 'Information Literacy as a Sociotechnical Practice.' *The Library Quarterly*, vol. 75, no. 3, July 2005, pp. 329–45, doi:10.1086/497311.

@tuuliel (Tuuli Lappalainen). 'Dear Fellow Scientists. The Next Time You're Going to Google for Info of the Husband or Wedding of a Female Colleague, Think Again. 1/6... I Want a Scientific Community That Treats and Thinks of Women as Professionals, Not as Objects of Desire or Wives of Someone! 6/6.' *Twitter*, 15 July 2017, twitter.com/tuuliel/status/88627253 3154103296?lang=en.

Tynan, Dan. 'How Facebook Powers Money Machines for Obscure Political "News" Sites.' *The Guardian*, 24 August 2016, www.theguardian.com/technology/2016/aug/24/facebook -clickbait-political-news-sites-us-election-trump.

Ulmer, Gregory L. *Internet Invention: From Literacy to Electracy*. Pearson, 2002.

UN Women. 'UN Women Ad Series Reveals Widespread Sexism.' *UN Women*, 21 October 2013, www.unwomen.org/en/news/stories/2013/10/women-should-ads.

Vaidhyanathan, Siva. *The Googlization of Everything (And Why We Should Worry)*. 2nd revised ed. University of California Press, 2012.

Van Couvering, Elizabeth. 'The History of the Internet Search Engine: Navigational Media and the Traffic Commodity.' *Web Search: Multidisciplinary Perspectives*, edited by Amanda Spink and Michael Zimmer, vol. 14, Springer, 2008, pp. 177–206.

Virno, Paolo. *A Grammar of the Multitude*. Semiotext[e], 2004.

Virno, Paolo, and Michael Hardt, editors. *Radical Thought in Italy: A Potential Politics*. University of Minnesota Press, 2006.

Walton, Mark. 'Many UK Voters Didn't Understand Brexit, Google Searches Suggest.' *Ars Technica*, 24 June 2016, arstechnica.com/tech-policy/2016/06/brexit-google-search-trends-t ech/.

Wang et al. 'Game of Missuggestions: Semantic Analysis of Search-Autocomplete Manipulations.' *Network and Distributed Systems Security (NDSS) Symposium 18–21 Feb 2018*, doi:10.14722/ ndss.2018.23036.

Wegner, Daniel M., Toni Giuliano, and Paula Hertel. 'Cognitive Interdependence in Close Relationships.' *Compatible and Incompatible Relationships*, Springer, 1985, pp. 253–76.

Wegner, Daniel M., Ralph Erber, and Paula Raymond. 'Transactive Memory in Close Relationships.' *Journal of Personality and Social Psychology*, vol. 61, no. 6, Dec. 1991, pp. 923–9.

Weird Things Humans Search For, Big Potato Games, 2018.

Weitzberg, Keren, Margie Cheesman, Aaron Martin, and Emrys Schoemaker. 'Between Surveillance and Recognition: Rethinking Digital Identity in Aid.' *Big Data & Society*, vol. 8. no. 1, 2021, doi:10.1177/20539517211006744.

West, Sarah Myers, Meredith Whittaker, and Kate Crawford. 'Discriminating Systems.' *AI Now*, 2019. Retrieved from https://ainowinstitute.org/discriminatingsystems.html.

White, Ryen W., Matthew Richardson, and Wen-tau Yih. 'Questions vs. Queries in Informational Search Tasks.' *Proceedings of the 24th International Conference on World Wide Web (WWW '15 Companion)*. Association for Computing Machinery, May 2015. pp. 135–6, doi:10.1145/2740908.2742769.

Williams, Raymond. 'Advertising: The Magic System.' *Problems in Materialism and Culture*, Verso Books, 1980, pp. 170–95.

Willis, Amy. 'Britons Are Googling 'what is the EU' After Voting to Leave It.' *The Metro*, 24 June 2016, metro.co.uk/2016/06/24/britons-are-googling-what-is-the-eu-after-voting-to-leave-it-5 965238/.

Wilson, Emily. 'Introduction.' *The Odyssey*, translated by Emily Wilson, W.W. Norton & Company, 2018, pp. 1–80.

Wilson, Theodore. 'Google Searches for 'What is the EU?' and 'How to Emigrate' Spike after Devastating Brexit Vote.' *The Mirror*, 24 June 2016, www.mirror.co.uk/tech/google-searches -what-eu-spike-8274842.

Wingfield, Nick, Mike Isaac, and Katie Benner. 'Google and Facebook Take Aim at Fake News Sites.' *The New York Times*, 14 November 2016, www.nytimes.com/2016/11/15/technology/ google-will-ban-websites-that-host-fake-news-from-using-its-ad-service.html.

Winkler, Mathis. 'Germany Pulls Away from Quaero Search-Engine Project.' *Deutsche Welle*, 21 December 2006, www.dw.com/en/germany-pulls-away-from-quaero-search-engine -project/a-2287489.

Wired. 'WIRED's Autocomplete Interviews.' *YouTube*, uploaded by WIRED www.youtube.com/ playlist?list=PLibNZv5Zd0dwjZFCTVZ8QdKq194CkwXjo. Accessed 22 July 2022.

Wittgenstein, Ludwig. *Tractatus Logico-Philosophicus*. 2nd ed. Routledge, 2001.

Yates, Frances. *Giordano Bruno and the Hermetic Tradition*. Routledge and Kegan Paul, 1964.

Yates, Frances. *The Art of Memory*. Routledge and Kegan Paul, 1966.

Yusuf, Nuhu, Mohd Amin Bin Mohd Yunus, and Norfaradilla Binti Wahid. 'A Comparative Analysis of Web Search Query: Informational vs. Navigational Queries.' *International Journal on Advanced Science Engineering Information Technology*, vol. 9, no. 1, 2019, pp. 136–41.

Zhang, Ying, et al. 'Time Series Analysis of a Web Search Engine Transaction Log.' *Information Processing & Management*, vol. 45, no. 2, March 2009, pp. 230–45, doi:10.1016/j. ipm.2008.07.003.

Zimmer, Michael. 'The Gaze of the Perfect Search Engine: Google as an Infrastructure of Dataveillance.' *Web Search: Multidisciplinary Perspectives*, Springer, 2008, pp. 77–99, doi:10.1007/978-3-540-75829-7_6.

INDEX

Index

Index

www.ingramcontent.com/pod-product-compliance
Ingram Content Group UK Ltd.
Pitfield, Milton Keynes, MK11 3LW, UK
UKHW020658280225
455688UK00004B/163